For Peter Alexander
Thanks for everything you do
for the FOUNDATION FIGHTING
Blindness

WINNING ☑
CAMPAIGNS
LOSING SIGHT, GAINING INSIGHT

KEN RIETZ

Foreword by
SENATOR WILLIAM BROCK

www.mascotbooks.com

Winning Campaigns, Losing Sight, Gaining Insight

The author has tried to recreate events, locales and conversations from his memories of them. He may have changed some identifying characteristics and details such as physical properties, occupations and places of residence.

For more information, please contact:
Mascot Books
560 Herndon Parkway #120
Herndon, VA 20170
info@mascotbooks.com

Library of Congress Control Number: 2016909678

CPSIA Code: PRBVG0716A
ISBN-13: 978-1-63177-769-1

Printed in the United States

For my wife, Ursula:
This song, sung by Kenny Rogers, says it best.

Through the years
You've never let me down
You turned my life around
The sweetest days I've found
I've found with you
Through the years I've never been afraid
I've loved the life we've made
And I'm so glad I've stayed right here with you
Through the years

And for my son, KC,
who inspires me every day with his zest for life.

Special thanks to my wife, Ursula, the best editor I know.

Thanks also to Colleen Hahn for her valuable contributions while helping me turn a rambling draft into a real autobiography.

A portion of all sales of this book will go to the
ANIMAL RESCUE FUND (ARF) www.arfrescueva.org
and to the FOUNDATION FIGHTING BLINDNESS
www.fightblindness.org

CONTENTS

FOREWORD

(By former Senator William Brock (R-Tenn.), who also served in President Ronald Reagan's Cabinet as U.S. Trade Representative and Secretary of Labor. He was Republican national Chairman from 1977 to 1981.)

A truly global economy, social media, Amazon and Apple—all these and more are clear signs of how radical is the transformation of today's world from that of our parents. People here and around the world are finding this incredible pace of change frustrating, even often frightening. Governments, particularly those we generally describe as industrial democracies, are finding it difficult (if not virtually impossible) to adapt at a pace even close to that required. For those of us who believe in the unique example of self-government that defines the United States, a world economy trembling with uncertainty and a seemingly dysfunctional national government are sufficient cause for profound concern.

Far too rarely do we pause to recall what an enormous gamble the creators of this nation took over two centuries ago, when they decided that the citizens of this land could be trusted to govern themselves without direction from kings, nobles, or landed gentry. Far too rarely do we pause to note the actions, attitudes, and achievements of those among us today whose lives validate daily that early gamble. Self-government, by its very nature, requires direct personal involvement—if not by every American every day, at least by the representatives they have chosen with their ballot. That's how the system worked when first I met a young man named Ken Rietz.

Having served for four terms as the member of Congress for the third district of Tennessee, I had set my sights on becoming the second ever Republican U.S. Senator representing the state of Tennessee. Clearly I needed help, and my best friend and most respected colleague in the U.S. House, William Steiger, recommended Ken Rietz. The challenge we were facing was considerable, but the chemistry between us was terrific. I doubt we ever discussed the process of self-governance, but the imperative of a successful race was to engage a majority of voting Tennesseans in our effort to give them a new United States Senator—one whom they could trust to share their values, reflect their concerns, and represent their best interests. A daunting undertaking in the best of circumstances, and this we faced together.

Tennessee is an interesting state; neither populist deep South nor industrial Midwest, it is a border between, or perhaps an amalgam of (as I believe) the best of each. Locals talk about the three states of Tennessee; in the east it is mostly mountains, with caring communities, Tennessee Valley Authority (TVA), and perhaps just a little bit of moonshine; in the middle it is rolling hills, horses, Nashville, and a lot of country music; and in the west it's a lot of cotton, corn, Memphis, and the Mississippi River. It's hardly a one-size-fits-all state.

Politically, this was not an easy time. Like the rest of our country, we had seen more than a decade of the distrust and division an unpopular war had generated. Our young men were drafted to fight in a country they had never heard of, for a cause they did not understand. They didn't have any voice, they didn't have any vote; they just went. In that same decade, they and their parents went through a time of dramatic change domestically—civil rights, voting rights, open housing, and the rest. Our task was to find a way to give each voter, in every community, in every county, a sense that they had a voice and that someone was listening. We needed them to decide they wanted such a voice, and act on that decision.

Ken crafted and led the effort. He gave us themes to raise the sights and restore the confidence of each Tennessean that they could influence the course and direction of their country and their own future. He led the creation of organizations at the neighborhood and community level, so that those who wanted to affirm their involvement could do so and measure the consequence of their efforts.

We won this election, and in doing so, we also proved something critically important about this country and its people—that the goodness of neighbors working for neighbors, every day, in every way, in every community, is no less ennobling than working with those same neighbors to strengthen their belief in themselves and their country through participation. That was a lesson learned and applied two years later, when we were given the opportunity to lead the development of a national organization of young voters for the president. (We won that one too.)

It was in those early years of the 1970s that Ken received horrifying news. He was going blind, and there was no known treatment. Without having any sense of underlying causes, he had had more than his share of stumbles, bumps against a door or chair, even close calls on the street. He had suffered those for years, thinking perhaps that he was clumsy, but not very different than the rest of us.

As the light faded until it disappeared, he persevered. Year after year, he went from challenge to challenge and opportunity to opportunity, building, growing, creating, and developing (as he aptly describes it) "insight," that critically important ability to discern value.

In my experience, most of us learn best when we see the consequences of life choices made by individuals whose challenges are far different and far more difficult than our own. The most valuable benefits usually come when we see individuals whose perseverance, determination, and character offer an example of what someone just like us can achieve in the face of very real adversity. Then the lesson is indelible.

PREFACE

When I first thought about writing this book, it was going to be about my experience going blind. I was diagnosed with Retinitis Pigmentosa (RP) forty years ago, when I was thirty-four. I have known since that time that one day I would lose my eyesight. During the past ten years, as I have lost more and more of my sight, I have begun to reflect on my various experiences and career choices along the way. Some of them came naturally, and others were forced upon me by outside influences. Throughout my life, I have been in places at moments in time where truth, facts, and agendas collided. Some of those moments fostered an environment where new ideas could make changes for the better, while others created friction and stumbling blocks. In many cases, history was being written.

As I reflect on all of my experiences and memories, it has led me to think of "losing sight" in its broader context. While I faced the challenge of losing my ability to see, I realized that many people I have known over the years lost sight in other ways. I have seen some individuals losing sight of their objectives and moral compasses. Others gained insight, affected change, and moved our world forward, regardless of obstacles. While losing my sight, I have gained valuable insights about politics and what it takes to win a campaign, about corporations protecting their reputations, and how my competitive spirit helped me overcome my disability.

With all the wonderful stories, interesting people, and incredible moments along the way, one of the most important things is that I learned everything on the job. I learned how to write a press release, how to write a speech, how to write and produce TV and radio commercials, how to produce a television show, how to develop an effective strategy, and the basics of management. My career in politics and business was shaped by learning on the job in my first few political campaigns.

I hope that young people reading this book will be encouraged to do the same. Politics and political campaigns have a very negative image; people are generally discouraged from getting involved as volunteers or staff. My experience was totally different. Political campaigns were challenging, interesting, and exciting. It brought out my competitive spirit and was more fun than most people have on any job. It took a lot of work. Campaigns are a twenty-four hour experience. Managing a campaign takes a total commitment of energy and intellect, 24/7. However, a campaign is a learning laboratory, and there is no bigger "high" than winning an election. As far as I am concerned, a political campaign is a lot like football; both take strategy, solid implementation, and dedication, but most importantly, you have to be able to take the lumps. As former Secretary of State Jim Baker has said, "Politics ain't bean bag. It's a blood sport."

There is nothing like winning a political campaign. After nearly a year of living on adrenaline, frenzied hours, tension headaches, no sleep, bad food, endless weather issues, and immeasurable effort, a campaign manager finds out whether the strategy was right or wrong. Election Day is exciting. The pressure and tension build, escalating into election night; in one announcement, you know victory or defeat. It is over. At that moment, you find out whether or not the strategy, the plan, the candidate, the commercials, and all the other elements of the campaign came together at just the right time. Suddenly, your tension headache is gone; celebrating a political victory is like nothing else I know.

The first step in creating a winning strategy is to do adequate research. This includes public opinion polling, opposition research, and discussions with local political leaders. From the research, a strategy can be written.

The tactics of a campaign will flow from the strategy. The timeline will be dictated by the strategy and the tactics. All three (strategy, tactics and timeline) become the campaign plan. Even today, on television and in discussions, I consistently hear people confuse strategy and tactics.

At times, a strategy can become a tactic. For example, in 1992, when James Carville (whom I consider the best Democrat strategist) came up with the slogan for Bill Clinton's campaign for president, "It's the economy, stupid," he was focusing the campaign on the most important issue. It was the right strategy. When he then put up a sign in the campaign headquarters with the slogan, it was a brilliant tactic. He focused the attention of the campaign volunteers, the media, and the public on the strategy. This was also a great example of message discipline, an essential element of a winning campaign.

The last element in an effective strategy is to have the courage to stick to it. At times this takes a lot of stubbornness. Every volunteer in a political campaign is an expert at two things: first, their own job, and second, how to run a winning political campaign. Finding a way to receive advice and criticism while sticking to the original plan takes real patience.

In each campaign I ran, I created a campaign advisory board. This is typically a group of about ten people, including the campaign co-chairs (usually a man and a woman), local volunteer campaign leaders, the finance chair, and the candidate. I also include someone close to the candidate, like a brother, sister, husband, or wife. This group becomes a sounding board for all plans and actions during the campaign.

Most competitive elections are decided by a small percentage of the total votes cast. This makes analyzing the potential electorate in any district or state extremely important. Analyzing the voters helps allocate the resources of the campaign, including volunteer activity, direct mail, advertising, earned media opportunities, and the candidate's schedule. The best person I know at this is Karl Rove.

Republican elections are usually decided by about twenty percent of the voters. These are the soft Republicans, undecided Independents and leaning Democrats. They are generally referred to as "swing voters." Understanding where these voters are and what will motivate them is crucial to any winning strategy. It dictates the timing of everything, from advertising to the candidate's schedule. In the 1960 presidential campaign, Richard Nixon made the mistake of promising that he would campaign in every state. In the crucial last weeks of that election, Nixon was in Alaska (where he was going to win anyway), instead of campaigning in one of the swing states.

I believe the most important period in any election is the final six weeks. That is when the swing voters begin to pay attention. A well-planned campaign will put the candidate where those swing voters are during this period, focusing on the most important issues. As an example, in Brock's campaign against Sen. Albert Gore, Sr., we found that the right to pray in public schools was a cutting issue. More than seventy percent of voters supported Brock's pro-prayer stance, while Gore had voted against prayer in public schools in the Senate. We had the choice of using this issue against Gore early or late in the campaign; because it was so powerful at the time in Tennessee, we used it during the last few weeks of that close election.

Issues are important in any election. The way candidates speak about the issues, and their abilities to articulate their positions, are vital. When I was running campaigns, we asked the candidates to describe how they felt about issues, and then we polled those answers. I have the feeling that today, candidates take polls first and then decide where they stand.

I found that the most important thing to voters is the candidate's character. Trustworthiness, believability, and likeability were paramount. If the voters believed they could trust the candidate, believed what he/she was saying, and they liked him/her, they were more likely to vote for that candidate. That is why, in many of the campaigns, I used "man on the street" interviews for TV and radio commercials. This allowed people interviewed to spontaneously endorse the candidate in their own words. This was particularly important in the Chic Hecht campaign.

Managing a campaign is a little bit of many things. You have to be an organizer, motivator, press secretary, writer, debate coach, driver, haberdasher, marriage guidance counselor, part-time shrink, and the candidate's chief counselor, while keeping everything running on time and in the right direction. I stuffed envelopes, swept floors, ran errands, and handed out thousands of buttons, matchbooks, bumper stickers, flyers, and other kinds of literature.

Still, it was the best job I ever had.

As the light is beginning to fade, and my ability to see is reduced to shadows and shapes, I contemplate the rich and often humorous experiences of my life. I hope to share those with you and, perhaps, set some facts straight along the way.

NOTE: Many of the events and conversations in this book occurred more than thirty years ago. I apologize if my memory has failed me in any of the details.

INTRODUCTION

In 1970, President Nixon signed the Voting Rights Act, which called for the voting age to be eighteen, the same age as the draft. That meant in 1972, for the first time in American history, eighteen year-olds could vote for president. This was significant, for young people as well as for the presidential election.

Based on my success managing Bill Brock's U.S. Senate campaign, where he carried twelve of fifteen college campuses, I was asked to create an effort to win support among young people for Nixon. This involvement gave me the opportunity for an incredible experience. It began in the summer of 1972 with a phone call from White House Chief of Staff Bob Haldeman.

Haldeman was a man of few words. He quietly posed the question, "Ken, could you be prepared to go to Camp David tomorrow and brief the president and his Cabinet?" The question was rhetorical; you didn't say no to Bob Haldeman.

He explained that he wanted me to give the president and his Cabinet the kind of briefing that I had done several days before for the White House staff. Since I believed in data and research, all of my White House staff briefings included charts, boards, handouts, and a variety of materials to back up the strategy and tactics we were using.

When I asked Haldeman about materials I should bring, he quietly answered, "Ken, this will be a casual dinner at Camp David. Your job will be to express your point of view, in ten or fifteen minutes, on the current status of the youth campaign and its potential success. You will have dinner, talk, and come back the same evening. We will send a car."

As I put the phone down and turned to my assistant, I must have looked like I had seen a ghost or just been fired. I was nervous and excited. How did a working class kid from Oshkosh, Wisconsin end up briefing the president? Although I thrived on a challenge, I thought this was something totally out of my league.

I spent the next few hours preparing and calling people I trusted. The first call was to my deputy, Tom Bell. The second was to George Gorton, who was running our mock elections on college campuses. I also called Bill (BT) Timmons, who had been Brock's congressional chief of staff in the '60s and was then working for Nixon as head of legislative affairs. Timmons and I were close. He led the conservative syndicate that controlled national young Republican politics. According to Pat Buchanan in *The Greatest Come Back*, Nixon had called Timmons a "managerial genius." In his usual straightforward manner, BT told me to "Just give them all the facts. Be yourself."

The next day, I was picked up in a black town car driven by a White House driver heading for Camp David. I was nervous, since I would not have my usual presentation charts and was losing track of time, going over all the information in my head. All of a sudden, I looked up and realized we were going the wrong way. As I looked out of the passenger window, I saw the car was pulling up to the Pentagon. I asked the driver, "Hey, aren't we going to Camp David?" The driver turned and smiled. "Yes, sir, you are, on Army One."

The pilot stood ready at the stairs as we pulled up. I tried to be as cool as possible as he welcomed the "kid" from Oshkosh. There on the brown leather seat was a place card that read "ARMY ONE, KEN RIETZ."

The thirty-minute flight took us to Camp David, where I was met by the Secret Service and escorted directly to the cocktail hour already in progress. I don't remember a thing about the cocktail hour or the surroundings. I was on automatic, smiling politely while running scenarios through my head. I was calm on the outside, but inside I was churning.

I was seated next to the president at dinner. He was a very charming host. While I expected him to ask me about the campaign, he instead asked the same questions he had before, when I had attended White House social functions. He would always inquire about my dating life, so the first thing he asked me as we sat down was, "Ken, who are you dating now?"

Once I covered a few small details about dating, Nixon switched the conversation to his daughter, Tricia. I had involved Tricia in the Youth Voters for the President (YVP) campaign and she had become quite an active spokesperson. We all enjoyed having her around. The president told me she was very happy participating in the campaign with our team.

Then we turned to politics. Nixon was the best political strategist I have ever known. He understood campaigns and what was needed to win. He also understood the Republican Party and where it was effective. He could name the Republican chairs in all the states and most of the counties. It was a challenge to keep up with him as he asked me questions about individual states. He introduced me to the Cabinet by leaning into the table and saying, "Ken, describe for our guests the Young Voters for President campaign and your progress."

I stood, paused calmly, looked around the table and began. This was a subject with which I was familiar. I knew the information and support data. The analysis was memorized because it had become such a part of my day-to-day life. I first discussed the need for our group to be independent from the rest of the campaign, and then outlined the importance of recruitment and our overall strategy to capture the youth vote. I pointed out that less than twenty-five percent of the "new voters" were college students. The balance had graduated from high school and either joined the military or went to work in their hometown. Our task was to find and persuade them to support President Nixon.

Although there were quite a few naysayers on Nixon's Cabinet and within the White House about our Young Voters for the President initiative, everyone around the table that night had the Republican National Convention in Miami on their minds. So, I took the opportunity to explain our plans for the convention and how the Cabinet might help ensure securing a larger percentage of the youth vote.

I told them that we had a group of 3,000 YVP participants who had agreed to attend the convention and pay their own travel expenses. We would help with finding airline deals and paying for lodging and meals in Miami Beach, but all the participants would work as volunteers. I pointed out that one of the important aspects of the program was giving the volunteers a real convention experience. We wanted Cabinet members to help out and participate in briefings, "meet and greet" activities, social events, and mini-convention experiences.

At the end of my presentation, I looked around the table and saw several smiling faces and nodding heads, including U.N. Ambassador George H. W. Bush, White House Counselor Bob Finch and Defense Secretary Mel Laird. I asked if there were any questions. There was silence. Nixon thanked me, and I was excused.

Two Secret Service agents came over and escorted me back to the helicopter. As I was strapping in and getting settled I felt a sense of relief. As I thought about the evening, Secretary of Defense, Mel Laird came up the ladder, smiled, and took his seat. Laird (a former Wisconsin congressman) and I knew each other. We had crossed paths a few times through Wisconsin politics. During the flight back, Mel made me feel at home. We chatted about politics and the coming election. He said that he thought the briefing had gone well and would be interested to see if we could make it work. I said that with the kind of support we hoped to get from the White House and the campaign, I didn't think we could miss. (A full description of the Young Voters for the President campaign appears later in this book.)

I really didn't know how well I did until a friend of mine, former Bush campaign manager Jimmy Allison, sent me a copy of a note he had received from George Bush. In it, Bush said, "Ken Rietz did a first class job at Camp David briefing Cabinet and staff. The only one to get applause.....— Damn good job —Thought you'd like to know it — GB."

On June 17 of that year, five individuals (White House operatives) were arrested for what would be the third attempt to "burglarize" the Democrat National Headquarters at the Watergate. At first largely ignored by the media, it would change my life as well as future political campaigns. I would willingly resign as deputy chairman of the Republican National Committee, put my political career on hold, and be implicated in false accusations that would take years to clear up.

Unfortunately, as I was regrouping and gathering my strength to build my second career, I never imagined what was coming next. At thirty-three, seated across from my eye doctor in Los Angeles, he looked me straight in the eye and said, "Ken, you have a rare eye disease called Retinitis Pigmentosa. There is no known cure, no medicine to take, no cause to identify, and no medical answers." Shocked, I asked him, "So what should I do?"

I will never forget his response. He paused, adjusted his gaze, and said, "See as much of the world as soon as you can."

CHAPTER 1
Values and Paper Routes

Except for the cold weather, Wisconsin was a terrific state in which to grow up. Back in the forties and early fifties, people knew about "being neighborly," especially in the Midwest. With our old fashioned, Midwestern values, most of our community was knitted together through a common sense of place. In general, we were all full of hope and inspiration that we could fulfill the American dream.

Life was simple. Kids played outside all year round. Summer was filled with creek and lake swimming, baseball, kick the can, and basketball. Fall was all about football—high school, college, and of course, the Green Bay Packers. Winter never slowed us down, even with below zero temperatures. Bundled up in layers, we went ice fishing, sledded, played ice hockey on any frozen surface available, and skied whenever we could. Childhood games were full of competitive spirit and sportsmanlike conduct. Neighbors became our teammates as we vied against each other with games like tag and hide-n-seek. This was a time when children spoke when spoken to, shook hands with adults, and used "Yes, ma'am" and "Yes, sir" for any inquiry from an elder.

The late forties and fifties were an interesting time in America. Post World War II, western countries had just come through the biggest, bloodiest war in human history. The United States became the world's strongest military power. The American economy was booming, and every American was touched by a new kind of prosperity. Cars, suburban houses, and a great variety of consumer goods were available for the first time. In general, Americans, especially American children, were untouched by events outside of their community.

I was born May 3, 1941 in Appleton, Wisconsin, at Memorial Hospital. My early years were spent in the city of Appleton, on Arnold Street. My dad, Howard Kenneth, and mother, Catherine, worked hard to see that my older brother Richard (Dick), two younger sisters Virginia (Ginger) and Martha (Marty), and I had all the basics. We were a working class family. Dad was our local mail carrier by day and drove a taxi at night for extra money. Mom was pretty much a stay-at-home mother during our time in Appleton. She and Dad were big believers in the YMCA programs. When I was around kindergarten age, my brother and I took advantage of the sports opportunities. Whether it was the influence of the YMCA or my natural instinct, my independent and adventurous nature started early in life. I swam quite early, and by kindergarten I was biking to school on a two-wheeler. I insisted, in my stubborn way, to take my bike and beat my older brother to school. I always wanted to be in front and get ahead. My two-wheel bike was just the start. The independence and mobility gave me a sense of freedom and a competitive edge that would continue through the rest of my life.

In Appleton, our family did not have a car. If we wanted to go somewhere, we would walk or ride our bikes. On weekends, we could use the taxi Dad drove during the week. Since we had an icebox instead of a refrigerator, we also used the taxi to pick up ice each week.

Throughout our childhoods and into our high school years, we were church-going Methodists. We attended church camp in the summer and went to Sunday school. I even sang in the choir at one point. Dad taught Sunday school and was an usher. Mom played the organ.

We were all involved in community activities. My brother Dick was a Cub Scout, although that was not for me. We lived the small-town, American way; our doors were never locked, we had no television, and we always had dinner together. Movies were rare, but a special treat when we could afford to go. I distinctly remember my first movie, *She Wore a Yellow Ribbon*, starring John Wayne, who was everyone's hero back then. He represented the strong, stand-up, action-oriented hero that young boys in America wanted to emulate.

When I was in second grade, we moved outside of Appleton to a rural area in Outagamie County. My father encouraged the move so we could experience country life. We moved into a former cheese factory that certainly had character. It was located on a two-lane highway, Route 41, which connected Appleton, Oshkosh, Green Bay, and Milwaukee. Except for the Butte des Morts golf course, located on the other side of Route 41, our rural part of the highway went for miles through Wisconsin dairy farms, peppered with a few roadside stops and farm stands. With the proliferation of automobiles and cheap gas, Americans took to the road on weekend trips. There were few places to stop, get refreshments, and buy gas in rural areas.

My mother saw an opportunity to try her hand as an entrepreneur. She and my father converted a room in the old cheese factory into a local corner store. She ran the business, catering to neighbors, workmen around the area, and the families taking road trips. Dick, Ginger, and I all worked in the store. We stocked the shelves and marked prices on the canned goods. We even took care of the cash register when Mom wasn't available.

For additional money, she converted an area upstairs into a renter's apartment, forcing Dick and me to use the attic as our sleeping quarters. One of the chores my brother and I hated most was going into our dark basement and shoveling coal into our furnace. It was difficult and scary in that dark basement. The furnace was not very efficient, and the steam heat it provided did not reach the attic. We learned how to get dressed in the morning while huddled under our threadbare Army blankets in the freezing cold.

All of us participated in 4-H. Dick raised ducks and I raised rabbits. The family had chickens, dogs, and a cat, so there was always something lively going on.

My brother, younger sister, and I walked or biked every day to the Badger School, a one-room schoolhouse located three miles from our house. The three of us attended school and learned together, despite our age range. Marty was too young, so she stayed at home. Our teacher was Mrs. Schimmelfinny, a robust woman with a kind heart who taught all six grades. She was patient, caring, and encouraging, each and every day. There were five or six children in each grade, and all six grades were taught in the same room. The best aspect of this arrangement was that once you finished your work, Mrs. Schimmelfinny encouraged us to listen in on the lessons for older students.

My brother and I had a paper route, and we thought this was an important job. We made extra money to help with our family expenses, and came to know each person on the route. The only negative was collecting the money; we would argue about whose turn it was to go knock on the door for it. We had to organize the pick-up from the distributor and make sure we delivered the paper, no matter what the weather, and it can get mighty cold in Wisconsin. We finally managed to arrange for the distributer to deliver the papers right to the Badger School. Dick and I walked or rode our bikes, delivering the *Appleton Post Crescent* on our way home, arriving at sunset.

Our family always gathered around the kitchen table for dinner. My mom was not the best cook because she had four children to take care of on a limited budget. She had a predictable menu, which included macaroni and cheese on one day, meatloaf on another, and Jell-O or pudding for desert. We all looked forward to having sloppy joes on Saturdays, but Sunday nights were special. On that night, all the family sat around the table listening to the Sunday night radio shows with homemade pizza, apples, and popcorn. Shows like *Amos 'n' Andy*, *Nick Carter Private Detective*, *The Green Hornet*, *The Shadow*, *The Lone Ranger* and my favorite, *Tom Mix*. Anything that had to do with cowboys was my thing at the time.

I don't remember getting a television, but I distinctly remember two things linked to it. One was the lovely Annette. Every young boy in America loved Annette Funicello from the Mouseketeers. She was my first big crush, and I would never miss her show on our small black and white TV. The other significant memory was focused around the Rose Bowl and the Rose Bowl Parade. My mother adored the Rose Bowl Parade. Each New Year's Day, the whole family gathered to watch the parade and then the Rose Bowl. One of the most exciting moments in my childhood was watching my mother's reaction when Dad brought home a color TV just before New Year's Day, so she could watch the parade in living color. Later in life, I would be able to arrange for my parents to sit in the reviewing stand at the Rose Bowl Parade in Pasadena.

I was a pretty good athlete throughout my youth and young adult life; however, there were occasional incidents that seemed totally inexplicable. When I was a young child, I was absolutely terrible at night games like hide-n-seek. My tag game went south once the sun set. Several times, while running through the fields with friends, I would careen into barbed wire while the rest of my friends would dodge it. We would all laugh, even though I was scraped up and bleeding. My parents chalked it up to being a boy. Another time, I hit an electric fence; although it was barb free, the charge dropped me to my knees. These little mishaps did nothing to slow me down. I just kept up with the rest and tried to outrun them. A couple of times at night, I ran straight into a tree. The most serious incident occurred when, with my dad watching, I walked straight into my brother's practice swing with his baseball bat. He hit me in the head, and I hit the deck.

As I only had my perspective, this was my normal. Back then, it was expected that boys got hurt. I had no idea my peripheral and night vision was unusual, nor did I know what other children could see. It was not until much later that doctors came up with instruments able to scan visual fields. Visual acuteness was on no one's mind.

Dick and I took up basketball. Dad put a basket on the garage, and we started to learn the basics. While I found I was a pretty good shot, I just could not dribble, as I really could not see the ground right under my nose. Although I made the teams, this lack of ability would follow me into high school and college.

In 1954, when I was in the eighth grade, we moved to Oshkosh. My dad had been promoted to the Regional Management Structure of the Post Office. Moving to Oshkosh was exciting for us, because it presented options. I wanted to be an athlete. In Oshkosh, there were baseball leagues, basketball teams, and in the spirit of the Packers, football organized sports everywhere. I played little league baseball, which had not been available in the country. There also were boating, swimming, and tennis lessons. Tennis would become an important part of my life and a significant indicator of my sight limitations.

Oshkosh was a city of about 30,000. It was a lumber, pulp, and paper town. The largest companies were Payn Lumber, Morgan Doors, and Buckstaff Hardwood, which made furniture. Other companies included Oshkosh-B-Gosh Overalls, the Diamond Match Company, Leech Garbage Trucks, and Rockwell Axle Company. While we were in Oshkosh, the

Diamond Match Company burned to the ground, and Oshkosh-B-Gosh moved to a Southern state. Every town in Wisconsin had a local beer, and in Oshkosh we had two: Chief Oshkosh and Peoples. This was long before the term microbreweries came into being.

Today, Oshkosh is best known for the annual Experimental Aircraft Fly-in. My brother Dick became involved in 1970 when the event moved to Oshkosh. He still works as a volunteer at the event every year.

In school and on the field as a boy in the '50s, you were called by your last name, a nickname, or something related to your father's occupation. I was called "Rietz" and my best friend, Tom Kelly, was called by his father's occupation, "Plumber." He followed his father into the business.

We had a drive-in movie, a Dairy Queen, one of the first McDonalds, and our local drug store had an old fashion soda fountain. Every Friday night, the entire town would turn out to watch Oshkosh High School football. The evening also included a fish fry at a local tavern and cruising Main Street after the game.

In eighth grade, I found my first opportunity to play an organized sport, and tried out for the ninth grade football team at Merrill Junior High, where Jim Bruins was the coach. I did make the team, but spent most of the time on the bench. The following year, I made the ninth grade team at Webster Stanley Junior High and played every play. Ken Potterton was my football coach and an important mentor. I can't remember the names of my academic teachers throughout those years, but I remember my coaches.

The summer between my eighth and ninth grades, I took a job with a traveling carnival that came to town. The tents, trucks, trailers, equipment, sideshows, rides, animals, and of course, the people, calling themselves "carnies," rolled into town each year. The people, from jugglers to barking vendors, fascinated me. Arcade games, where players tossed a ring over a bottle and won a fish, or knocked over two Coke bottles with a ball to win a prize, were all so exciting. This was great fun, and I wanted to be part of it.

I befriended a "carnie" who steered me to the game where you had to hit two Coke bottles with a ball and knock them over. It was legit, and I, good with a baseball, quickly became adept at it. I became a "barker." I would encourage and entice people walking by to come and play the game.

I became a good salesman. My strategy was to find a really cute girl and let her try the game; even if she did not win, I would give her a prize. I gave out large stuffed animals that would grab the attention of potential players. The girls would then become my sales representatives, encouraging others to play. This was my first experience dealing with the general public. It taught me selling, recruiting techniques, and how to encourage people to participate. This would serve me well in my political career.

One day I took my "carnie" friend home to meet my parents. He thought that he could persuade my mom and dad to let me go on the road with the troupe. I really wanted to go. He was older, tattooed, and road-worn, but gentle and talked of good money to be made. My mother never batted an eye at having a guest over, and he was polite throughout dinner. I believe he thoroughly enjoyed a traditional home-cooked meal. After he left, my parents laid down the law. I stayed home the rest of the summer.

In the ninth grade, I was elected to the Oshkosh Youth Council (OYC), which would turn out to be a significant step toward my ultimate career in politics. The OYC was created by the city fathers to give the young people of Oshkosh a voice in city activities. Each junior high school had a representative, as did each class in high school. We met each month in the city council chambers and conducted our meetings according to Robert's Rules of Order. The major project OYC took on each year was to conduct a citywide canvass for the March of Dimes. We recruited volunteers, organized the canvass, and walked door to door. My brother's best friend, Bill Steiger, was president of the OYC when I was first elected to it. Bill would later become a very important mentor. His future wife, Janet, followed Bill as president of the OYC. I was elected president in my junior year of high school.

I was a straight A student all through the ninth grade. Academically, things came easy to me. In high school, I became so involved with OYC, the Wisconsin State Youth Committee to which I had been elected, and sports that I neglected my studies. I soon became a B and C student. Sports, which had always been a priority, now took the majority of my time. In the tenth grade, I made the first team of the football, basketball, and baseball teams. I also played some tennis. The sports priorities shifted, based on the season and the sport.

It was the time of James Dean, crew cuts, and letter jackets. Kids my age started driving and drinking beer. Compared to today that all seems tame, but back then parents were worried. Rather than set up curfews, the OYC became an important part of focusing the energies of young people toward community impact. OYC instilled a sense of civic duty through the various volunteer activities, including community events, charities, and politics.

Bill Steiger and I became quite close while he was president of OYC. He taught me much about leadership, and introduced me to Young Republican activities. Bill was from one of the more wealthy families in our area. His family was in the lumber business. He always seemed to create opportunities wherever he went. During the summers, Bill worked as a DJ at our local radio station, WOSH. This would later affect him in a positive way when he ran for the state legislature.

Bill was active in the College Young Republicans at the University of Wisconsin. He was elected chairman of the National College Young Republicans. When he came home from college during the summers, he worked at WOSH. I would visit him at the station and spend hours with him talking politics while records were playing. This would help set the stage for my later political career.

Between tenth and eleventh grades, I had a job at the local Coca-Cola bottling plant. It was great money and they paid us overtime, even though I was not in the union. Every two weeks, I would bring a paycheck home to my mother, and it would go into the family coffers. I learned one of my biggest life lessons during this time. I was so excited about making all this money. It felt so good, contributing to the family funds, that when football practice started in August, I declined to join my teams and kept working. This set up a chain of events. My coach called my brother, my junior high coach, and my parents, but I could not be persuaded to change my decision. The money was exhilarating. Of course, by September, school was in full swing, the summer job ended, and I was sitting in the grandstand, watching all my friends play without me. It was painful. The money had not been worth it. I felt that I let the team and coach down. I vowed not to choose money over other things ever again.

Between my junior and senior years in high school, my dad was once again promoted. He was sent to work in the new Regional Office of the Post Office Department in Minneapolis, Minnesota. For most kids, that would have been hard, but I welcomed the change. Once we heard the news, I decided I would play all three sports, football, basketball, and tennis, at my new high school. I earned a letter in all three in my senior year. My football coach called me Oshkosh. The name stuck, and the kids called me that for the rest of the year.

During this time, I also realized that I wanted to go to college. Neither I, nor my parents, could afford it. Luckily, I heard about a program called the Naval Reserve Officers Training Corps (NROTC). It was highly competitive, but if you scored high enough on their test, you could go to college, and the scholarship would pay for your tuition, room, and board.

Despite all my C grades in high school, I scored amazingly well on the test. I had my choice of schools that had the NROTC program. I knew right then and there that I wanted to go anywhere where it was warm. I hated the cold weather in Wisconsin and Minnesota. I decided on Vanderbilt in Nashville, and was all set to go when Cong. Walter Judd called and said there was an opening at the U.S. Naval Academy, if I went in as a football player.

So, upon graduation from West High School, I received an appointment to the U.S. Naval Academy and headed to the East Coast. It was the ultimate in a "free ride," including books, tuition, room, board, and a clothing allowance. I even received a paycheck, as a mid-shipman in the Navy.

CHAPTER 2
Naval Academy and GWU

People close to me were not surprised by the turn of events that led me to the Naval Academy. When I wanted something bad enough, my competitive nature and extreme focus were evident to all those around me. Although my grades had improved in my senior year while in Minneapolis, I was not an A student. I really wanted to go to college, and this was my best chance. I was committed to the challenge.

The Naval Academy had an extremely competitive football team. I was excited, not only to have the chance to play football for an American institution like the academy, but to be on a winning team. At that time, Navy was always in one of the major bowl games. I also dreamed of someday being a Navy pilot.

I passed the Navy physical with ease. I had 20/20 vision, but they didn't test me for night vision. The peripheral vision test was simply to extend my arms out to my side and wriggle my thumb. I could see movement and passed. There was no test for vision below my nose. Years later, I would discover that lack of night vision and diminished peripheral vision were the first signs of Retinitis Pigmentosa (RP). By reviewing my activities in my early years, doctors would discover that I'd had RP in my childhood.

I arrived at the Naval Academy in July 1959. The Navy's academic year was very different from most universities and colleges. When you were admitted to the Naval Academy for plebe summer, you were assigned an upperclassman as a guide and mentor. Because I was going to play football for Navy, I was assigned an upperclassman football player named Joe Bellino. I had never heard his name, and was unaware that he was one of the all-time great Navy football players. He would win the Heisman Trophy in

1960. Joe came into my room and introduced himself to my roommates and me. He then said to me, "I am your second classman, and I will look out for you." He motioned me to follow as he led me through the halls and outside. He took me on a tour of the monuments and buildings that make up the campus (they call it the "yard"). As we walked, an officer came up and we saluted. The two of them started talking about the upcoming football season. Joe finished his conversation and we walked on. I turned to Joe and asked, "Do you play football?" With that, Joe stared at me and commanded, "Underclassman walk three steps to the rear." He never spoke to me again. I had lost my one "friend" at the Academy.

I spent the first few weeks in plebe summer boot camp, learning the basics of military life, enduring the typical upperclassmen harassment. It was rigorous. As a fourth classman, I became keenly aware of the hierarchy and protocols. Throughout the first weeks, I couldn't wait for football practice to start.

Unfortunately, my stay at the Naval Academy would be brief. I had a series of medical conditions unrelated to my eyesight that would end my military career and my ability to play football. The medical condition that followed me throughout my life began with an innocuous jump off the top of a bunk bed. It caused a hernia and required an operation. There were complications, and the result was a dull pain in my side. A series of surgeries followed as doctors tried to correct the problem. I spent most of the next few months in the Naval Academy Hospital without success. Finally, the Naval Academy doctors sent me to Bethesda Naval Hospital for additional examinations; specialists there were more experienced in these matters. The prognosis was that some nerves were compromised during the initial operation. The problem was never fixed, and I still have that pain to this day.

Although I continued to keep up with my studies, I had missed two to three months of military training and my football career was on hold. Finally, decisions had to be made. My options were outlined by my company officer. I could try to stay on and catch up with military training; I could drop out and come back the next year to start over; or I could just drop out of the academy all together. I chose the last option, and in December 1959, I left the Naval Academy.

During my time in the Naval Academy, changes had taken place back at home. My dad had been promoted yet again, and his new position relocated him to the Post Office Headquarters in Washington, D.C. When I packed my bags and left the academy, I did not return to Minneapolis, but headed to Alexandria, Virginia to join my parents.

Now I had to work. Although I was still hoping to go back to college at some point soon, I needed an income. Living at home, I took a job as a reservation agent with United Airlines working at National Airport (now Reagan National). I worked full-time throughout the spring and summer, and in the fall I enrolled in George Washington University (GWU) in D.C. Since I was paying for my education, I needed to work a full forty-hour workweek, which I was able to do by taking the midnight shift.

GWU was a fertile ground for my interest in volunteer activities and politics. There were many students involved with politics, and because of the school's proximity to Capitol Hill, there were many jobs and internships available. Political conversations took place on a daily basis. Many fellow students were directly connected to the activities on the Hill through their internships. I also joined a fraternity, Phi Sigma Kappa; I was determined to get into more political committees. After six months of working the United Airlines job, a fraternity brother, Bill Carter, recommended that I apply for his job after he graduated from GWU. That spring, I went to work in the office of Sen. Earnest Gruening, a Democrat from Alaska. I was excited. This would enable me to see inside the workings of Capitol Hill. It was the kind of job I had hoped for. My position on the totem pole in Gruening's office was pretty low, but my enthusiasm was high. The senator gave the first speech on the Senate floor against the Vietnam War. He and Sen. Wayne Morse were the first to vote against the Gulf of Tonkin Resolution, which authorized an expansion of U.S. involvement in Vietnam. I did not agree politically with Gruening, but I loved the job.

In those years there were no faxes, copy machines, or computers to help with documentation and overall communication. For outreach and updates, political office holders relied on letters, letters, and more letters. They were drafted, edited, signed, copied, and then sent to the basement to be put on automatic typewriters. Once copied, the automatic letters were signed by an automated pen, and stuffed into envelopes to provide direct connections with constituents. These letters addressed issues, had commentaries, and sometimes included educational materials for specific regions. The entire process of the auto-letter was considered very important. They kept the communication lines open between an elected official and his constituents.

I was in charge of Gruening's "robo-room." This sub-basement office in the Russell Senate Office Building contained a room full of the automatic typewriters. I spent four hours each day keeping them typing form letters addressed to Alaska residents. Each afternoon, after class, I would go to the robo-room. This was my job for two and half years while at GWU.

One of the advantages of this job was that it gave me complete access to the Capitol. This was before there were any security problems or precautions.

I could walk to any part of the Capitol, and with my Senate pass, get into any room. Before or after work hours, I would sit in the Senate Chamber watching the debates. This was in the day of Hubert Humphrey (D) and Everett Dirksen (R). These articulate Senate leaders would debate each other for hours. I was fascinated.

In general, my schedule was grueling, but I was young and had the energy. I took six classes a semester, worked a part-time job in the afternoon, and was president of my fraternity. Still, I wanted to be more involved in Republican politics. My commitment to school and work prevented me from devoting more time volunteering in the 1960 Nixon for President campaign. Although I was sorry Nixon lost the election, it did not affect me the way losing an election would affect me later in life. Since I was only a some-time volunteer and not actively running the campaign, it was not the end of the world for me. Later, running a campaign and losing would be very difficult for me to accept. I was not a good loser.

The 1960 election was unique in many other ways, and would even be shrouded by accusations of fraud. It was the first election in which the incumbent, President Dwight D. Eisenhower, was not eligible for re-election, having been elected the maximum two times allowed by the 22nd Amendment. He was the first president affected by that amendment. This also was the first presidential election in which voters in Alaska and Hawaii were able to participate; both had become states in 1959. It was also the first time a candidate in an American presidential election had lost despite carrying a majority of the states. Nixon carried the majority of states, but Kennedy won the Electoral College vote 303 to 219. Many believe Mayor Richard Daley's Chicago was the key to the difference.

At GWU, I had a wonderful girlfriend, Karen Dixon, who would later become my wife. Karen's mother ran the office at a powerful Democrat lobbying firm, which had been involved in the Kennedy campaign. She had tickets to the inaugural ball, and since Karen wanted to go, she asked me to accompany her. So, my first inaugural experience was for Kennedy, a Democrat.

I clearly remember the day of the Kennedy assassination. When I first heard the news, I was driving to work at the Senate building. The radio emergency signal went off, and reporters announced that Kennedy had been shot. Hearing the news and then sitting in the Capitol listening to updates was very moving. There was a feeling of fear and apprehension. Our sense of security had been shattered. As I was based in D.C., I received many calls from home asking about anything I might know that had not been reported in the news. All of my friends were looking for answers, which did not exist.

The day of the funeral was somber for every American. I distinctly remember the funeral procession from where President Kennedy had been lying in state in the Capitol, down Constitution Avenue to Arlington National Cemetery. Karen and I, along with thousands of people, stood along the route. What I remember most was the total silence and hallowed quiet except for the hoof-clicks of the seven white horses leading the caisson, followed by a black, rider-less horse taking President Kennedy to his final resting place. It was heartrending.

CHAPTER 3
Unlocking the Mystery

By now, all the inconveniences of Retinitis Pigmentosa (RP) had become part and parcel of who I was. I had not even heard of RP, but had instinctively learned to compensate for the problem. I thought everyone experienced the same field of vision. There were innumerable examples throughout my life that demonstrated how difficult this disease was to diagnose. I had great hand/eye coordination, straight ahead 20/20 vision, and had passed the Naval Academy tests. Except for small anomalies, there was little evidence of RP.

It is a degenerative eye disease, about which little was known. The early stages of RP cause night blindness and tunnel vision. As I was growing up, I had no way of knowing that this was unusual. I wasn't very good at games after sunset, and I could not see anything below my nose. The first clue for me that something was wrong was when I watched other kids dribbling a basketball. I knew I could not do the same thing. It was frustrating, but I never asked anyone about it. Only years later, when questioned by the researcher at Jules Stein Eye Clinic at UCLA, did I realize why, as a kid in the country, I couldn't safely run through the fields with the other kids.

RP refers to a group of inherited diseases causing retinal degeneration. The cell-rich retina lines the back inside wall of the eye. It is responsible for capturing images from the visual field. People with RP experience a gradual decline in their vision because photoreceptor cells (rods and cones) die. In most forms of RP, rods are affected first. Because rods are concentrated in the outer portions of the retina and are triggered by dim light, their degeneration affects peripheral and night vision. When the more centrally located cones, responsible for color and sharp central vision, become involved, the loss is in color perception and central vision.

Night blindness is one of the earliest and most frequent symptoms of RP.

It is typically diagnosed in adolescents and young adults, and is a progressive disorder. The rate of progression and degree of visual loss varies, but most people with RP are legally blind by age forty. An estimated 100,000 people in the U.S. have RP, mainly caused by gene mutations (variations) inherited from one or both parents. In my case, I am the only member of my family with any evidence of RP.

About thirty years ago, my friend and mentor Gordon Gund, along with Steve Wynn, founded the Foundation Fighting Blindness (FFB) organization. Foundation-funded researchers are currently working towards treatments for RP and other eye-related diseases. This organization has helped many, including me. My sight deteriorated over a long period of time. For Gordon, it happened in a matter of months.

CHAPTER 4
The Fire is Lit – Wilbur Renk

Leaving GWU in my senior year was not what I had planned. I was doing okay in school, liked my college life, and especially enjoyed the fraternity activities and my job on the Hill. In the spring of 1964, Bill Steiger, who had been elected to the Wisconsin State Legislature, called with an interesting opportunity. He knew of my desire to become involved in a political campaign. Bill asked me if I would like to spend the summer working as a driver for a Republican named Wilbur Renk. This would provide an opportunity for me to be involved in the Renk for Senate campaign in Wisconsin. Bill explained the situation and then added, "Ken, you would be his driver, only staff member, and you would be paid." I didn't wait for summer. I jumped at the opportunity. That week, I dropped out of GWU and drove my car to Oshkosh.

Renk was opposing incumbent Sen. William Proxmire (D), who had been an unsuccessful candidate for governor of Wisconsin on more than one occasion. He was not a Wisconsin native, and was later known to have said that he left the East Coast and moved to a Midwestern state (Wisconsin) to more easily pursue his political career. In a special election on August 28, 1957, Proxmire was elected senator to fill the remainder of the term vacated due to the death of Sen. Joseph McCarthy, (R). On the Senate floor, Proxmire was called a maverick, and was sometimes considered disruptive and inconsistent. Campaigning tirelessly was Proxmire's greatest gift. He was a champion with what was called "hand-to-hand" campaigning, or "retail politics."

Wilbur Renk was from Sun Prairie, Wisconsin. His father served as commissioner of agriculture, not a small title in the Dairy State. His family operated a very successful hybrid seed company called Renk Seed, which is still in business today. In addition, Renk had been head of the University of Wisconsin Board of Regents. He played a major role in many agricultural and educational initiatives across the state, and was one of the first Wisconsin Republican leaders to support Eisenhower in his election campaign. He had headed the State Citizen Committee for Eisenhower in 1952. Nicknamed the "farmer-businessman," Renk had strong Republican support, and being a native of Wisconsin, he knew the issues near and dear to the voters in the Dairy State.

Interns, schedulers, researchers, and deputies were not part of this campaign. This was in the day when one person did all of those jobs; each campaign had few staff. The campaign driver was one of the most critical roles, as it meant hours on the road with the candidate. From driving in the car, to staying in the same motel room and eating all our meals, we did everything together.

Renk spoke with me about his schedule. We discussed the issues. He rehearsed speeches to me. He had me relay messages to the advertising agency we were using in Milwaukee. He dictated press releases for me to type on our portable typewriter, so we could distribute them at newspaper offices and radio stations. It was my first campaign job, and I was learning constantly.

As there were no computers, cell phones, Internet, or fax machines the only communication device available on the road was a pay phone. At each campaign stop, while Renk shook hands with voters, I would search for the nearest phone and call his secretary back home for messages or changes in our schedule. I would also call the ad agency to keep them informed.

Renk was a tireless campaigner. We would get up at 4 a.m. each day and head for the nearest plant. Standing outside the gate, Renk would greet the workers and shake their hands. I would hand out matchbooks. In the days when most workers smoked, we knew they would make good use of them. They contained Renk's name and a few sentences about him. We did this day after day, hitting the early shift in the morning and the 3 p.m. shift when a new group of workers arrived.

As Renk had been quite an influence in the Eisenhower campaign, the former president was willing to come to one of our rallies (something he did not do for Goldwater). With Eisenhower's support, we all thought we could win.

Our campaign materials also included car top advertisements, billboards, signs for store windows, flyers, bumper stickers, and yard signs. We carried whatever we could in the trunk of our car and distributed materials to our volunteers. As the campaign progressed, my role kept expanding. I would give my insight to the agency on the status of the campaign, relay some of the details and comments from voters, and discuss what was working and what was not.

This was the era when "retail" or "hand-to-hand" campaigning was critical to a candidate's success. Voters wanted to get to know the candidate. As there were few TV stations, voters were reached through newspapers, radio, and most importantly, person to person. Shaking hands and speaking directly to the voters were vital to a successful campaign. Some politicians did this extremely well; Proxmire was one of them. He understood the importance of connecting to his constituents, and he was prepared to take the time to do so. We knew we had our work cut out to make sure we reached as many voters as possible, or Proxmire would have the edge. There were county fairs, town hall meetings, and Rotary and Kiwanis clubs, all requiring a candidate's attendance. It was essential to go out and connect with as many people as possible. We did, using whatever means necessary, from walking to driving in cars and buses.

It is hard to overestimate the powerful impact of a faithful core of volunteers. In a campaign, they are essential. Since Renk and I grew up in Wisconsin, we tapped into the strong community groups embedded in each town. As we had limited access to phones on the road, we were obliged to borrow someone's house line. Back then, many houses in rural areas had party lines. We had to wait for the line to clear before using it. Even pay phones were rare, mostly located in city centers and gas stations. Our tools of the trade were typewriters with carbon paper to make copies. The wire or telegram services were the only ways for a quick connection, but were only used for emergencies. In states where campaign funds were limited, the use of television was sparse or non-existent. It was radio that was a significant influence and communication vehicle to reach those people in larger demographic areas, especially in rural communities. We focused on radio talk shows, interviews, and quick ads to reach voters both urban and rural. Our materials were printed quickly, and banners and signs were put up in as many windows and yards as possible.

Car top signs were large, similar to what cab drivers have now. The basic car top was a picture of the candidate, his name and, if possible, a quick line or message. Supporters and volunteers would place them on top of their cars and park outside plants, events, fairs, and meet and greets. Funds permitting, we would hire someone to drive around neighborhoods and events to spread our message. Catchy slogans were seldom used, except in newspaper ads.

We developed a "play book" for every town. Prepping the volunteers prior to our visit and using them as our ambassadors to the region was extremely valuable. They would organize an informal coffee hour for Renk to meet potential supporters. Generally, we would notify the local newspaper and radio station of our upcoming visit to their town. When we arrived, we would visit the radio station so Renk could be on the air interviewed by the local DJ. We would then stop at the local newspaper office for a quick visit, and Renk would speak at a local Rotary or other service club. Finally, we would campaign door to door on Main Street and visit the major plants and manufacturing operations. Renk hoped that if he visited every shift at every plant around the state, he would win. Time spent and the distances covered were vast. The unforeseen and astonishing factor was Proxmire's genius.

Wisconsin is Green Bay Packer country. A beloved team, owned by the people—if you were not a Packer fan, you could not be from Wisconsin. In the early years, the Packers played some of their games in Milwaukee, so their fan base ran from Milwaukee all along Highway 41 to Green Bay. On game day, Highway 41 was bumper-to-bumper with Packer fans, wearing their "Cheese Hats," heading for Green Bay. Proxmire brilliantly took advantage of this traffic jam. Instead of driving to the game, he hitchhiked. Starting in Milwaukee, he would catch a ride with Packer fans and go only four to five miles. He would get out of the car, stick out his thumb and catch another ride. In this way, he met a variety of voters all the way to and from the Packer game. He also created a lot of buzz in the stadium, with people telling other fans about their encounter with Proxmire. While he was in office, it became a Packer fan tradition to see who could pick up the Wisconsin Senator.

In 1964, Goldwater was swamped, nationally, by President Lyndon Johnson. In Wisconsin, Goldwater lost by more than 400,000 votes. Swimming against the tide, Renk was edged out by Proxmire, only by the margin provided by the state's biggest Democrat stronghold, Milwaukee.

This experience with Renk was educational. It had not been an easy lesson, but I thrived. This was the first of many campaigns in which I would work as a paid staff member. It was the beginning of a process that would lead me to a career as a political consultant. The things I learned in that first campaign about candidate scheduling, press release drafting, the creation of campaign materials, the long campaign hours, and the interaction with volunteers were things I would not have learned in any college class available at the time.

CHAPTER 5
Bill Steiger

Having learned more on the road in Renk's campaign then back in D.C. at GWU, I realized that returning to school was not necessary. I decided to stay in Oshkosh. Although I had not studied it in school, I thought I would try my hand at public relations. I found a cheap, one-room office in downtown, and with a typewriter and a telephone, opened up for business. It was fortunate that the Winnebago County Republican Committee was looking for someone to help them with a PR program. They became my first client.

In short order, I had other paying clients that included Hoffmaster Paper Company and the National Right to Work Committee. With my company launched and money coming in, my college girlfriend Karen Dixon and I were married in Washington, D.C. She joined me in Wisconsin that winter, where she taught school.

I had settled in Wisconsin, started my business, and had paying clients when I received another call from Bill Steiger. I trusted and respected him. We set up a meeting, and Bill asked my opinion about him running for Congress against the incumbent, John Race (D), who had been elected in the 1964 Johnson landslide. The 6th Congressional District had traditionally been Republican, so I encouraged Bill and said that I thought he could win. He then surprised me by asking if I had any interest in running for political office. Bill explained that if he ran for Congress, he would recommend that I run for his state legislative seat. Always very thoughtful when it came to his professional plans, he continued to say that he would endorse me if I were interested. I was quite flattered at the offer and, at the time, I thought it might be a good idea. After taking it all in and mulling over the prospects, I sent out a press release announcing that I would be running for the state legislative seat. Once the press release went out, the political campaign process started to roll. I began attending a variety of functions and pre-planning events, including visiting Bill at his office.

That plan lasted only a few weeks. Although I had deep respect for those who held office, becoming involved with my own campaign, I realized what I loved best was working behind the scenes. I just could not picture myself holding political office. Campaigns had a beginning, middle, and end. On Election Day, there was instant gratification or immediate disappointment. I wanted the excitement that only a political campaign could give, but not as a candidate.

I decided to withdraw and help Bill Steiger with his campaign for Congress.

John Race, a former union leader, had been elected during the an-ti-Goldwater landslide. We decided we would run Bill's campaign much like that of Renk. Our focus would be on public appearances around the district at local service clubs and a healthy volunteer grassroots mobilization. Bill was young, smart, and had great personal presence. He was a good per-son-to-person campaigner, with a good memory for names and faces. His experience campaigning for the legislature introduced him to a large portion of voters he would need to win the congressional seat.

Bill had married Janet Dempsey. The three of us had served together on the OYC and were good friends. We hit the campaign trail together. Bill had a very serious case of diabetes, and it was Janet's job to keep him healthy during the rigorous campaign.

Our first move was to mobilize our volunteer core, called "Steiger's Tigers." We established organizations in our three major cities—Oshkosh, Fond du Lac, and Sheboygan. The organizations were built on Bill's past relationships and networks. Bill, who was twenty-eight, looked young for his age. Young women loved him, older women mothered him, and men respected him. He was a relentless campaigner, and the perfect candidate in many ways. He could connect with people young and old, and reach out to farmers and urbanites alike.

He understood their issues and concerns. He was up before dawn to hit the local factories and afterward walked Main Street, going from shop to shop.

Summertime in Wisconsin is filled with fairs and festivals, which provided terrific campaign opportunities. We took advantage of many people being in one place at the same time. To maximize this situation, we developed a system.

The focal point of every festival or fair was the beer stand. That would be our first stop. With a $10 bill slipped to the bartender, he would allow us to put up a "Steiger for Congress" sign somewhere on the stand. We would then work our way out from the beer stand, putting up signs along the way. The result was that people approaching the stand could not miss a "Steiger for Congress" sign. Bill would spend an hour there, shaking hands and greeting people. Then we would move to our next event, leaving behind signs, volunteers, and materials.

The other thing on which we relied heavily throughout our campaign was radio. Since Bill had worked for the local radio station, WOSH, earlier in his career, he understood its impact. As a former DJ, he could go to any station and while discussing music, mix in a little politics. This was invaluable in the communities where he was not as well-known as in Oshkosh. Aligning our radio campaign with the only television station in Green Bay helped us reach a greater audience. As the station did not cover local events outside the Green Bay area, we made the fifty-mile drive to get Bill on the air.

Finally, our big coup was getting Nixon to come to the district in support of Bill. This massively boosted our credibility. Nixon's participation was part of his "rehabilitation tour" of the U.S. He campaigned for dozens of Republican candidates that fall, and this effort helped him launch his 1968 campaign for president. It was the first time I would meet our future president. I found him intense, but incredibly polite and charming.

We won, and in 1966, Bill Steiger was the youngest person to be elected to Congress. It was my first taste of a campaign victory, and I loved it. Karen and I headed back to Washington, D.C., to work in his office.

The two years I worked for Bill Steiger in the Longworth House Office Building were fascinating. I had been on the Hill before as a college intern, but this was different. I was on the inside with a high level position, working directly for a congressman and managing his communications. It was an exciting time for young politicians. There was a vibrancy and hope of change on the Hill and in D.C. Bill soon formed alliances with other young members of the House of Representatives, including George H.W. Bush, Bill Brock, and Don Rumsfeld. The White House scholar assigned to work with us on the House Education and Labor Committee was Dick Cheney. During this time, I had my first introduction to the former FBI investigator John Buckley. He would become known as "Fat Jack" during the Watergate investigation. It is also where I met Jimmy Allison, who worked for Cong. George H.W. Bush and would later become my business partner. Jimmy had been a newspaper publisher in Midland, Texas. He had managed Bush's unsuccessful Senatorial campaign and later his winning congressional campaign.

In 1968, while I was in Wisconsin working on Bill's re-election campaign, I received a call from Jimmy. He and Harry Treleaven had a new campaign consulting firm, and were working on Sen. Ed Gurney's re-election campaign in Florida. Harry had been the creative director at J. Walter Thompson Advertising, and had designed the campaign introducing the Ford Mustang. He had created the advertising in both Bush campaigns. Because Harry was also doing the creative work on the Nixon for President Campaign, they were shorthanded and needed someone to go to Florida to supervise the production of television commercials for Gurney. I told Jimmy that I had no experience in television production and would need Harry to give me a quick tutorial.

Harry was working on television and radio commercials for Nixon in New York. I flew there and met Harry in the studio for an afternoon briefing. I was learning on the job again. Although Harry was very patient with me, I was swimming in deep water. He explained the results he wanted from the television production, gave me a few scripts and sent me on my way.

I knew they were counting on me, so I headed to Florida to do something I had never done before. This was not unusual in the world of politics that I was getting to know.

Harry was keen on using real people and capturing sound bites. The scripts he had given me took that approach. I asked the Republican chairman in Orlando to line up people for my "man on the street" interviews. These were going to be regular people and we would have cue cards. The chairman came through, and we had quite a group of volunteers for our interviews. The problem was that these people were not used to reading cue cards. Several takes did not go well, so I came up with an alternate idea. I would stand behind the camera and ask a series of questions until we found a usable answer. To my surprise, it worked like a charm. We could not have planned it better. Real people using their own words came through as believable. We recorded them saying things we would never have been able to script. This "man on the street" interview technique would become a standard method for me in future campaigns. By editing several people's comments together into a thirty-second spot, we were able to capture a powerful endorsement.

CHAPTER 6
Bill Brock

Jimmy Allison was a hard-drinking, five-pack-a-day smoker, an engaging personality, and one of the most politically savvy people I knew. I really liked him, and more importantly, he had the respect of many politically powerful individuals. Originally, Jimmy came to Washington with Bush in 1966 to work in his congressional office. A year later, Jimmy and Harry set up one of the first Washington, D.C. based political consulting firms—Allison and Treleaven. After the successful Steiger re-election campaign, they asked me to join the company as an associate. I was happy to be working with these two friends and political pros.

Unfortunately, it was at this time that my marriage broke up. Politics is tough on any relationship. It is twenty-four hours a day, with total focus on winning at the expense of everything else, including family. This would be the first of my three marriages lasting only four years each.

In early 1969, Jimmy joined Rogers Morton at the Republican National Committee as deputy chairman. He asked me to join him as communications director, and Harry Treleaven worked with us as a consultant.

Except for the presidential election of 1968, the Republican Party had fallen on hard times in the post-Goldwater era. Rogers Morton was determined to change that. He wanted the party to be more youth-oriented and attractive to young people and minorities. He asked us to come up with a new look for the party, plus some programs to accomplish his goals.

Working with Jack Frost, the committee's in-house artist, we designed a new Republican symbol—the red, white, and blue stylized elephant that is still used today. We also developed a monthly magazine called *The Republican* and a weekly newsletter called *Monday*. These glossy publications were designed to tell the party faithful the accomplishments of the Nixon administration.

These efforts were not without controversy. When we retired the old gray elephant symbol and introduced the new one, our phones rang off the hook with complaints from members of the Republican National Committee (RNC). Morton stuck to his guns, and in January we introduced the new symbol at the RNC committee meeting. At the press conference that followed, I was grilled by the news media about the meaning of the various elements of the new symbol. Why were there three stars? Why were the stars on end, rather than positioned the way stars are normally positioned? Why was there no tail on the elephant? Members of the press probed for the hidden meaning of the redesign. The truth was, it just looked good. None of the elements were designed to mean anything.

That summer, Jimmy and Harry asked me to become a partner in their firm, and we became Allison, Treleaven and Rietz. The first client of the newly named firm was Bill Brock's campaign for the U.S. Senate in Tennessee.

Tennesseans take their grits, whiskey, and politics seriously. The home state of Jack Daniels has spawned a range of national political figures, including Davey Crockett, Vice President Andrew (Old Hickory) Jackson, candidate for Vice President Sen. Estes Kefauver, Senate Majority Leader and former White House Chief of Staff Howard Baker, actor/Sen. Fred Thompson, Vice President Al Gore, Secretary of Education and now Sen. Lamar Alexander, Sen. Albert Gore (the father of the vice president), and Bill Brock.

When I met Bill Brock, he was a fourth-term congressman from Chattanooga. He had been the chairman of a committee to find a congressional candidate from his district in 1962, and when none could be found, the committee convinced him to run. To everyone's delight, he agreed. He was only the second Republican elected to Congress from that district in a hundred years. He was re-elected in 1964 despite the Goldwater disaster, won re-election in 1966, and won again in 1968, with over sixty-five percent of the vote.

In his 1962 campaign, Brock had recruited more than 4000 volunteers, contacting through them 300,000 Tennesseans; he also created the "Brock-ettes," the first and by far the most effective women's campaign team in Tennessee—which helped immeasurably over the following four campaigns and the 1970 Senate campaign.

During his eight years in Congress, Brock led the effort to build a state-wide effective Republican party, and to recruit Republicans to run across the state, including Dan Kuykendahl. The Brock organization played the most important role in assuring the election of Howard Baker to the Senate and Dan Kuykendahl to the House.

As young members of the House of Representatives, Bill Steiger and Bill Brock became good friends. They worked together to recruit a group of young members of Congress, with the goal of visiting fifty college campuses to determine the cause of, and find solutions to, the campus disruptions surrounding the Vietnam War. The result of their efforts was a proposal to President Nixon to support the eighteen year-old vote and end of the draft, both of which were accomplished.

In 1969, several Tennessee Republican leaders asked Bill Brock to run for the U.S. Senate in the next election against Sen. Albert Gore. Gore was a senior political veteran, who had served in the House of Representatives and then in the Senate for three terms. Cong. Brock asked our firm to handle his campaign for the Senate.

We began the process by doing a careful analysis of the voting history in Tennessee. We broke the vote down by county, party, and candidate, and looked at Gore's voting record in the House and Senate. Armed with this in-formation, I went to Tennessee during the summer of 1969 and interviewed approximately a hundred Republican Party leaders, potential supporters, and friends of Bill Brock.

I returned to Washington, where Harry and I wrote a campaign strategy and plan, which we presented to Brock. He agreed to the plan and urged us to move forward.

Except for my Brock related interviews, I had never been to Tennessee. In the fall of 1969, I drove my car south through the mountains with a trailer full of everything I owned, thinking about the challenge that lay before me. I was twenty-eight, recently divorced, and had never run a statewide campaign. At this point, Sen. Albert Gore had been in the Senate for seventeen years and had always been re-elected by wide margins. All the pundits thought of him as a virtual shoe-in in the next election, but I had research and a new poll revealing weaknesses in Gore's positions in the Senate.

In the survey taken by our pollster, Tully Plesser, the elements on which most Tennessee voters focused, describing their image of the ideal senator, were: "keeps in touch with the people, honest, sincere, experienced in Tennessee affairs, experienced in national affairs, aggressive/gets things done and statesman-like." While Brock was relatively unknown statewide and comparisons were hard to ascertain, he received high marks in all these areas in the 3rd Congressional District, which he had represented for eight years.

Gore, on the other hand, received low marks statewide, which was in line with the feeling that he had grown out of touch with his constituents. All these thoughts were running through my mind as I drove to Tennessee. Once I arrived, I was put up in a small apartment, not far from the campaign headquarters. In that apartment, in my two-day old travel clothes, unpacking my boxes, I had only one thought—now, what the hell do I do next? Then came a knock on the door.

As I opened the door, I was staring into a light and right down the lens of a TV camera, with a reporter to one side who said, "Welcome to Nashville. We came to ask how you expect to win against the very popular Senator Gore?" I'm not sure what I said. I do know that at that moment, for better or worse, I entered the big leagues of American political consulting.

As candidates, the two men were drastically different. Gore was a personable, outgoing, hand-to-hand campaigner. Brock was a studier and thinker. When he spoke with voters, he took his time and really listened to their concerns. On the stump, Gore was a good speaker, but arrogant. He looked down his nose at people and tended to lecture, rather than speak to them. Brock was, on the other hand, low-key, a term to be used so often in describing him that he soon became known as "low-key Bill" within our organization.

Until the last stages of the campaign, Brock seemed unable to warm up his audience. He spoke without notes and gave the same talk, which was an "I love America" speech. He talked of the Bible, home, family, and America. He said he was tired of being pushed around, and that what he wanted was a country in which his children could grow up without fear. He looked deep into the audience and said he "wanted to be your Senator because I believe in you and we believe in the same things." (Thus, the campaign slogan became "Bill Brock believes in the things we believe in.")

It was an unmoving speech, except when it was over. There were no applause lines. The audience did not stand and shout as they would during other political speeches. They did not elbow each other or smile and clap. They sat and listened. At the end, they applauded and talked about his sincerity, his honesty, and his straightforward approach.

Bill Brock was not the typical Southern political speaker, nor did he want to have the ranting/shouting speaking style so often employed by some Southern candidates. It was just not his style; he also believed that a candidate would win more friends and be able to draw the audience into listening more carefully with a quiet voice. He was and is sincere about the challenges the average person faces in this country. While his quiet speaking style was effective with the voters, it was not endorsed by a few established politicians involved in our campaign.

At one of our major fundraising dinners, our statewide finance chairman, David K. (Pat) Wilson, who was one of the wealthiest and most influential businessmen in Nashville, cornered me in the back of the room. In the middle of Bill's speech, he announced his intention to resign as finance chairman if I didn't "get that guy some speaking lessons." Pat was so upset that he and Ken Roberts, a key supporter who had previously run for the Senate, insisted on leaving the dinner with me, Pat saying, "We don't have to hear any more of this speech." In the middle of this important function, the finance chairman and the campaign manager left the dinner early to commiserate and discuss ways to solve the problem. After three or four drinks, I had Pat calmed down and back on board.

Brock's style would never change. The politicians would hate it, but the voters would believe in it, be impressed by it, and be influenced by it. The style was discussed often between Brock and me, and we decided not to change it. I felt that an attempt to change his style would have put Brock on unfamiliar ground. It would have made him uneasy and unnatural, and that's something the voters can see right through.

Originally, Gore had been elected as a "man of the people," in the best traditions of a Southern Democrat. He was a Tennessean who would fight big government and fight for the people. However, throughout the '60s, Senator Gore sought the national spotlight that had shone on so many Tennesseans. He came out against the war in Vietnam, and attended anti-war rallies where the American flag was burned. This was a position foreign to the state that, dating back to the Civil War, consistently sent more young "volunteers" into combat than any other state. Gore also came out against prayer in public schools, which was not a popular position in this Bible-proud state. He had also begun voting with the Northeastern block of liberal Democrats on spending and social reform legislation. His actions were no longer aligned with those of the people of Tennessee.

We knew from our poll that these issues would resonate with Tennessee voters. Our problem was how to effectively find a way to communicate Gore's Eastern liberal positions. We also faced a well-organized Democrat state that had only elected one Republican Senator in modern times—Howard Baker. The Democrat grassroots organization was strong and effective. On the other hand, the Republican Party was confined to three Eastern congressional districts and one district in Memphis. In the east, Congressman John Duncan represented the district around Knoxville; Jimmy Quillen represented the area that included Johnson City, and Bill Brock represented the district that included Chattanooga. Dan Kuykendahl represented the district in Memphis.

Brock had worked with Quillen and Duncan in the House and had supported Kuykendahl in his successful campaign, earning the support of each. Our challenge in east Tennessee was dealing with continuing jealousy between the Brock political organization and that of incumbent Senator Howard Baker. It was our sense that many among Baker's team had encouraged a country singer and movie star, Tex Ritter, to run in the Republican primary against Brock. Ritter had never played a role in politics, but was a popular figure in Tennessee. Even though the Nixon White House encouraged Brock to run and President Nixon had talked to Bill about the race, Tex would not be deterred.

Nevertheless, we felt the issues were on our side, and Bill Brock was a candidate able to raise money both within the state and nationally. Our job would be to carefully navigate the primary in September, just eight weeks before the election. We would have to develop a statewide grassroots organization while creating a communications strategy.

One of our most successful tactics was our statewide bus tour. We loaded a bus (sometimes two) with volunteers and drove the state, from Memphis to Johnson City. Most of our staff and volunteers were young; I was the oldest at twenty-nine. With all the fanfare, the bus captured a lot of attention as it went from town to town, loaded with signs and, of course, with pretty "Brockettes" leaning out the window as we pulled into sleepy Southern towns. At each stop, our staff and Brockettes would flood Main Street, going from store to store with signs and materials as Brock spoke with groups of voters.

As we continued to build momentum, the national press corps began to pay attention to the race. A number of them decided to cover the bus tour as something rare in campaigns at the time, but small town after small town soon grew monotonous for them. As we pulled into Johnson City near the end of the tour, Roger Mudd of CBS News, who had fallen asleep in his seat, took a look around, and said to me, "Rietz, wake me up when we leave this joint."

To capture the difference between Brock and Gore, and to emphasize the distance Gore had been putting between himself and the voters, Harry Treleaven, working with our pollster Tully Plesser, developed the theme "Bill Brock Believes." Captured on billboards across the state, these three words led the press and public to wonder the obvious question: what does Bill Brock believe? The response was, Bill Brock believes in you, he believes in Tennessee—"Bill Brock believes in the things we believe in." This slogan, although considered too long by many pundits, then appeared on billboards and signs across the state. It was used on the side of our bus and as a theme-line in all of our commercials. And it worked.

The theme began to be played back to us by volunteers as they joined our campaign. Most importantly, our polling showed Brock's popularity rising. We had started the campaign, as we told the media, just below undecided. Both Gore and Ritter had been well ahead of us. Our billboard campaign and bus tour had a strong impact in west Tennessee, and by the summer of 1970, we had pulled even with Gore and well ahead of Ritter.

The campaign was working particularly well in rural west Tennessee. This was a conservative Democrat stronghold, never before carried by a Republican statewide candidate. As it turned out, Brock would be the first Republican to ever carry west Tennessee, and he did so handily.

Tennessee was really three states in one. The industrial east is the area traditionally fertile for Republican candidates. To win the election, we needed to strengthen this support and win it by a substantial margin. Middle Tennessee was dominated by Nashville. It was the new South and Democrat. In later years, Cong. Al Gore Jr. would represent this area. Although we expected to lose this part of the state, our goal was to contain that loss to less than our margin of victory in east Tennessee.

West Tennessee is the Mississippi Delta, dominated by Memphis. Our strategy was to win the west and thereby carry the state. We felt we could win this rich, rural farm country, because it was where Gore's change in positions really caused the most heartburn among voters. The area was fiercely in favor of the war in Vietnam and school prayer. Voters in that area did not like big spending liberals, and they didn't mind letting you know.

Brock had asked country music star Johnny Cash to support him. Cash agreed, but within two weeks, he had endorsed Tex Ritter. Brock asked if he had changed his mind. The story goes that Cash replied something to the effect that of course he would support Bill, adding that Tex was also a friend, so he had to support him too. Everybody was happy.

One of our challenges throughout the campaign was fundraising. This would be the most expensive campaign in Tennessee history, and one of the most expensive Senate campaigns nationwide that year. By today's standards, of course, it would not even be in the top tier. Spending two million dollars on a Senate race in 1970, however, made it number one.

Our finance chairman, Pat Wilson, did a great job of shaking the trees for money, both in Tennessee and nationally. That was before the campaign finance laws brought about by Watergate, and we could accept contributions of all kinds. It was not unusual for me to receive paper bags with cash in them as I traveled the state. People would just hand me cash and say "Remember me to Bill when you see him." In fact, carrying the cash given to me on trips became so problematic that I began bringing an empty briefcase, where I could stash it.

One day, just back from a trip, I walked into the headquarters, threw my briefcase on my desk, and asked my field director, Tom Bell, to go to lunch with me so we could talk about the campaign. In the middle of lunch, I told Tom I had to make an urgent call. I had remembered that my briefcase, which I had casually discarded, contained $15,000 in cash. I made a quick call to my secretary, and the briefcase was put in my desk drawer.

As the campaign went on, the bags of cash kept coming. I did not receive many calls from the White House in those days, but when I did, I was always asked if we had enough money; we even received cash from Bob Haldeman's famous safe at the White House.

President Nixon had a personal interest in the race. He did not like Albert Gore or the principles Gore represented. Nixon wanted him out of the Senate. He decided to make a campaign stop in the state for Brock, just before the election. We had just defeated Tex Ritter by a big margin in the September primary, and had a lot of momentum going into the last few weeks.

Working through Bill Timmons, who had been Brock's congressional chief of staff in the '60s and now worked for Nixon as head of legislative affairs, we nailed down Nixon's appearance in Johnson City. We felt we needed to energize our base and maximize the Republican turnout. The place to do that was east Tennessee. So, after working out logistics and outlining our strategy with the White House, we scheduled a late morning outdoor rally.

After weeks of preparation led by Tom Bell and the head of the White House advance team, Ron Walker, the morning of the event arrived with a major storm warning. After all the planning and work, it was going to rain on our outdoor rally. Having received the weather report, Bob Haldeman called me at about 9 a.m. to see if we wanted to cancel the event. I told him we already had thousands of people waiting, standing in the rain with umbrellas; some had already been there for two hours. "Well, be sure you have a canopy for the president to stand under," he growled. That sent all of us scrambling. We had less than two hours to find and erect a canopy of some kind. By 10:30 a.m., the canopy was in place and the sun was shining.

Haldeman called again from Air Force One. They were thirty minutes out and he wanted a weather report. I told him the sun was shining and everything looked great, including the canopy. "Canopy," he yelled, "if the sun is shining, get rid of the canopy." So we did.

The president's plane arrived just before 11 a.m. Over my walkie-talkie, I could hear, "Rietz, Rietz, where the hell is Rietz, it's raining for God sake." And it was. The canopy was gone, and the president was about to get drenched as he spoke to a crowd that was now more than 50,000.

President Nixon stood, with an umbrella held for him by Tom Bell, and spoke to a huge, enthusiastic crowd holding umbrellas. The pictures were fantastic. The television coverage was terrific. We had taped it and produced a five-minute program that aired statewide the same night. The whole thing created the kind of momentum we needed. As Air Force One left the runway, Haldeman called me one more time, to congratulate me on a really terrific event. No mention was made of the canopy or the rain.

The advertising used by both sides drew a real contrast between the two candidates. I'm sure that was not intentional for the Gore camp, but it was for ours. A key element in our TV campaign was our "man on the street" interviews. Natural light and people's own words all helped turn Brock's understated, soft speaking style into an asset. The Gore TV commercials were highly produced and slick. In one, he rode a white horse with music swelling in the background. His early commercials did not show him with people, and seemed to emphasize what we were saying. In thirty-one years in the House and Senate, he had lost sight of the positions significant to the people of the state.

Our commercials featured lots of people. We taped Bill talking to regular folks about their concerns. One of the best of these clips happened spontaneously. While talking to a small group of people in a parking lot, Brock said to them, "I think Albert Gore has misrepresented the people of Tennessee… and I want to come home, and I'm gonna listen. Not talk down to you, but listen to you. And when you tell me, this is what we like, that's what I'm gonna try to do, because you're paying the bills."

One of the men standing to the left of Brock said, "Congressman Brock, I think that's why people all over this state of Tennessee are beginning to get on the Brock bandwagon at this time right now. Honestly, because of the statement you just made. I've voted Democrat for many, many years. But the time has come and gone. This time it's for Bill Brock. One hundred percent, all the way down the line." Brock replied, with a smile, "Appreciate your testifying, brother."

It was magic. Once the cameraman gave me the thumbs up, I breathed a sigh of relief. I then worried all the way back to the studio, hoping we had it all on film. We did. After a quick editing session, we rushed the finished spot to the TV stations. This was one of our best commercials. It was extremely effective against Gore sitting astride his white horse.

During the final stages of the campaign, Gore put on another commercial that misfired. We were having trouble figuring out why our polls were showing a sudden move from older voters to Brock. Then, during some of the open-ended questions, people starting referring to the fact that Gore was going to take away their Social Security. That rang a bell.

Gore had a new commercial on the air that was meant to attract older voters. He was shown playing checkers with an older person, surrounded by senior citizens. As his opponent jumped a number of his pieces, the senator looked at him and said, "Do that again, and I'll take away your Social Security." This was followed by laughter all around.

I'm sure Gore's campaign thought this was a charming spot that showed a lot of personality and his ability to relate to older people. It was and it did. However, the take away by a lot of viewers was that final line—"I'm going to take away your Social Security." It was a good lesson for me. In future years, I always looked carefully at the words in commercials we were producing, to make sure that there were no unintended innuendoes.

Our most effective TV commercial was a scroll on the screen with an announcer who said: "On gun registration, Tennesseans said no, but Albert Gore voted yes. On busing of school children, Tennesseans said no, but Albert Gore voted yes. On school prayer, Tennesseans said yes, but Albert Gore voted no. On Carswell and Haynsworth, Tennesseans said yes, but Albert Gore voted no. Isn't it time Tennesseans said no to Albert Gore?" We used this commercial during the final weeks of the campaign. We took full-page ads in the newspapers with the same message. In addition, we printed thousands of flyers that said the same thing and distributed them through our volunteer organization. When anyone called our headquarters during those last few weeks and offered to help, we sent them flyers and urged them to canvass their neighborhood. We complemented these attacks on Gore with positive speeches by Brock on the environment, the economy, and education.

All our efforts were bearing fruit, and the national press realized something special was happening in Tennessee. *Meet the Press* invited Gore and Brock on the Sunday program. Brock came out afterwards smiling, saying that he knew he had Gore from the moment the senator walked on the set, intense, uptight, and carrying a large sheaf of papers to which to refer. This was another moment when Brock's easy, low-key way was a real advantage. From that program on, we knew we had Gore on the ropes.

The most talked about part of our advertising campaign was the radio effort. We decided that we needed a way to make Democrats comfortable with voting against Gore and for Brock, particularly in middle and west Tennessee. One of the people endorsing Bill was a well-known Democrat from middle Tennessee, Alf MacFarland. He had served in the administrations of two Democrat governors. We created Citizens for Brock to attract disenchanted Democrats, and announced Alf MacFarland as the chairman. He had a real down-home Southern voice and drawl. It was so distinctive that one night, when I was calling him "person to person" (you did that in those days), the operator said, "Oh, he's that nice man on the radio."

The radio commercials Harry Treleaven put together were sixty second attacks on Gore's positions. Each began the same way, "Hello, I'm Alf MacFarland from Lebanon, Tennessee. I've been a Democrat all my life, but this time I'm voting for Bill Brock." One of the commercials continued: "Now, this may sound a little paradoxical, but I have been angered, as a lawyer, at Sen. Gore's vote on the Supreme Court nominee. As a sportsman, I have been dismayed by his vote on the gun control bill. As a Tennessean, I've been frustrated, angered, and dismayed by his persistent and consistent vote with the ultra-liberal Democrats of the Northeast who have apparently captured the Democratic Party. As a Tennessean, I urge you and all Tennesseans of whatever persuasion, to support Bill Brock for the United States Senate." In other commercials, he talked about Gore's position on school prayer and Gore attending an anti-war rally where they burned the American flag. As we flooded the air with commercials, calls of support came in.

We did have vigorous debates in our steering committee as to the larger aspects of campaign tactics and even strategy. When I presented the advertising campaign, Bill's father looked at me and said he wanted only positive messages, without overt criticisms of Gore. I was twenty-nine and looked around the table at the committee. They were all senior to me in age and knowledge of the state. I thought, "What should I say? How should I defend what I believe?" Fortunately, Bill broke the silence. He stood up and told his father that he believed in the campaign plan, and we were going forward with the ads.

Election nights are always exciting, but this one would prove to be one of the most exciting and interesting I would ever experience. Even political reporters were unsure who would win; a poll done by the *Nashville Banner* showed eleven reporters picked Brock to win and ten picked Gore.

Bill had decided he wanted to be in Chattanooga with his family and friends. I wanted him in Nashville at our headquarters, where the news media and volunteers would be waiting. Although the polls were showing us neck and neck, I was more confident than Bill. I thought our west Tennessee strategy would work, and our volunteers there would not let us down. Bill Morris, a close friend of Bill's, had been our volunteer organizer in the west, and had done an exceptional job. He had even called black preachers the weekend before and convinced some of them that Bill would be the better senator.

We were also doing better than expected in rural middle Tennessee. Our chairman there, Don Sundquist (later to be elected to Congress and then governor), had built a solid grassroots organization. I thought he would be able to reach our vote goals.

To get out the vote in the east, we did what the Republicans had done for years. We used "walking around money" and Jack Daniels miniatures to make sure we drew out every last Brock vote. Walking around money was used in northeast Tennessee to pay election-day campaign workers. The county Republican chairman would receive the money and distribute it to the workers. We were never sure how much of the $30,000 we delivered, in cash, to the chairman actually reached the workers. It was the tradition, however, and we had to live with it.

Bill and I reached a compromise. He would stay in Chattanooga until enough of the votes were in to determine the direction of the outcome. This plan would work, because even though Nashville is an hour away by plane, the time zone cuts right through the middle of the state. It is an hour later in Chattanooga than Nashville. That meant the polls would close an hour earlier in the east, giving us an indication of what was going to happen.

For those days, we had set up a fairly sophisticated vote tracking system and established vote goals for each precinct and county. We had people in the courthouses calling us with totals as they came in. At 9 p.m. in Nashville, I was following the western vote closely. We were exceeding our precinct vote goals, and it looked like we were going to win. That was 10 p.m. in Chattanooga, where the TV was carrying just the opposite prediction. The eastern and part of the middle Tennessee votes were in, and all the pundits were predicting we would lose based on those results, presuming we would lose the west. I felt just the opposite. We were doing well enough in middle Tennessee to make the west the deciding vote.

I called Bill and asked him to go to the plane and come to Nashville.

While in the air, Bill took the lead in the vote count, and the networks declared him the winner. I met the plane and was able to say, "Congratulations, Senator." Of course, he didn't believe me until he turned on the radio.

Brock defeated Gore by a little over 42,000 votes, or by a margin of 51.3 to 47.4 percent. He lost middle Tennessee, won west Tennessee, and carried east Tennessee by a substantial margin. Bill Brock became only the second elected Republican senator from Tennessee. He was one of only two Republicans to defeat an incumbent Democrat senator that year. The next week would find him on the cover of *Time Magazine*.

Many people who have analyzed this campaign came to their own conclusions. Some in the media, perhaps seeking to find some rationalization for the defeat of a Southern liberal, have implied there may have been some underlying racist feelings that lent support to our campaign. We had absolutely no evidence of that. Certainly Bill Brock, in every aspect of his public life, demonstrated a deep and profound commitment to equal rights and equal opportunity for every American as an essential part of his values, a commitment validated by his every act as a congressman, senator, secretary of Labor and Republican national chairman. There was no racial tone to this campaign, nor would he countenance it in any other in which he was involved.

Some have said we won because we had a strong Republican west Tennessean running for governor on the same ticket. There may be some truth to that. Understanding the value of a candidate from that critical part of the state, Brock had actively pressed for a strong gubernatorial candidate from the Memphis area and helped recruit a popular and attractive local leader, Winfield Dunn. Lamar Alexander (later elected governor and then senator) ran a great campaign for Winfield Dunn, the dentist from Memphis. Winfield won, and the fact that Lamar and I worked closely together helped both campaigns.

The truth was that Gore himself was his own worst enemy. He had lost sight of the reason he was elected to the Senate in the first place—to represent the people of Tennessee. Gore had caught Potomac fever. He had decided he wanted to play on the national stage at the expense of working for his home state, and the positions he had taken in the mid '60s were no longer compatible with the views of Tennesseans. In trying to become a national figure, Gore had lost sight of the interests and opinions of people he had represented for eighteen years in the Senate.

On the other hand, Bill Brock's position on the issues agreed with the majority of Tennesseans. In the final months of the campaign, he became an excellent candidate. He was relaxed with voters and they were comfortable with him. He listened to their questions, looked them in the eye, and responded forcefully. In addition, we were able to recruit a large volunteer force of mainly young people. The state Republican Party, at the time, was divided and ineffective. It was controlled by the country club set, and ignored energetic young people who were anxious to be involved in the political process. Bill was under forty and I was only twenty-nine. We vigorously recruited young people for our campaign, and ended up with thousands of volunteers. We also created a research-based campaign plan and then stuck to it. The result was not only victory in 1970, but a complete change in the make-up of the state Republican Party, which would bring victories to the party in Tennessee for years to come.

Truth be told, I had a terrific year in Tennessee. I made life-long friends, had lots of fun, worked hard, and the culmination was a hard fought, well-deserved win. That is politics' greatest reward.

CHAPTER 7

Back to Washington – Bill Mills

During the 1960s, St. Thomas in the Virgin Islands was the place where all the political consultants went after an election campaign. It was their reward after the hard won war, or it was respite to ease the pain of defeat. Whatever the outcome, the months of all-nighters, grueling schedules, and traversing geographic areas took their toll, win or lose. Once the mission was complete, you needed to recharge. So before I was to head back to Washington, D.C. for my next move, Tully Plesser and I took a six week vacation to the Virgin Islands.

During the vacation, I would have time to think about Bill Brock's offer to come back to D.C. to be his administrative assistant in the Senate Office. I liked Bill, and his campaign had been quite extraordinary. We had become a team, with great respect and a good understanding of how we worked together. Previously, I had worked with Bill Steiger on Capitol Hill in communications and, although I had enjoyed the time there, I had missed being in the action of running a campaign. Bill Brock was offering me another role on the Hill, and in an even higher position. This was a nice compliment for all the hard work and success we had achieved. Of course, I still had my office at Allison, Treleaven and Rietz, to which I could go back and pick up where I left off. So, with a few cigars, dinners, and nights out recharging, I spent the trip mulling over my options.

As the vacation came to an end, I knew the answer. Although it would be a privilege to serve on the Hill with Bill Brock, I was hooked on one thing—running political campaigns. When Bill had offered me the extraordinary position, I had already decided against working in any legislative capacity. I was not a policy wonk; I was a campaign strategist. I declined the offer from Bill Brock, and told him I would be more help to the Republican Party as a political consultant. Bill, of course, accepted my no as graciously as any gentleman could. Bill had such strong character and with it a deep, intuitive sense of how things should be run.

This would not be the only time in my career when a wonderful position, working directly in government, would be offered to me. There would be many other offers later in life. In each case, I would politely decline. I was a campaign strategist, and I would look for the next opportunity to work as one.

Once back in Washington at Allison, Treleaven and Rietz, it wasn't long before my opportunity came along. Cong. Rogers Morton, for whom I had worked when he was Republican national chairman, had been appointed by President Nixon to the Cabinet as secretary of the Department of the Interior. That meant he had to resign from his seat as a member of the House of Representatives. There would be a special election in his district (1st Congressional District) on the Eastern Shore of Maryland.

Secretary Morton wanted us to help elect his administrative assistant, Bill Mills, to replace him in Congress. While Bill Mills was earnest, hard-working, and willing, he was no Rogers Morton. Rogers cut quite the swath both intellectually and physically; he was striking, tall and impressive, and at times seemed larger than life. Rogers' constituents loved his sense of humor, his easy-going manner, and the way he could turn a phrase. His voters would miss him, and Bill Mills had some big shoes to fill.

Mills had been a telephone lineman before meeting Rogers Morton during his first campaign. After Morton was elected to Congress, Mills joined his staff and ultimately became his top aide. He knew the district well. He had the Morton organization behind him, and the new secretary of the Interior would campaign for him. Despite Mills' lack of charisma and his clumsy campaign style, he was well financed, and we mounted an effective campaign. There was no television station on Maryland's Eastern Shore at this time. We had to use radio, direct mail, lots of volunteers, and strategic special events.

Bill was a tireless worker on the campaign trail. He was a committed and an honest man. He and I spent day after day traveling the Eastern Shore, from Easton to Salisbury to Westover to Princess Anne, shaking hands, meeting the voters, and hearing about their concerns. Maryland, especially the Eastern Shore, had an economy built around the water. Ports, sailing, boating, commercial and recreational fishing, supplies, crabbers, and shrimpers comprised a large part of the economy. These watermen loved Bill. He knew many of them by name, and had spent time with them working on issues. This group was a powerful influence in the election. As in all special elections, the voter turnout was light. It was close, but we won a hard fought campaign.

Money has always been the mother's milk of politics. In more than one case, it has been the downfall of a politician. The so-called "scandal" began innocently enough, with a phone call to me from Morton. He said he wanted to see me about the Mills campaign, and asked if I would stop by his office at the Department of the Interior. I was happy to do so. I had stayed with him at his home in Easton and played more than one game of tennis with him. I never missed an opportunity to spend time with Rogers. He had such a big stake in this race, as it was his district. When I arrived at his office, "Rog" greeted me and then closed his office door. He said he had an envelope that he wanted me to give to the Mills campaign treasurer. When he handed me the envelope, he said in a straightforward, matter-of-fact voice, "Be careful with this, because it contains $25,000 for Bill's campaign." I said of course I would, thanked him for all his advice, and left. In 1971, two full years before Watergate would become a household word, this was everyday business for most political campaigns, both Democrat and Republican. I did not even give the entire situation a second thought. I had a campaign to win.

In the days before the Watergate scandal, accepting cash was perfectly legal, as long as it was reported. It wasn't until the summer of 1974 that I learned the contribution that was given to me by Morton had not been reported by the Mills campaign. Unfortunately, it was also in 1974 that I learned that the money had come directly from Bob Haldeman's safe in the White House. It was the front-page story of *The Washington Post*, and Cong. Mills called me in California, very distraught. This would develop into a real political scandal. The Mills campaign and Watergate would be interconnected, and bring about a tragic end.

CHAPTER 8
Young Voters for the President

In 1971, the voting age for president in the U.S. was reduced from twenty-one to eighteen, a change that had been proposed by Sen. Brock and Cong. Bill Steiger. The 1972 elections would include a new group of young voters, able to participate in a presidential election. The Nixon inner circle had some concerns on what the impact of this would be on his re-election campaign. From a public opinion standpoint, eighteen-year-old voters could present a very big problem for President Nixon, who, at the time, was viewed as anything but pro-youth.

Sen. Brock had a conversation about these first time voters with the president in May 1971. President Nixon was interested in the large number of young people Brock had recruited for his Senate race, and wanted to know if the same could be accomplished in the upcoming presidential campaign. Brock said he was sure it could be done, and told the president he would work on a plan. The president responded that if his Attorney-General John Mitchell agreed, he would implement it. When Bill called me to discuss, I agreed to help.

I contacted Jeb Magruder, who was setting up a skeleton staff for the re-election campaign. He invited me to a meeting at the new campaign headquarters, where we agreed that I would join the campaign and work on a young voters plan with Brock. I left my position at Allison, Treleaven and Rietz and moved into the re-election campaign headquarters as an advisor to Jeb Magruder, to start the process of developing a youth strategy. This was exactly the kind of challenge I sought.

Brock and I, along with Tom Bell, who had joined his Senate staff, worked on a plan focused on creating an independent youth organization within the re-election campaign. We felt young voters would not be attracted to either the Nixon re-election campaign or the Republican Party. We wanted a separate identity and independence from the main campaign. Our plan was put into operation through the Young Voters for the President (YVP) organization, created July 1, 1971.

Early research showed that the president's policies, except for the war in Vietnam, were popular among young people. There was substantial media-created peer pressure preventing them from supporting the president. It had become an "in" thing for them to be publicly against President Nixon. It was at this peer group pressure that the YVP campaign was aimed. The initial YVP plan stated the objectives clearly: "young people will work for the President if we ask them and they will vote for the President if enough young people are working for him." The essence of the plan was to use the residual support for the president among young people to attack the peer group pressure by involving thousands of them in the campaign in as public a way as possible.

Our research showed that only twenty percent of first time voters (age eighteen to twenty-five) for this presidential election were college students. The other eighty percent were working. Our challenge in recruiting would be to locate the non-college young people. Our plan focused more than half of our resources on them.

The good news in our research was that a large number of first-time voters wanted to be involved in the political process. In other words, if we asked them, they would join. The YVP campaign plan called for involving 500,000 people under age thirty. This volunteer base was to be used for the real campaign work—voter registration drives, door-to-door canvasses, telephone surveys, etc. Emphasis was to be placed on public involvement. This would force the media to initially report that all young people were not against the president, and in the final stage of the campaign, that the majority of young people were for him. We felt that only through this public exposure would a majority of young Americans ever become comfortable voting for Nixon.

By the end of August 1971, Sen. Brock and I completed a fifty-page YVP strategy and campaign plan. It included targeting of specific states, cities, counties, and college campuses. Our budget was $2.5 million, with a paid staff nationwide of fifty. (By the end of the campaign, we would also have over one hundred full-time volunteers.) Brock would serve as chairman of a congressional advisory committee comprised of young members of Congress. We would recruit a well-known young person to be YVP chair, while I would serve as the full-time director of the YVP campaign.

Brock and I flew to Key Biscayne, Florida to present the plan to Attorney General John Mitchell, who Nixon had chosen to chair the re-election campaign. He and Nixon were taking a few days off and had invited us to meet with them. We were pleasantly surprised when Mitchell approved our entire program.

There were only a few of us in those early days of the Nixon campaign. Jeb Magruder was the day-to-day campaign manager, with a staff of about six. There was the beginning of an advertising group under Peter Daley called the "November Group," an advance team, and fundraising arm. The main Nixon campaign headquarters was located one block from the White House, at 1701 Pennsylvania Avenue. My office was situated just a few doors down from Magruder's office. Over the next few months, this small team would grow into a staff of several hundred. Nixon's team would eventually bring in Fred Malek to share the day-to-day operational responsibilities, working with the campaign chairman, John Mitchell.

I suggested that it was very important for the office of the YVP to be autonomous and not be shoved into the same office space as the senior campaign officials. We were following through with the idea of independence that we outlined in our original proposal: independent office, independent budget, and independent strategy. That way, the YVP team could conduct their meetings and have young volunteers stream in at their own pace. Across from 1701 Pennsylvania Avenue was an empty storefront property I thought would make the perfect location.

Marilyn Johnson, whom I knew from her work on the Brock campaign, was my assistant. During Brock's campaign, Marilyn had worked for Lewis Dale, who had helped with Brock's fundraising. She had the look and style of a librarian, but was extremely attractive, smart, and diplomatic in every situation. Marilyn was one of the most efficient people with whom I have ever worked.

I had only been with the campaign for a few weeks when Jeb came into my office looking nervous. He closed my door and asked, "Ken, in those campaigns that you worked on previously, had you ever 'infiltrated' another campaign?" My answer was no. After a pause, he continued, "Would you know how to do it if someone asked?" I thought about it for a minute, paused, and then said, "I could probably figure it out."

Over the years, I have often thought long and hard about this answer. Why hadn't I just passed? I was hired to create a youth campaign, excitement enough for a thirty year-old political consultant. There was plenty on my plate, and we were having a run of success. Yet, standing in front of me was Jeb Magruder, from the White House inner circle, asking me to help. Had I answered the way I did because I was anxious to please those invisible people at the White House, or was it just plain ego? I'm not sure. But I took on the challenge. It was a mistake that I would pay for, in many ways and for many years.

Political pranks or dirty tricks have been a part of American politics since the beginning of our party system. They can be traced back to Jefferson, and there are lots of examples in the political history books. The 1960s were rife with those types of antics. It was common knowledge, inside the Beltway, that the Johnson Democratic campaign team had run one of the most corrupt elections in 1964. The team had infiltrated the Goldwater campaign with CIA Agent E. Howard Hunt. He posed as a volunteer, where he gained access to advanced copies of Goldwater's speeches and fed them to the Johnson White House. This caused Goldwater to complain that whenever he put forth an initiative, the White House immediately trumped it.

Each campaign had opposition research staff as part of their team, and they would come up with pranks. These were standard tactics at the time. Some were more serious than others, but most were just nuisances. For instance, we sent pizzas and other fast food to Gore's receptions during the Brock campaign to create confusion. We also had Senator Gore paged at football games on Saturdays all across the state, knowing Tennesseans would boo politicians announced on the loud speakers at sporting events. Pranks, nothing more.

When Jeb asked me to find someone to work in the Muskie campaign headquarters to let us know what was going on, I didn't think too much of it. Obviously, from his tone, it was important. Jeb said the White House wanted us to do it, so I felt justified.

While I had worked for Cong. Bill Steiger, I had met a former FBI investigator named Jack Buckley. Jack was an investigator for one of the House committees. He and I had lunch together from time to time, and were on friendly terms. I didn't know much about what he actually did, although I had heard a lot of stories from him about the old days in the FBI. I called him and asked him to meet me for lunch at The Palm. This was a convenient meeting spot, as the Allison, Treleaven and Rietz offices were in the same building. At the end of the lunch, I asked Jack if he would be able to help me find someone to work as a "volunteer" in the Muskie campaign. He said he would think about it and get back to me.

Since I was under a lot of pressure to develop a nationwide YVP strategy and plan, I quickly forgot about my meeting with Jack and moved on to the real matters at hand—the young voters.

Several weeks later, while I was still working on some details alone in my office, there was a knock on my door. It was Jeb. He stuck his head into my office and asked me if I had had any luck. He added that it seemed the 'folks across the street' (code for the White House) were getting anxious about the idea of planting someone in the Muskie campaign. They wanted to get someone in there sooner rather than later. With all my work on the youth campaign, I had almost forgotten about the request and my conversation with Jack. Since it had been a few weeks, I thought the idea had been forgotten. I told Jeb that I would look into it and check with my contact. I called Jack, who suggested we meet again over lunch at The Palm. (No wonder my friend's nickname, later provided by Gordon Liddy, became "Fat Jack.")

Over lunch, Jack told me he had been successful in recruiting a former informant of his, who now drove a taxi. This man was willing to be a volunteer to the Muskie campaign for $500 a month, which would have to be paid in cash. The fee or compensation was required, Jack explained, since the work would require a lot of time with the Muskie campaign and it would be taking time away from his taxi driving. As we discussed the limited details that I knew about, I told Jack I needed to discuss the compensation details with Jeb Magruder, since this was his request, and that I would get back to him. Once Jack heard the mention of Jeb's name, he paused as if there was something else. As I looked up, Jack became very serious and said, "Ken, there are a few other requirements that I think are very important." He continued, "First, Ken you should never know the taxi driver's name, second, my name should remain unknown to Magruder or anyone within the White House or the campaign team. Third, Ken, I insist that my name should never come up in conversation, and you keep me out of this." While I thought this was a bit odd and perhaps dramatic, especially since this was just a prank job, I took it as a remnant, left over from Jack's spook days. So, I agreed.

When I reported back to Jeb, he was excited. Immediately, he said, "They will be pleased with this. Let's move forward." I let Jack know and continued with my real work on developing our campaign. While I went back to work trying to figure out how to win the new youth vote for the president, Jack Buckley and his taxi driver went about their business. I was busy building a campaign around the research we had compiled and connecting with both college and working young Americans. Our days were long and our schedules busy.

Brock and I had received approval from Mitchell for our plan, strategy, and budget. I believe that Jeb and the White House accepted our concept because they really didn't know what else to do, and it was better than doing nothing at all about the new youth vote.

The Nixon campaign had hired Peter Dailey and Associates to form an in-house ad agency called the November Group. They created all the advertising for the campaign and were helpful in designing the YVP logo and basic materials. Later on, I believed we needed someone independent who was more in touch with youth culture to design our campaign posters and materials. For this, I hired a California agency experienced in marketing movies to young people and asked them to handle some of the additional work.

Working with Tom Bell, we were able to learn some of the key issues that concerned young people. We used opinion polls, research, and focus groups. Our information was showing that peer pressure had a lot of influence on who young voters liked as a candidate. When they talked about

Nixon and his strengths and weaknesses while in groups, they were extremely negative about his personality and style. However, when they were questioned alone, young people would discuss some of the positive aspects of his presidency. We knew this was important, so in order to recruit the volunteers our campaign strategy called for, we would have to attack this peer pressure against Nixon.

The overwhelming issue was the war in Vietnam. On this, young voters were divided. Most in college were strongly opposed to the war. The majority of those in the workforce were supportive of Nixon and his efforts in Vietnam. In each group, the issue was emotional. This became a critical point for all of us, working on the strategy and developing the tactics to reach both groups. Research in the early '70s showed there were more young people in the workforce than in colleges and universities. This provided a roadmap for us. The data allowed us to divide our youth campaign into two segments. One was to be aimed at non-college students, the other targeted at the campuses. We focused on those in the workforce first.

One interesting fact that came up in our focus groups was that most young people did not care much for the existing political establishment. This was true for both workforce and college student demographics, but particularly with college students. This information did not go unnoticed by the campaign of George McGovern. His political team used this attitude, labeled "anti-establishment," to ultimately fuel his campaign. College students were anti-establishment, anti-political parties, and anti-war. We knew we would need a well-planned mechanism with creative tactics to get around this "anti" culture. We thought long and hard about how to do that.

As I had spent my campaign life steeped in building volunteer efforts, I knew that our volunteer core would be critical to our campaign. To manage and promote this effort, we needed key people around the country. Our strategy seemed simple and it was: recruit a large volunteer base of young people, and put them in front of all campaign events where the president was in attendance. We wanted to surround Nixon with young people, especially whenever he was on TV. This was intended to impact the peer pressure young people were feeling. We needed to change the general perception, in both media and among young voters.

I also believed having young people voting for the first time would be a historic moment for our country. We wanted to encourage all young people, not just Republicans, to vote and to join the YVP. Our volunteers would be youth-ambassadors to educate young people on how to vote, encourage voting, and getting involved with politics regardless of party affiliation.

We set the 1972 Republican National Convention at Miami Beach as our pinnacle moment to complete our recruitment of young voters. With all the news coverage of the convention, we knew that if we could have young people visible, it would have a great influence on the outcome of the election. We wanted our young voters program to peak at the convention, and we put the timing of our campaign together so that it would.

In the beginning, I am not sure Jeb thought we could actually win the youth vote. He was operating under White House orders from Bob Halde-man to create a campaign "to satisfy the old man." In a short time, I became used to this shorthand for Nixon. Without ever mentioning his name or saying "the president," dozens of people at the White House would invoke the power of the presidency every day. I believe that invocation of power was a factor that ultimately destroyed the Nixon presidency.

By late fall, McGovern, who had been viewed as the Democrat dark horse, was starting to pick up speed on college campuses, gaining on Muskie. While he was not viewed as a serious candidate at that time, there was growing concern in the White House about his success on campuses and our ability to counter his up-tick in the polls.

Jeb called after a few weeks and asked me how it was going with the Muskie volunteer and if we were finding anything out. This being the last thing on my mind at that point, I had to confess that I really didn't know. Sternly, he said, "Look into it."

I called Jack to arrange a meeting. Of course, he insisted on meeting at The Palm for lunch. I asked him how things were going with our volunteer, and he said they were going very smoothly. Our taxi driver had been well received, and he was acting as a courier and sometimes even drove Sen. Muskie. His main job was taking memos and letters that needed the senator's signature from the campaign office to his office on Capitol Hill. From time to time he picked up the Senator's dry cleaning, and actually even joined Muskie for a sandwich after driving him home. As far as real information was concerned, we weren't getting much. Jack then handed me an address list intended for Christmas card recipients from the Muskie campaign, plus the senator's schedule for the next week. And that was that.

When I reported back to Jeb, we had a good laugh about the dry cleaning errands and the sandwich at Muskie's home. With that, I gave him the two documents—the senator's schedule and his Christmas card list. Then I went back to the job I was hired to do, the youth campaign.

Time Magazine, in an article titled, "G.O.P. Reach to Youth," described our efforts this way:

> In the offices of the Committee for the Re-Election of the President (CRP), the official campaign headquarters, some of the desks are still empty awaiting the arrival of a staff—including Attorney General John Mitchell, who is expected to take up his old post as campaign manager. But one part of the Nixon drive has been operating at full tilt for weeks; the G.O.P. Youth Division is wasting no time going after the 25 million young men and women eligible to vote for the first time this fall. The early activity is spurred by the sound premise that the youth vote could be the key to a second term in office for President Nixon…
>
> There a staff of twelve professional political workers—all pointedly under thirty—directs the most sophisticated youth campaign of any candidate. Its goal: to organize young volunteers across the country for doorbell ringing, voter registration, and grassroots organizing. With registration among the young currently running two to one Democratic, the G.O.P. hopes that its youthful volunteers can persuade enough of their contemporaries to vote Republican to offset the Democrats' nominal advantage.
>
> To identify potential volunteers—and voters—the Youth Division relies on computerized analyses of young voters. The result is a carefully laid out plan that, unlike the strategies of most of the Democratic candidates, does not rely primarily on college students.

Like their parents, non-college youth are primarily interested in the less glamorous economic issues: mortgage interest rates, unemployment, taxes for schools, government services. To reach them, the G.O.P. will send battalions of organizers into areas where new housing construction—and young families—is concentrated. G.O.P. statisticians have discovered that in California, for example, 2.4 million of the 2.5 million new voters live in ten of the state's fifty-eight counties. G.O.P. bigwigs will visit vocational schools as well as universities.

By December, we had a small nucleus staff. YVP was starting to catch on. George Gorton, a young college activist from California, had joined us to organize the college campuses. Tom Bell, who had been with me in the Brock campaign and preceded me to the Nixon campaign, was setting up a field organization. The volunteer and recruitment programs were taking off. Angie Miller (who would become my second wife and mother of my son, KC) was organizing the Nixonettes (young females) and Nixonaires (young airline stewardesses).

Ken Smith was working on research and analysis, Angela Harris was handling communication, and David Chew was working as a deputy to Tom. We also had Bob Haldeman's son Hank, John Ehrlichman's son Peter and daughter Jan, future President Gerald Ford's son Jack, as well as future Cong. Tom Davis. It was a terrific group of young people. All of them have had successful careers since and remained friends throughout the years. As the campaign grew, others would be added, but this was the team that brought it all together. We had developed a plan that included holding mock elections on college campuses, organizing non-college young people in the targeted states, recruiting celebrities, and having a major presence at the national convention in Miami.

We knew that young people did not trust Nixon, but our work connecting the young voters with our young recruits was going well. We felt it important that Nixon's connection with youth be consistent, and include younger members of Congress and staffers on the Hill. To lead that effort, Sen. Brock chaired a national advisory committee made up of young members of Congress, which included Congressmen Bill Steiger (WI), Bill

Archer (TX), Don Rumsfeld (IL), Ed Biester (PA), William Whitehurst (VA), Lou Frey (FL), Manual Lujan (NM), Jerry Pettis (CA), and Bill Frenzel (MN). These young congressmen were regulars on college campuses, and knew how to present our campaign mission and the president's values in ways that would resonate.

Our speakers' bureau started an aggressive effort to book them into venues on campuses, where they would deliver speeches about current issues and the policies of the Nixon administration. In most cases, the Republican Party was not mentioned. At the end, the speaker would talk about the need for young people to be involved in the political process. They stressed the importance of first time voters participating and voting in the upcoming presidential election. Finally, they would mention how to become a volunteer at the YVP.

The role of surrogates became extremely important in our campaign as well. Using young celebrities and high profile individuals as the faces of YVP in various outreach efforts, the tone of Nixon's campaign began to shift. We would use them in advertising, news events, as speakers, and to give talks when they were available. We recruited young celebrities to assist in this effort. These included actors Clint Eastwood, Chad Everett, Kathy Garver (*Family Affair*), Stanley Livingston (*My Three Sons*), Gary Collins; former Miss America, Mary Ann Mobley; Miss Texas, Brenda Fox; and Miss Teenage America, Janene Forsyth. We recruited young athletes, including ice-skaters Dorothy Hamill and Jo Jo Starbuck (1970-72 U.S. Pairs Figure Skating Champion Team); Olympic track star Lacey O'Neal; and football stars Howard Twilley, Nick Buoniconti, and Robert Griese (Miami Dolphins); Lance Alworth (Dallas Cowboys); Marlin McKeever (LA Rams); and Tommy Mason (Washington Redskins).

To lead our surrogate effort, we recruited a young actress named Pam Powell, who was the daughter of actors Dick Powell and June Allyson. We eventually named her chair of the YVP, and she went to work for us full time. Her message was the same: YVP offered young people an opportunity to get involved in the political process and make a difference. Here is *Tribune* staff reporter Sharon Lacey's description of Pam:

> Although Pam Powell stands approximately 4 feet 11 inches, she is one of President Nixon's 'biggest' supporters. And although

she's 24, and feeling 'quite old', she is on a campaign tour throughout the United States in her capacity as the National Chairman of
the Young Voters for the President persuading 18-year-old voters
to re-elect the President.

Our goal was to recruit several hundred thousand young volunteers nationwide by the time the national convention took place, and we had to build
those efforts state by state. Tom Bell was great at recruiting responsible and
passionate young people to lead our state campaigns. Without the support of
cell phones, Internet, or even phone banks, we used lots of face-to-face time.
Once we had a lead in a state, it was the state YVP chairman's responsibility
to take control and involve the young person. For many of these individuals,
this was the first time they were exposed to the political process.

With the YVP staff, I was relentless about recruiting. Each week, we had
staff meetings. I would go around the table and ask questions like: "When
you gassed up your car, did you speak to the attendant and tell him about the
election?" "When you see a young person, do you ask them if they registered
to vote?" "How many YVP volunteers did you recruit last week?" I emphasized that we had no litmus test for YVP recruits. We wanted first-time
voters in our organization, regardless of their political persuasion. Involving
them in the process and allowing them to feel the power of political activism,
they would recognize the importance of our cause.

At times, it was difficult to keep this philosophy going. There were
political leaders in Washington who wanted us to turn the effort into a
Republicans only program. We knew this would fail. The key to recruiting a
large number of new voters was to keep the effort pro-involvement first, and
pro-Nixon second. Our youth oriented surrogates were key to this effort. We
found the "working" new voters by going door-to-door in neighborhoods
known to have large numbers of new residents. We organized block-can-
vassing parties and, in most cases, took the media along to show them our
recruitment efforts. Even the materials we used to recruit were youthful and
did not mention the Republican Party. They were focused on the new law
allowing eighteen year-olds the right to vote for president and the nationwide organization we were building.

It worked even beyond our hopes. As our early focus groups had shown, young people were excited about being involved in the electoral process. If we could keep them from getting into ideological debates and focus their attention on being involved in a new movement, they would respond. To this day, I still meet people who thank me for giving them their first taste of political activism.

Internally, our team was dynamic and full of opinions. The anti-war protests were growing across the U.S. and in Washington. When we arrived at our campaign headquarters, we had demonstrators in front of the building yelling and spitting on us. It wasn't unusual to be criticized by our peers and the news media. Behind closed doors, we also had many debates about Nixon's policies.

Each week, Jeb had a senior staff meeting for all of us responsible for departments within the campaign, to keep apprised of our work. It was in early December 1971, at one of these meetings, that I met G. Gordon Liddy. Jeb introduced Gordon as our new campaign lawyer. Then he turned over the meeting to Gordon so he could introduce himself. Gordon started with a brief bio on his work history and then, without warning, he took out a lighter, lit it, and held his palm over the flame, stating that he wanted to show us how tough he was. He added that he would do anything to get the president re-elected, and said we should all stay out of his way. Nothing could have prepared us for this. No one really knew what to make of Gordon. From then on, we all tried to do what he had asked us to do—stay out of his way. Since my office was just around the corner from his, I would run into him on a regular basis. I tried to avoid him and focused on work.

Shortly after Liddy arrived at the campaign, Jeb called me into his office and said he didn't think we were getting our money's worth out of the taxi driver. He decided that I should turn control of that operation over to Liddy. I was relieved and readily agreed. Not only did I have no interest in controlling this project, but I also thought it unnecessary and a distraction from the work I had at hand with our YVP campaign. I thought if Nixon could win the youth vote, he would be re-elected, and that was how I wanted to spend my time. Jeb said he would tell Gordon to see me.

My first and only real meeting alone with Gordon Liddy was right out of a spy novel. He asked me to meet in his office, because he had just had it swept for listening devices. He was really serious, and spoke in a low, unemotional voice. He asked me about my contact working on the inside. Finally, Gordon stated he wanted me to turn over the names and relationships. Remembering that Jack Buckley did not want people to know his name, I said I would have to see if I could set up a meeting. Liddy went on to tell me how I should arrange the meeting: my contact should meet him at the corner of Pennsylvania Ave. and 19th St. the next day at 3 p.m. Liddy added that my contact should look for someone wearing a trench coat and carrying a rolled up newspaper. I thought this all highly dramatic. At the time, I had important work to do on the New Hampshire primary, as it would be the first real test for our YVP campaign. So, happy to get out of this situation, I called Jack and he agreed to meet Liddy. The meeting took place, and that was the last I heard of the matter.

It was not until later, during the Watergate Senate hearings, that this all became known as the "Fat Jack Operation." It would be some time before I would know about the details of this meeting and its implications. In fact, it was not Liddy but Howard Hunt, subsequently one of the Watergate burglars, who met with Fat Jack. Later, when Jack testified during the hearings, he stated that under the direction of Liddy and Hunt, a studio had been set up with a desk full of listening devices and photography equipment, and the "agents" were required to take photos of all the people and correspondents that the taxi driver was transporting. They had also begun recording conversations that Sen. Muskie had while riding in the taxi.

CHAPTER 9
New Hampshire (and Beyond)

For most of us, 1972 was a year of extraordinary, rollercoaster events. On one hand, it seemed full of promise. There was hope for peace, new innovations in space and technology, and new policies on human rights, women's rights, and the environment. From a political perspective, the potential for peace seemed attainable, or at least the escalation of war seemed to be held in check. The last draft lottery took place. President Nixon spent eight days in China meeting with the People's Republic of China's Mao Zedong. Nixon and Leonid Brezhnev signed the SALT I treaty, as well as the Anti-Ballistic Missile Treaty. Kurt Waldheim was elected as the new secretary general of the United Nations. The U.S. and seventy other countries signed the Biological Weapons Convention, an agreement to ban biological warfare, and the United Nations Conference on the Human Environment was held in Sweden.

Here in the U.S., the 92nd Congress sent the proposed Equal Rights Amendment to the states for ratification. Shirley Chisholm, the first African-American congresswoman, announced her candidacy for president on the Democrat ticket. Women were finally allowed to compete in the Boston Marathon. Bob Douglas became the first African-American elected to the Basketball Hall of Fame. The FBI hired female agents for the first time. The first financial derivatives exchange opened in Chicago as the International Monetary Market.

There were massive leaps on the technology and innovation fronts. President Nixon ordered the development of the space shuttle program, and Apollo 16 launched. Apollo 17 was launched, and would be the last of our manned missions to the moon. The first paper on recombinant DNA was published, revolutionizing biotechnology and the way we look at genes and viruses.

On the other hand, 1972 was a year of terrorism, death, natural disasters, and fear. Several tragic terrorism events occurred in 1972, including the Munich Massacre at the Olympic Games, the Burundian Genocide of 500,000 Hutus, and the Portuguese Army killing of four hundred Africans in Mozambique. After the British Army gunned down fourteen unarmed nationalist civil rights marchers in Londonderry, Ireland, the Irish Republican Army (IRA) retaliated with Aldershot, Bloody Friday, and Claudy, to name a few. There were four hijackings, one in the U.S. and three in Europe. Of eleven significant plane crashes, which killed more than seven hundred people, one included the incredible story of the Uruguay rugby team, which survived harsh conditions by cannibalism. More than 5,000 people died as a result of earthquakes in Iran. In the U.S., the Black Hills Floods in South Dakota killed 238, coal sludge spills in West Virginia killed 125, and Hurricane Agnes killed 117.

In the spring of 1972, the streets of Washington, D.C. were full of unrest. The number of protesters and picketing grew around the White House, the Capitol, and the city, and there was a crescendo of tension. Nixon had ordered the mining of Haiphong Harbor in Vietnam on May 8th, which set off a series of protests, especially among young people, who began to take to the streets and congregate.

The 1972 New Hampshire primary was scheduled for the first Tuesday in March. From the perspective of our team within the YVP, this would be our first significant test. I wanted to make sure that all our activities and tactics were right on target in the months leading up to the event. This field test would prove to the White House inner circle and the doubting pundits that the strategy we had developed in the fall worked. In his book *An American Life*, Jeb Magruder points out that pollster Bob Teeter told the White House:

> On the basis of his first-wave polls, had recommended that we halt all activity among young people, lest it prove counterproductive. He was concerned (as were many others in the Republican Party) that if we registered young voters, we would just

be registering people who would end up voting Democratic... Furthermore, there was the risk that activity by young Republicans would only inspire a greater amount of counter-activity among young Democrats.

At this point, there were additional external pressures bearing down on the campaign team, and even rumblings within the Republican Party that Nixon might be challenged. Eventually, liberal Pete McCloskey of California and conservative John Ashbrook of Ohio entered the race. McCloskey ran as an anti-war and anti-Nixon candidate, while Ashbrook opposed Nixon's détente policies towards China and the Soviet Union. In addition, McGovern's campaign was picking up steam as he continued to build momentum among anti-war youth, especially around colleges and universities. With Gary Hart as the campaign manager, McGovern also focused more on the state caucuses and less on the primaries. Our goal was to outperform them, take away voters from McGovern, and continue to make the Nixon campaign as youth focused as possible. Although most of the pundits thought Nixon would not attract any of these new young voters, we hoped to prove them wrong.

Our first activity in New Hampshire was aimed at college campuses. George Gorton had developed a mock election model for college campuses, designed to help us come out looking good. He hoped that once it succeeded in New Hampshire, we would implement it in various other states with universities and colleges. The system was very simple. He would ask an official organization on the campus, like the student council or fraternity council, to sanction the election. Then, he would have all the candidates listed and open the election to all students. The key to our success was voter turnout.

Working with volunteers he recruited, George developed a sophisticated turnout effort aimed at getting dormitories, fraternities, and sororities to vote. George went after the body of influence on a campus. At the time, college students were not used to voting, and a large percentage of them were not interested. The mock elections helped educate them on the election process. If we could get our voters to vote during the two or three-hour period when the mock election poll was open, we had a good chance to do well.

It worked. With a few weeks left before the New Hampshire primary, we started winning mock elections on college campuses across the state. Normally, this would not have been news. But in that year, with college students having the right to vote for the first time, and those same students being viewed as anti-war and anti-Nixon, to win on college campuses was real news. As the press continued to pick up the story, it helped us back in Washington, where some of the cynics in the White House started to become believers.

Our other goal in New Hampshire was to make young people highly visible in the campaign. For this, we focused on the election eve rally that the campaign was sponsoring in Manchester, NH. We wanted to surprise the press and media and the general public by turning the event into a youth rally, with tons of young people front and center, supporting Nixon. This meant that instead of having VIPs seated in the front rows, we would put in young people, so the press and television could capture the images as Nixon addressed the crowd.

The question was where to get enough young people to show the Nixon team, the public, and the competition that we were gaining ground. We had a great volunteer core in Boston, New York, and Connecticut, so we decided to bus them to New Hampshire. Our Northeast coordinator, Cathy Bertini, took on the logistics. She assured me that buses would arrive on time and we would fill the hall with young people. (Cathy's amazing organization skills would ultimately take her to the U.N. as head of the World Food Program.) Once we knew our logistics and had a plan, I went to Fred Malek to outline what we were proposing. He had joined the campaign as deputy campaign manager and was my new boss. Fred was responsible for New Hampshire, and knew that an empty hall the night before the election would be trouble in the press. It was risky, but we knew we had the Nixon supporters in the right age range, and they were willing to stand up and be counted. Fred was on board, and gave us the go ahead.

The one thing we had not planned on was the weather. Sure enough, on the day of the rally, not only did it snow, there was a major storm. I knew immediately that Fred would be upset. A West Point grad, he expected you to deliver. Throughout the day, he and I waited together, anticipating impending doom. Having no cell phones at the time, we had no way of contacting the buses regarding their locations. We received updates from local officials on the weather and the conditions, but nothing from our team.

Fred and I stood at the back of the auditorium as it filled up with older voters and the front rows stood empty. The clock was ticking. Nixon was backstage. Members of the news media had gathered in the hall. Magruder was asking us every few minutes, "Where are the kids?" I just kept saying over and over, "They will be here."

Cathy was true to her word, and thirty minutes before the scheduled rally, buses started to arrive from New York and Boston. Our new voters for president began to file in, cold and somewhat tired, but filled with enthusiasm. And then the chanting started—"Four more years, four more years." Suddenly, the room was full of energy.

Our young volunteers would stay in New Hampshire and help turn out the vote for the primary the next day. Our total young volunteer strength in the state would be more than 1,000 young voters.

The plane that was scheduled to pick us up to fly back to D.C. was barely able to land in the terrible storm that had developed. As it tried, it weaved to and fro. The takeoff was very scary for all of us as we clung to our armrests. We held our breaths and concentrated on the fact that our rally had been a big victory for us.

Safely back on the ground in D.C., I knew another challenge lay ahead. Our New Hampshire success had to be amplified across the U.S. between now and the convention. From now on, all tactics, outreach, and recruitment would be focused on the convention. Our volunteers had been invaluable, and we hoped that by the November elections we would be able to recruit over 500,000 volunteers nationwide.

By early spring, the YVP campaign was going very well. We had won eighty percent of the mock elections on college campuses across the nation. Our recruitment program was ahead of schedule, and the media had started to pay attention to the Nixon youth campaign. We were also giving the McGovern campaign some heartburn. After New Hampshire, it was clear that Nixon's campaign was gaining traction with young people. It was covered on television, press outlets were writing articles, and people were talking about it on Capitol Hill.

A Council Bluffs, Iowa newspaper described our progress:

> An efficient 15 member Washington staff, plus numerous field operatives, a speakers bureau, a college directorate, a convention section and the Nixonette program to enlist young women are all part of the youth campaign…But the guts of the operation, and the key to hopes of a November victory, lie in the 125,000 young volunteers which Rietz says have been signed up by organizations he has established in thirty states. All fifty states will be organized by fall.

In fact, it was going so well that the president himself couldn't believe it.

As the YVP campaign continued to make progress, Haldeman called with an unusual request. He wanted to know if I could get a few of the "campaign kids" to meet with the president. "He wants you to come over and tell him why things seem to be going so well with the YVP. He's having a hard time believing the reports," he said. I said yes, and asked him when. He said in about an hour. I said, "Mr. Haldeman, you understand that our campaign team has a casual dress policy. I can't guarantee that any of them will be wearing a tie." He said, "Even better." Having never seen the president and his staff in anything but suits, I worried and thought, "This will be interesting."

When I called the team to prepare for the meeting, I wanted to make sure we had charts and graphs to back up our success. Most importantly, I wanted the team to be honest with their comments and recommendations to the president. I knew that if we were going to succeed, this was the time to show our president the real personality of the YVP.

An hour later, I joined members of the YVP staff in the Oval Office. They included Ken Smith, Angela Harris, George Gorton, Angie Miller, Lea Jablonsky, and Tom Davis. This was a lively, smart, polite group, committed to the cause, which I was proud to introduce to the president. At his request, we were joined by Tricia Nixon and Ed Cox. Later in life, George Gorton would continue his career in political campaign strategy and helm the efforts in Russia of Boris Yeltsin's campaign for president. He would also manage Pete Wilson's campaigns for the Senate and governor of California. Tom Davis later served fourteen years in Congress.

Haldeman's briefing to the team was quick: "The president wants a general description of the campaign and where we stand. Give him the data to back up all the work the YVP group is doing so we can justify the effort." He added, "You only have twenty minutes, so make it count."

I started out with a brief outline of the campaign, and then George Gorton talked about the mock elections and our technique. Nixon was fascinated by our college efforts, and asked a lot of questions. At one point in the discussion, Nixon directed a question to George Gorton, and without hesitation, George looked at the president and said, "Mr. President, young people don't like you. And we are trying to change that." I took a deep breath, waiting for the reaction. Nixon laughed, we all laughed, and then we quickly returned to the discussion. Nixon seemed satisfied with what he was hearing. Then he looked around the room, smiled, and launched into a fascinating discussion about China. In February of 1972, Nixon had made his historic trip to China. It was on his mind, and he wanted to talk about it with young people.

Our allotted twenty minutes grew into thirty, and then an hour. Haldeman was shuffling in and out of the Oval Office, looking at his watch and giving me signals. I could only imagine the scheduling problems we were causing, but this was a once in a lifetime opportunity, and I wasn't about to end the meeting.

Nixon talked about his trip, and the role he felt China would play in the future. He talked about Vietnam and his concern about bringing that war to a close. He asked how young people felt about his China trip and his efforts on the war. He expressed great concern about his unpopularity with young people and what he might do about that.

We were frank with him, and told him that young people just did not relate to him. George Gorton said, "Mr. President, sometime when you are at San Clemente, take a walk on the beach in a windbreaker. Let young people see you in something other than a suit." This, of course, set the stage for Nixon's famous walk on the beach. There he was, on the cover of *Newsweek*, on the beach in his windbreaker, dress slacks... and black wingtip shoes.

Good idea. Bad execution. The picture came to symbolize President Nixon's awkwardness when not in coat and tie. It failed in its purpose. Young people did not relate; they snickered.

We spent almost two hours in the Oval Office with the president that day. He listened and we talked. He talked and we listened. When we left, we were enthusiastic about the president, the campaign, and the future of the country with him at the helm. We had seen a rare glimpse of a candid, dedicated Nixon. We saw a man devoted to peace, and to building a bridge to China aimed at stabilizing the world. More than a year later, that meeting would make the disappointment of Watergate even sadder.

There were those at the White House who wanted to misuse our volunteers. Jeb Magruder came to my office one day and told me he was getting pressure from "across the street" to do something about the Daniel Ellsberg rally planned on the Capitol steps later that month. Ellsberg had authored the "Pentagon Papers," which had been released to the *New York Times*. They had given a negative view of the conduct of the war in Vietnam, and infuriated Nixon and the White House.

"Charles Colson wants me to see if you can get some of your kids to stage a counter-rally to Ellsberg," Magruder said to me. This was fairly typical of the requests coming from Colson, and it was the kind of thing I wanted the YVP to stay away from. I refused. A few days later, Jeb was back. This time it was "the old man" that wanted something done about the Ellsberg rally. This was something that happened on a fairly regular basis; you had to try to interpret the code. Did this really mean the president wanted something done, or was it just Colson invoking his name?

I was, of course, too junior to call the president, and I knew better than to raise the issue with Haldeman. If I refused Magruder, he could find someone else to run the YVP effort. I knew that creating a counter-rally would not be in the best interests of the YVP effort, so I offered a compromise. We would send a few volunteers wearing Nixon buttons to stand quietly at the rally, in full view of the press. This seemed to satisfy the folks "across the street."

CHAPTER 10
Camp David, Watergate, and the Draft

To most of us in the campaign, Watergate seemed like a third-rate burglary. We paid it little attention, except for the involvement of James McCord mentioned in the papers. He was the head of security at the campaign headquarters, and the majority of us knew him and, in fact, really liked him. It was quite a surprise when we heard the news. Most of us shook our heads and asked each other "Why?" As little bits of news came out through the summer, I kept an ear to the ground, finding it a bit troubling. In fact, when I thought about it, I had growing doubts about it being an independent operation by a group of misguided operatives. But I was busy running the YVP campaign.

We had our sights set on the convention. Our YVP footprint had grown across the country, thanks to the commitment of our volunteer core. We had designated state chairmen who were building grassroots coalitions county by county. The enthusiasm was contagious. We were gradually shifting the perception of Nixon among young people.

Following our meeting with the president, Bob Haldeman asked me to brief the White House staff on the YVP campaign. He told me the president was impressed and wanted to be sure the entire staff knew of our progress and our goals. Tom Bell and I briefed the White House staff and answered their questions. There was still much skepticism, but we thought we had made progress in helping them understand our campaign.

It was a few days after that briefing when I received a call from Haldeman asking me to go to Camp David and brief the president and his Cabinet. That amazing experience is described in the introduction of this book. It provided me with an opportunity to solicit support and participation by Cabinet members in our convention program.

Sometime during late June or early July, Jeb Magruder called me into his office. Jeb had been a volunteer in several congressional campaigns, but had never been involved in the management of any campaign at any level.

Therefore, he often sought my advice on sensitive political issues. He asked me for my views on the Watergate break-in. I was straightforward. I told him that if the campaign or anyone involved with the campaign had been involved, we should admit it and take whatever disciplinary action was required. I told him that the campaign was going extremely well, and that we were going to beat McGovern unless this break-in grew into a full-scale scandal. I said, "At this time, we can take the hit. Let's not let it get out of control."

I later learned that Jeb was the person who, after the approval by the attorney general, had authorized the funding of the break-in. Jeb had plans to run for office in a few years, and was not about to damage what he considered a bright political future. He had asked me if I would be willing to run his campaign for secretary of state in California. Admitting a campaign link to the break-in, he would have to admit his involvement.

Although I don't know why the plan was developed, I think I know when it was approved. It was during a weekend that Nixon and his inner circle went to Key Biscayne. Because we had requested an additional budget for the convention, I was asked to go to Florida and stand by, in case there were questions regarding the YVP campaign. Nixon stayed at what reporters called the winter White House, a retreat owned by Bebe Rebozo. Charles Gregory "Bebe" Rebozo was a Florida banker and businessman who became one of Nixon's close friends and confidants.

Jeb Magruder was at the Nixon compound at Key Biscayne, and we planned to meet for dinner in Miami on Saturday night. I was to call Jeb and schedule a time and place. During the day, I spoke with him on three different occasions to determine the time to meet. Each time we spoke, he was more irritated. It seemed that things were not going well in his meetings with Mitchell. It wasn't until 9 p.m. that we finally met for dinner.

Jeb explained that he had brought a file of plans for the campaign to be approved by John Mitchell. However, each time they tried to discuss campaign matters, Mitchell was distracted. "Martha [his wife] was creating a nightmare for the poor guy. What should have taken us an hour took us all day," Magruder said. "I don't even think he read half of the stuff I gave him to approve. He seemed to be preoccupied, and just signed off on documents as they moved across his desk."

The only plan in which I was interested at the time was the YVP convention budget. Jeb assured me that it was approved. It was years later that I learned the funding for the Watergate break-in plan might have been one of the documents Jeb took to the meeting for approval. I have never been convinced Mitchell knew what he was approving. So, I believe there was a plan created by the "darksiders," in the White House, taken to a meeting by a very ambitious Jeb Magruder and approved by a distracted attorney general.

I did not have much to do with Martha Mitchell. She was one of those individuals in the administration who we all tried to avoid. Volatile and unpredictable, she was John Mitchell's cross to bear. Martha would pick up the phone and call any reporter, at any time of the day or night. She would discuss campaign plans, criticize people involved in the campaign, and attack members of the press corps and politicians. These calls usually happened after she'd had too much to drink. Nixon's inner circle was deeply worried about her. They were trying to devise a plan to get her away and out of the spotlight. Magruder had proposed to send her on a two months cruise, but she would have none of it.

Since I had not spent much time with her, I was surprised one day when my assistant, Marilyn Johnson, told me Martha Mitchell had come to the headquarters to see me. "Really?" I thought to myself, "What could this be about?" Of course, in typical unpredictable Martha fashion, when I walked into the reception area, she greeted me and handed me a parrot in a cage. "I'm going out of town for a week," she said. "Be sure you take good care of him until I get back." She turned on her heels and walked out, leaving me standing dumbstruck and holding a parrot.

I was shocked and more than a little irritated. However, my feelings were nothing compared to those of Ken Smith. When I called him to my office and delivered the parrot to him, he stood there just as dumbstruck. Then I warned him to keep it healthy until Martha returned, or there would be hell to pay.

The Watergate break-in was just what it had been called: a third-rate burglary. If the campaign had treated it as such and admitted to being involved, it would have cost a few people their jobs, and perhaps some people would have served some brief jail time. It would not have become the scandal it did. Nixon would still have won the election. There would not have been a cover-up that cost so many people their futures and led to the resignation of a U. S. president.

Later, in 1973, I was advised by my attorney to leave Washington due to the Watergate investigation and all the press surrounding it. I was lucky not to have been sucked into the cover-up scandal. Magruder told me several years later that when he and Haldeman were talking about people in the campaign that could be trusted to go along with the cover-up due to their loyalty, I was high on the list. Fortunately, I was not asked.

During the campaign, whenever Magruder did talk to me about Watergate, I told him the same thing—get the truth out before the election, and we would still win. Regrettably, here was an example of losing sight. Instead of looking at what was best for the campaign and the country, Jeb was worried about his personal future and the future of his allies in the White House. People looking out for themselves and their friends are what I believe caused the cover-up and ultimately cost the presidency. Magruder was protecting himself and being loyal to Haldeman. Haldeman and Ehrlichman were being loyal to Nixon. Nixon was protecting and being loyal to his longtime friend, John Mitchell. In the end, they all lied and paid the price.

The summer of '72, before the Republican National Convention most of us spent very little time thinking or worrying about the Watergate break-in. We were focused on the campaign and on what needed to be done to win. Our YVP campaign had grown into a major force in the re-election effort. We now had hundreds of thousands of volunteers we could count on. We had celebrities and athletes speaking on our behalf, and a national convention plan that would focus attention on the youth support for Nixon.

One of the biggest concerns of the campaign leading up to the convention, was how to address the planned demonstrations by anti-war activists. Nixon's inner circle was so concerned that they approached me, in their usual fashion, to see if I could get a handle on the situation. Jeb Magruder had come to me with one of those requests from "across the street." At the time, a group of young anti-war activists were camped on the sidewalk outside the White House. Magruder and others were convinced that these "hippies" were planning to disrupt the convention. Magruder wanted to know if I had a young person who could spend a couple of nights on the sidewalk with the protesters and find out what they were talking about. Against my better judgment, I said yes.

I asked George Gorton to find someone who was willing to sleep on the streets. George found Ted Brill. George specifically said that Ted wanted to be paid. I told George, rather off-handedly, that it was okay to pay Ted, but to please make sure it was in cash. Then I went to Bart Porter, the campaign cash master, and got a few hundred dollars to give to George. Only when the Watergate investigation was underway did I learn George had converted the cash into a check, which he then presented to Brill. So much for stealth.

Meanwhile, we were progressing well on our plan for the Miami Republican National Convention. We were continuing to build our momentum, and we started getting names of people who would attend.

Bob Haldeman's son Hank had come to work in the campaign. With his youthful exuberance and shoulder length hair, he was nothing like his crew cut, straitlaced father. Hank was an anti-war Nixon supporter. His views were typical of many of our new recruits. He fit the mold of what we were trying to do with the YVP movement; young people, although they felt like they did not fit in with conservative Republicans, came to us wanting to be involved in the campaign. One summer night, Hank invited a few of us to his home for dinner. He said his dad loved to make Mexican food and wanted to cook for us, as Hank's mom was going to be out of town.

None of us wanted to turn down this opportunity, but we were nervous about accepting. The Bob Haldeman we knew was the strict perfectionist. I had heard his wrath over the walky-talky in Tennessee when I was putting the Nixon/Brock event together. He was known to chew people out for everything from appearing in a photo of Nixon (staff were not supposed to be seen), to drafting a memo that was too long or too confusing. We had no idea what to expect.

He was charming and a good cook. The food was great, and the non-alcoholic Christian Scientist margaritas were fantastic. We talked about the campaign, about his trip with Nixon to China, and the war in Vietnam.

Then came a moment I will never forget. Haldeman looked at me after a sip from his margarita and said, "What is the one thing the president can do before the election that will have an impact on the first-time voters?" I said, without hesitation, "End the draft." Hank quickly echoed my statement, as did George Gorton. Haldeman listened, and then went on to other topics. A few weeks later, I received a rare telephone call from him. He simply said, "I can't tell you about it but, you will be very interested in the Presidential Proclamation we are issuing tomorrow." That was it. He said goodbye and hung up.

The next day, President Nixon ended the draft. To this day, I don't know whether or not the few of us having dinner at Bob Haldeman's home that night really had anything to do with the change in policy. I like to think we did, and I feel pretty good about that.

CHAPTER 11
The Convention

San Diego, California had originally been selected as the host city for the 1972 Republican National Convention, to be held August 19th to 23rd. Then columnist Jack Anderson discovered a memo written by Dita Beard, a lobbyist for the International Telephone and Telegraph Corp. (ITT), suggesting the company pledge $400,000 toward the San Diego bid in return for the U.S. Department of Justice settling its antitrust case against ITT. Once this story broke, the Republican National Convention had to make a last minute change.

This was a logistical and communication challenge for all of us involved. Since Miami Beach had hosted the previous convention, it was the logical choice. The pressure was on to produce an event that would positively impact the electorate. Generally, planning for a national convention took about a year; in this case, we only had three months. In addition, the change in venue and location would impact transportation, accommodations, schedules, celebrity participation, and police protection. One advantage was that most of the Nixon convention team, led by Bill Timmons, felt strongly that Miami Beach might be a better choice, as it would be easier to control potential anti-war protesters. By this time, the Youth International Party, or Yippies, had grown their grassroots mobilization and were hoping to take a stand at the convention. With the disastrous anti-war riots at the 1968 Democrat Convention in Chicago in mind, we knew special precautions would have to be taken.

With all of these considerations, it was felt that the geographic location, experience of the police, and the overall political support made Miami Beach a good decision. The mayor's office, police department, and other local officials of Miami Beach would be much more cooperative in controlling crowds. Also, because of the causeways and bridges, it was easy to control access on and off various locations around Miami Beach. Of course, as the convention began, this type of access had a negative effect, since it was so crowded that at times it was difficult to move key people around.

Our East Coast YVP membership was strong. Now, with the convention on the East Coast, we had a better chance of mobilizing those individuals.

While for most of the other divisions of the campaign the convention was the beginning, for us it was our final objective. We felt that if we were successful in demonstrating to the nation that there was youth support for the president, it would dramatically reduce the youth peer pressure against Nixon. We would undercut McGovern's effort to be seen as the new voter's candidate.

As our convention program began to take shape under the leadership of Tom Bell, we noticed that many more volunteers than we originally thought possible were signing up. Our goal had been to recruit 2,000 YVP volunteers to pay their own way to the convention, and we would cover the cost of lodging and meals. We planned a program of speakers, entertainment, and political briefings. Each volunteer would have the opportunity to attend the convention. Tom was so successful that we ultimately had to accommodate 3,000 YVP volunteers.

Despite the press comments at the time, we were not paying young people to attend the convention. Dan Rather went on the air and, referring to Chicago Mayor Daley's political machine, compared our YVP volunteers to Chicago sewer workers, who were encouraged to participate in local politics while on the city payroll. We felt Rather and the press had unfairly tarnished these young volunteers.

One of the important aspects of the program was to give the young volunteers a real national convention experience. Like all such conventions, the one in Miami Beach was crowded, with space on the convention floor tightly controlled. With the convention manager, Bill Timmons, we worked out a system for our YVP volunteers to rotate into the gallery seats and get some experience on the convention floor. This put them all in the convention hall at one point or another. Every single one of them was able to go home having been in the hall and having participated directly in the 1972 convention.

We also put together a series of YVP events outside the hall, which included speeches, briefings, and meetings with our congressional surrogates, Cabinet members, and celebrities. We held an exhibition tennis match between Stan Smith and Peter Curtis. A youth rally was held as the final experience of the convention.

Regrettably, the accommodations were a big disappointment. Today, one of the jewels of South Beach is the Delano Hotel. In 1972, it was in a state of advanced decay. It was rat infested, moldy, and dirty, and unfortunately it had been chosen, probably due to its low tariff, as the YVP headquarters. When it was assigned to us by the RNC, we had no idea of its condition. Initially, I wasn't aware of just how bad the hotel was, as I was staying with the rest of the senior staff at the campaign headquarters hotel, which was the Doral Beach. After the first night, Tom Bell asked me to visit the Delano to calm everyone down. When I did, I found a very unhappy group of young people, most of whom had decided to go home at that point. Once I spoke with them about what was in store, the coming events, and the experience they had before them, the vast majority decided to stay.

Moving the 3,000 young volunteers around Miami Beach was no easy task. We rented buses to shuttle them between the hotel, convention center, and our special events. The buses never seemed to be where they were supposed to be. Almost any time of day, I could hear one of our staff on the walkie-talkies calling for Bill Russo, our man in charge of the buses. "Russo, Russo, where the hell are the buses?" Sooner or later, Bill always delivered. In fact, one late night when our rented buses did not appear, Bill and John Stamps, who had worked for me on the Brock campaign, commandeered a city bus. They convinced the driver of the importance of the convention and put it to work, taking our volunteers back to the hotel. For many years after, when I ran into Bill Russo, I would say, "Bill, where the hell were those buses?"

One of the advantages for the senior staff was transportation on the water. As part of the presidential group, we had access to a variety of boats and docks. Instead of taking buses or ground transportation to the convention hall, many of us used boats. This was especially helpful because during the convention, most of the roadways were crowded and at times impassable.

Throughout the convention, we had anti-war demonstrators doing their best to disrupt it. Several times, as I arrived at the convention hall, I would have to walk through tear gas, armed police, and spitting protestors. We had not learned anything of value from Brill's overnight sidewalk sleepovers outside the White House. The anti-war protesters were well organized. They had walkie-talkies for communication and seemed to know as much about the schedule as we did. They tried to disrupt everything from our YVP meetings, to the sessions in the convention hall, to press interviews. On more than one occasion, the tires on our buses were slashed.

Timmons managed the Republican presidential candidate's convention operation in 1968 and again in 1972. One of the things that he always did was assign his various directors, of which I was one, floppy red tennis hats so everybody could identify us. We looked ridiculous, but we could readily tell who was responsible for specific activities. There we were, in a room full of adults, sitting at our desks with our red hats on, looking ridiculous.

In addition to the visibility our young people would have in the convention hall in front of the TV cameras, we planned a final youth rally at Miami Marine Stadium. The idea was that after Nixon was re-nominated and gave his acceptance speech, he would go immediately to our YVP rally. Nixon would be in front of 3,000 young people with the TV cameras rolling. The whole nation would see that Nixon was acceptable to young people. The problem we faced was that the White House would not commit to Nixon attending the rally. We decided to go ahead and hope for the best, and continued planning the rally without guarantee the president would be there.

We asked Mike Curb, the president of MGM Records and YVP volunteer, to line up entertainment for our rally. Mike delivered. He did a terrific job, recruiting entertainers including Sammy Davis Jr., the Mike Curb Congregation, and an entire cast of celebrities.

Finally, it was the last day. We had worked all day on the staging and rehearsals, and were about to get the rally underway when we heard from the escort we had assigned to Sammy Davis Jr. that traffic was a nightmare, and Sammy was stuck in it. He was our keynote entertainer. It would take him at least an hour to get to the stadium, long past his scheduled appearance. We wanted to have the rally fully underway when Nixon delivered his acceptance speech in the Convention Hall. We needed Sammy on stage at a specific time, and as Marine Stadium was on the water, we decided to bring him in by boat.

The problem was that I forgot to tell the Secret Service. As we prepared to get the show underway, I saw the boat carrying Sammy approaching the stage. I felt relieved until suddenly several Secret Service officers rushed by me with their guns drawn. "Stop," I yelled, running after them, "that's our boat!" Finally, after a few tense seconds, we drew a sigh of relief as the guns were holstered. In my head, I saw tomorrow's headline, "Secret Service shoots Sammy Davis Jr." Thankfully, the crisis was averted.

We started the concert with a stadium full of young people. All the networks were covering our event. No one could believe we had done it. We still did not have a commitment from Dwight Chapin and the presidential advance team that Nixon would appear. So, I took a chance and told the media the president would be attending our rally. I could not believe, after all those months, that the White House would let us down. The only way I could keep the press committed and interested was to tell them the president was coming after his speech. I figured if he didn't, what was the worst that could happen? We needed the network cameras, and nothing was going to stop me.

As I watched the president's acceptance speech backstage on a monitor and saw it coming to a close, we put Sammy Davis Jr. on stage to begin his performance. The call I had been waiting for came, and I crossed my fingers. Dwight Chapin said, "Ken, the president will be there immediately following his speech, and he wants you to escort him onto the stage."

Initially, I was excited that the president would attend and had asked for me. Then I realized my clothes were unacceptable for the privilege. I was wearing a t-shirt and jeans, in case I had to pitch in wherever needed. I had worked in the humid, ninety degree Miami heat since early that morning, and had been moving equipment and setting up the production area. There was no time to shower and change. What the president needed was one of our YVPs, and who better than our chairman, Pam Powell. I quickly said, "Dwight, I am honored, but I think Pam Powell, our chairman, is the right person."

Pam Powell and the president walked on stage as Sammy Davis Jr. and the Mike Curb Congregation were performing. The audience went wild. The chant started: "Four more years, four more years." The kids were standing and cheering. The TV cameras were rolling, and the flashbulbs popping. We had worked and planned a year for just this moment; then Sammy and Nixon made it magic. First, Sammy pulled out his camera and took Nixon's picture. Then Nixon took the camera and took Sammy's picture. The following week, Nixon taking Sammy's picture was the cover of *Time Magazine*. The nation saw a playful Nixon with one of our leading entertainers, in front of thousands of cheering kids chanting, "Four more years, four more years."

The strategy worked. The next day, Nixon left Miami for a tour of key states, and everywhere he went, there were cheering young people at his rallies. While we recruited many, most of them were new voters who just wanted to be involved. They now found their interest in Nixon acceptable. Ultimately, this would contribute to a Nixon sweep in the election. More than fifty percent of the votes he received were from new voters. On election night, both Bob Haldeman and John Ehrlichman told Tom Bell and me that without the youth campaign, the election would have been much closer. "You gave us the sweep," Haldeman said.

As in any election, I don't think you can look at any one event or activity and say that is the reason for the win or loss. I do know we had a good strategy, a good plan, a great team and many dedicated young people having their first experience in national politics. By the end of the campaign we had recruited more than 500,000 young volunteers. The result was not only a winning campaign, but also many young people thrust into leadership roles for years to come.

CHAPTER 12
The Elephant Wins

At the convention, we accomplished what we had set out to do. The pictures of Nixon surrounded by young people would continue to appear throughout the fall and into Election Day. We changed the perception of Nixon, not only with the media, but with the voters. We encouraged young people to vote and participate in the political process, regardless of party affiliation.

Since most of our team had worked tirelessly for a year, we were all exhausted after the convention. Having barely slept over the previous few months, I was exhausted and needed peace and quiet. I wanted to be totally removed from anything political. I flew to Nashville for a few days of rest and to visit a friend. Since I really wanted privacy, I did not tell anyone where I was headed, not even my assistant, Marilyn Johnson. Imagine my surprise, when I entered the terminal and someone was waiting for me, yelling, "Ken, Ken, over here. The White House is looking for you. The president wants to talk to you."

I went to a pay phone and dialed the White House switchboard. I was surprised when the White House operator said, "Ken, the president is anxious to speak with you, but he is in a meeting." I left a message with the operator saying I would call back with a number when I was in my motel room.

Arriving at the motel, I called back and left the number with the White House operator and thought I would hear back another day. A little wine, a beautiful woman, and some R&R was the plan for the night. About 30 minutes later, when completely undressed, the phone rang. It was a White House operator. She asked me to wait, and then the president came on the line. He asked me what I was doing and I told him. He laughed out loud, and asked me to describe my date who was with me in the room. After a brief description, we began discussing the reason for his call. He thanked me and told me how grateful he was for all the hard work of the YVP team. He talked about all his post-convention campaign stops throughout the country, and said that at every rally there were lots of young people shouting, "Four more years, four more years." With a smile in his voice he said, "Those young people have really energized our campaign."

Once I returned to D.C., I continued to monitor the media and press coverage. We focused the YVP campaign on recruitment and organizing for the autumn get-out-the-vote effort. To help recruitment our California ad group put together a youth-oriented series of posters. We distributed thousands, and asked our volunteers to post them wherever young people congregated.

The first one was a 22" x 44" color poster. A bald eagle was pulling at a huge, unfurling banner that read, "For the first time in 20 years we are spending more on human resources than on defense." Centered under the banner was a large photograph of President Nixon sitting casually on some White House steps. He was smiling broadly, chatting with a blond little boy dressed in a red jacket, white knee-highs and black shoes. Surrounding this central picture were eight circles, each featuring an illustration accompanied with wording pertaining to the illustrated subject.

During the heat of the fall campaign, most of us didn't think much about Watergate. We didn't talk about it, but it was always there in the back of our minds. In those days, campaign headquarters seemed to have two distinct factions: Fred Malek was one faction, and Jeb Magruder the other.

Fred Malek was an amazing person and a wonderful mentor. Having graduated from West Point he was a successful businessman who specialized in operations and efficiencies. He served in Nixon's first administration as deputy under-secretary of the Department of Health, Education, and Welfare, under Secretary Robert Finch. Nixon's team positioned him to serve as deputy chief of the Committee to Re-Elect the President in 1972. Fred was running the day-to-day operations, and I reported directly to him. Throughout the process, I learned a lot from Fred on how to streamline the roles and responsibilities of people, and how to stay focused on milestones. He really was a great manager, and the campaign ran a lot more smoothly due to his influences. With the entire operational infrastructure aligned and the success of the convention behind us, there was a positive feeling in the air, and we were confident of victory.

On the other hand, Jeb Magruder and his staff were becoming more removed from the day-to-day campaign and more secretive. I would see Gordon Liddy moving in and out of closed-door meetings in Jeb's office. When I talked to Jeb, he seemed disconnected from the campaign. He started to look like he had the weight of the world on his shoulders, and he probably did.

Looking back, there were little things that gave me pause. Many things were just blips on the radar, and the frantic pace of the campaign gave us little time to stop and ponder what was happening around us, like the day I took Fred LaRue to the airport.

LaRue was an experienced Mississippi politician. He was one of the architects of Nixon's Southern strategy. He was the political advisor to John Mitchell, was consulted by the Nixon inner circle, and was part of the re-election team. Since he had many contacts in the South, he was constantly traveling back and forth to the region. In his role, Fred was secretive and did many things for Mitchell he never discussed. Fred was a true Southerner. He was very social, enjoyed his whiskey, and loved talking about my favorite subject, politics. He and I spent many evenings together discussing politics, strategy, and some of the challenges of the new Southern strategy. We soon became good friends.

During the fall, LaRue asked me to take him to the airport for a trip that he was taking to Mississippi. As we arrived at the airport, Fred said he was carrying a briefcase that he didn't want to take through security. In those days, they hand searched all carry-on bags, as there were no screening devices. With that, Fred handed me the briefcase and added, "Take good care of this while I am gone. It's important." He smiled, said he would see me in a week, and left me with the mystery briefcase. I drove back to the campaign office, put the briefcase in my trunk, and promptly forgot all about it.

During that week, as I went about my usual routine, working long hours during the day, grabbing drinks at various bars at night, I parked that car wherever I could find space. I often ran late, so many times it was in a no-parking zone or near a fire hydrant. One time that week, I carelessly left my car parked, overnight, in downtown Washington.

When LaRue returned later that week, he anxiously asked me for his briefcase. "Oh yeah, the briefcase." I paused, "Actually, Fred, I left it in the trunk of my car all week. I kind of forgot about it." He looked at me, stunned. "Go get it, Ken," he said sternly.

When I returned with the briefcase, he was obviously relieved, so I asked him what was so important about it. He opened it and showed me $30,000 in cash. It had been riding around in my trunk. I was shocked, but was relieved that I did not lose it. When I asked him where he got the cash, he gave me that little LaRue smile that said nothing and meant mind your own business. Based on subsequent events, it may have been part of the hush money paid to the Watergate burglars.

A few weeks later, LaRue was headed out of town again. This time, he brought a woman's dress on a hanger in a plastic cleaning bag, and asked me to look after it while he was away. He winked and smiled, then said, "This time, don't leave it in your car."

This time, my curiosity would not allow me to resist a closer look at the mysterious dress. I found bunches of $100 bills carefully pinned inside. Throughout the week I took good care of that dress, and upon his return, delivered it back safely to LaRue. He was later branded, by the news media, the "campaign bagman."

He was a friend and I was saddened, years later, when he was convicted and served six months in prison for his involvement in the events surrounding the Watergate cover-up. He had shredded financial documents of the re-election committee, and was convicted for obstruction of justice.

Throughout that fall the campaign continued to pull ahead. You could feel the buzz, not only around our offices, but throughout the nation.

An article, dated Friday, Sept. 15, 1972 in *The Honolulu Advertiser*, described our success:

> The myth that young people are solidly behind McGovern has been shot full of holes by all the recent nationwide polls,' says the leader of Hawaii's Young Voters for the President.

Fred Hemmings Jr., cited this week's Gallup poll showing President Nixon leading McGovern 61:36 among voters under thirty years old.

'Hawaii's young people are helping to dispel the McGovern myth. We have around 200 young volunteers campaigning for the President and more are joining us every day.' Hemmings said.

As for the president, he was confident of victory, and was beginning to focus on the next four years. One day, late in September, Haldeman called me to ask if Sen. Brock and I would meet with the president that week. Bill and I were scheduled to meet with him in an office he kept in the Executive Office Building for non-official meetings. Nixon felt people were more relaxed in the Executive Office Building than in the Oval Office. Nixon wanted a candid discussion, and felt this to be the right setting. We all discovered later that there were no recordings made of meetings in that office.

Bill and I didn't know what the meeting would be about; however, whenever you were asked to meet with the president, it was exciting. Since Bill and I had worked together and he was the chair of our YVP National Advisory Committee, we assumed it would be about the final days of the re-election campaign. In the next few days, we put together some information and status updates so we could be prepared. That morning, we met at my office to iron out any outstanding issues, and then walked across the street to our meeting.

Once we settled into our chairs, we were both surprised when Nixon, sitting with his feet up on the coffee table, started talking about the RNC. Nixon was a pretty formal man, so this was his way to relax and put us at ease. As he continued, he said the RNC had become old and out of date. He said if we were ever to become the majority party, we needed to do what we had done in the Brock campaign and the YVP campaign—appeal to young people. He wanted something fresh and new. He talked about the current leadership very disdainfully, and said that we needed to "get the old guys out and put some young people in. We need to do what you did in Tennessee and the YVP." He went on to ask us to write a reorganization plan for the RNC that would "move us toward the majority in my second term."

We were both surprised and honored to be asked, and this was something both Bill and I really wanted to do. As we were leaving after an hour and a half discussion, Nixon asked us to deliver the document to him before the November election so we would be ready to implement it at the beginning of the second term.

Bill and I left the meeting excited by the prospect of actually making changes that would help our party move in a new direction. Both of us realized the meeting was an extraordinary experience. We heard our president, without any outside interference, talk about the country and the future of our party. It was in this casual atmosphere that we both saw a very candid and determined Nixon. We were impressed with the fact he was thinking about the future of our party and wanted to embrace change.

Bill and I agreed that I would draft the document based on the meeting. We would discuss ideas on the phone while we both focused on our present jobs. After numerous discussions, Bill and I presented the final plan to Bob Haldeman before the election.

On October 30, 1972, we delivered a twenty-five page memorandum for the president. It included,

1. Redefinition of the role of the RNC as one of achieving a national "New Majority" identification by:
   A. Recognizing it is only the President who has achieved a new majority, and he should be its principal spokesman.
2. Reorganization of the RNC to focus its activities solely on the election of the "New Majority" by:
   B. Specifying the role of the Chairman of the RNC as the President's full- time political staff director.
   C. Centralizing all national political activities, including the Senate and House Campaign Committees, Finance Committees, and patronage, under the Chairman of the RNC.

D. Professionalizing both the RNC and State organizations.

E. Professionalizing House and Senate candidate recruitment and election campaigns.

The last few months of the YVP campaign were hectic. We organized a '50s Nostalgia Concert Tour to help with our volunteer recruiting program. The concerts were free to those willing to sign up. One of our California volunteers was Tom Campbell, a well-known disc jockey. He worked with us to package the tour and was the M.C. of the shows. Performers included the Coasters, Bobby Lewis, Gary U. S. Bond, Danny and the Juniors, and the Five Satins. All the entertainers donated their time. In Chicago, our concert featured the Osmonds and Frank Sinatra.

We asked our state chairs to merge our volunteer recruits into the voter turnout program of the Committee for the Re-Election of the President. We encouraged all involved to join the voter canvas programs.

From the Sunday, September 17, 1972 *Milwaukee Journal*, "Senator Goes a-Calling at Grass Roots":

As a topless Glendale man discovered Saturday, you never know who's going to come calling when an election campaign is underway.

In this instance, it was a United States Senator from Tennessee, William Brock, accompanied by two Nixonettes and trailed by assorted cameramen and reporters.

The man, who had stripped part way down to wash his car, seemed more interested in how his bare chest might look on television than in politics. But he told Brock he planned to vote for President Nixon.

In fact, in a door-to door tour of 10 houses on N. River Forest Dr. north of W. Silver Spring Rd., the chairman of the Congressional Advisory Committee of Young Voters for the President found no George McGovern backers at all.

An October 24, 1972, article in *Newsweek Magazine* described our success in organizing the youth vote:

> At the beginning of this year's presidential campaign, it was generally thought that Sen. George McGovern would capture the majority of the college vote. But according to a recent *Newsweek* poll Richard Nixon now commands fully 48 per cent of the campus vote.

The results of our nationwide voter contact efforts were reflected in the article "YVP makes Door-to-Door Canvass" from the Myrtle Beach (SC) *Sun-News*:

> Young Voters for the President (YVP) and other youths are in the process of making a door-to-door canvass of every household in Horry County to determine who is for the President and who is going to vote Nov. 7.
>
> YVP, a youth branch of the committee to Re-Elect the President, is headed up in Horry County by Mrs. Kyle Macrafic of Myrtle Beach Air Force Base.
>
> 'These youths are asking people if they are going to support the President on Nov. 7,' Mrs. Macrafic explained. 'They are also going to ask them if they are registered and in cases where they are not, they will explain the voter registration process and offer assistance to get everyone registered.'

Nixon won in a landslide, with sixty-two percent of the vote. As we celebrated the victory, I could not help but think about all we had accomplished. Our small team of under-thirty year-olds had built, from scratch, a nationwide campaign organization of more than 500,000 young volunteers. Most people and pundits in 1972 had thought it would be impossible to get the new voters to support President Nixon. We proved them wrong. On Election Day 1972, we monitored eighty precincts with a high concentration of young voters; fifty-nine of those precincts reported. Of those, the president carried forty-six. It is my firm conviction that the president won the eighteen to thirty year-old vote.

In looking back, the Watergate break-in had no impact on the election. It didn't hurt the campaign, though it certainly didn't help. To this day, I do not understand why anyone thought it was necessary. When I think about it now, I only think about people losing sight of their real objective.

CHAPTER 13
The Inauguration

At this stage in 1972, I was not aware of any problem in my eyesight. It was hard for me to see in dark restaurants and bars, but bumping into tables and chairs as I moved through a room did not seem out of the ordinary to me. It was several years later, when I was diagnosed with Retinitis Pigmentosa, that I learned the loss of night vision is one of the early signs.

Following the election victory, a number of the campaign staff were asked to move to the inaugural committee. Jeb Magruder and Fred Malek took up the reins as chairmen, and I joined the team as a group director. In that role, my job was to produce all of the public events, except the swearing-in ceremony and the parade. This meant I was in charge of the inaugural balls and concerts and the receptions. To assist me, I moved most of the YVP leadership to the inaugural committee. The group of us had become close, and we worked well together under pressure. We were committed to Nixon and the party, and felt honored that we continued to have a place on the president's team. We had only a little more than two months to plan and implement all the activities and events that surrounded Inauguration Day, set for January 20, 1973. There was no time to decompress from the election as we started on our next mission.

As we continued to put our inaugural plan together, Thanksgiving was rapidly approaching. I received a call from the White House. Our YVP group was going to be acknowledged during a dinner for Republican Party leadership and the Cabinet. There would be a reception and dinner, followed by entertainment. We were invited for the entertainment after dinner. While all the VIPs were seated up front, we were in the back, thrilled just to be there. Little did we know what the president had in mind. During a pause in the entertainment, he took the stage and asked the members of his Cabinet to join him in a standing ovation for the YVPers. The president, the Cabinet, and all the formal guests, without hesitation, stood up and applauded, giving us all a moment we would never forget.

During December, all of the hotel workers in Washington were on strike. The inaugural balls became a particular challenge. The idea of arranging them in hotels with limited or no staff was not an option. On top of the general strike issues, Nixon had not been a friend of organized labor, so the strikers were not cooperative. On more than one occasion, there were threats to make a total mess of the inauguration activities.

As I faced this dilemma, wondering what I could do, I received a phone call from Bob Haldeman, who said, "The president does not want to cross a picket line to attend an inaugural ball." He asked, "Would it be possible to move the inaugural balls to public buildings?" When Bob Haldeman made a suggestion, you just didn't say no. I responded, "It could be done." He told me to prepare a plan and we discussed possible sites, including the newly opened Kennedy Center, the various Smithsonian museums, and the long forgotten Pension Building (now the National Building Museum).

As I hung up the phone, I thought about the challenge ahead. We would have to put in dance floors, bars, bands, stages, coat checking, valet parking, and VIP boxes for big contributors, in addition to all the other things that would be necessary to make this inauguration special. We would also need to staff each venue as if it were a hotel ballroom, which would require us to hire carpenters, electricians, sound engineers, and set designers. Bars would have to be stocked with liquor and champagne, with all of the glassware provided. An orchestra in each of the five ball sites would be necessary. An estimated 30,000 guests were expected to attend. All of this, and we had less than two months; it was a job for which only Tom Bell would be capable.

I met with Tom to ask him to manage the balls, and explained what we had been asked to do. He responded, "You're kidding." I told him that Haldeman wanted us to do it, and we needed to just find a way to meet the challenge.

Throughout the next few weeks, Tom and I looked at numerous potential sites. Once we saw the old, rundown Pension Building, we knew it had possibilities. It had been a site of inaugural balls in the 1800s. Historically a significant piece of architecture, the layout included a big open space suitable for dancing, with lofty spaces above. It now was an office site, which had fallen into disrepair. It had good bones, beautiful potential, and there was something about it that was quite elegant. However, it would take a considerable amount of work to put it to good use. We put it last on our preference list.

The sites Tom and I suggested to Bob Haldeman included the Kennedy Center, which was new and had never been used for a ball; the Museum of Natural History, next to the Republican Party symbol—a life-size elephant; the National Gallery of Art; and the Pension Building. A youth ball could be held in a designated hotel. Bob Haldeman liked the plan and approved it. Tom went to work to put together the first modern-day inaugural balls held in public buildings.

In the end, we would accommodate 10,000 people at the Kennedy Center ball.

One day, Tom came to me and said he had a problem with the Kennedy Center location. He said the building was not designed nor built to hold 10,000 people attending a dance. He was concerned about the parking; this was long before there was an underground garage. In fact, the layout was designed for valet parking. As Tom put it, "If we do not do something drastic to remedy this issue, Washington, D.C. will have the all-time worst traffic jam." He suggested closing the E Street Tunnel (which is located in close proximity to the building), and using it as a parking lot, then building a walkway so people could safely get to the Kennedy Center.

I thought, "This is a presidential inauguration. We should be able to solve this problem." I said to Tom, "Call the Park Service and see if they will build us a walkway." He did, and they did. Can you imagine a couple of young guys getting a special walkway built in six weeks? That was what it was like in those Nixon days. You could get a lot done if you had the guts and used the right kind of language, like, "The White House wants…"

Our other challenge was organizing the inaugural concerts. The Kennedy Center had not been available for previous inaugurations. Haldeman wanted to have three simultaneous concerts—one for American music, one for classical, and one geared to young people. Nixon had been re-elected overwhelmingly, and there was no shortage of performers who wanted to participate in our concerts. We had Frank Sinatra, Sammy Davis Jr., the Osmonds, Wayne Newton, the Mormon Tabernacle Choir, the Philadelphia Philharmonic Orchestra, and Van Cliburn. The challenge was the logistics, not the entertainment.

President Nixon and Vice-President Spiro (Ted) Agnew wanted to attend each of the concerts. The Secret Service, however, did not want both Nixon and Agnew at the same concerts, or moving from one concert hall to the other, at the same time. That meant the president and vice president had to change concert halls at different times.

I worked with the Secret Service on a very carefully orchestrated and coordinated plan. The president refused to walk out on any performer, so intermissions were added. This allowed for him to leave in such a way that he and the vice president could enter without passing each other in the hall.

It was 1973; there were no cell phones, and communicating with three theaters at the same time was going to be difficult. I asked the communications folks at the White House to install direct phone lines backstage in all three theaters, and connect them to three telephones in a small room in the basement of the Kennedy Center. This would be my headquarters. There, I could make sure that the shows ran on time, with intermissions, in order to get the president where he needed to be. He would go from the classical to the American music concert, and end with the youth concert. The vice president would start with the youth concert, then follow the president to the classical music and the American music concerts.

All went very smoothly for the first change of theaters. The Secret Service was happy, and everything was running according to plan. The president was in the American music concert and Wayne Newton was on stage. As soon as he finished his number we would go to an intermission, and the president would leave and go to the youth concert.

Anyone who has seen Wayne Newton in Las Vegas can imagine what happened. "One more time," he yelled, and went into another song and then another. My phone began to ring. My walkie-talkie from the Secret Service began to chatter. Magruder was on the walkie-talkie, then Malek and then Haldeman, wondering what the hell was I going to do to get Newton off the stage. The president would not walk out on him. He was in his third "one more time," and we were in trouble on the schedule. The Secret Service was ready to move the vice president, but he could not be in the hall at the same time as the president.

I made a decision; I called my stage manager in the hall where Newton was performing, and told him that as soon as Newton finished the song he was singing, he should drop the curtain. "You're going to drop the curtain on Wayne Newton?" he asked.

"I have no choice," I said, and the curtain came down. As expected, Wayne Newton went ballistic. "In my entire career, no one has ever dropped a curtain on me," he yelled. "I want to see the person responsible." Fortunately, I was in the basement, and the president and vice president were both on the move. We were back on schedule.

CHAPTER 14
RNC Turmoil

Throughout the pre-inaugural planning, Bob Haldeman and I talked on a regular basis. With the new format, use of public buildings, and the list of concerts and celebrities, he wanted to make sure we were all on the same page. He was particularly interested in the VIP dinner the president would be attending at the new Kennedy Center. During one of these discussions, he asked me if I would be interested in heading up the Peace Corps. I was flattered, of course, but not interested. I told him my interest was in the political process and campaigns, not policy or policy positions.

One day, Haldeman called me at the inaugural committee headquarters. "Ken, you know, we have been talking recently to the president about the Republican National Committee. The president was extremely impressed with the plan that you and Bill Brock put together before the election. To move us forward, we think we need a youthful look to the RNC. We are interested in having you become the next Republican national chairman. I don't want you to say anything to anyone right now about this." I asked him what they planned to do about Sen. Dole, who was then serving as RNC chairman. Haldeman said, "Leave that to us. For now, we just wanted you to know, you are the number one choice to be the next Republican National Chairman." It was later reported in *All the President's Men*, by Carl Bernstein and Bob Woodward: "Ken Rietz, thirty-two, was Haldeman's choice as the next Republican National Chairman."

I was thrilled about the potential opportunity. It would make me the youngest ever to hold that position. I was especially excited since Haldeman pointed out that the plan Bill Brock and I had submitted in the fall had been well received at the White House, and the president wanted it implemented.

The plan called for changing the role of the chairman to that of a full-time position. This would be modeled after the days when Ray Bliss served as full-time chairman and enjoyed real success in rebuilding the party in the '60s. Since then, the RNC chairmen were part-time, Cong. Rogers Morton and Sen. Robert Dole.

Bill and I believed a part-time chairman had not been effective, and in our plan, we proposed that Nixon be the spokesperson for the Republican Party. We thought the chairman's main role should be more of a professional mechanic who helped recruit candidates and put campaigns together. The RNC should be the mechanism to help build, support, and align resources for national, state, and local Republican campaigns. As Bob Haldeman requested, I did not say anything and waited patiently.

One early Sunday morning, my housemate, Stan Anderson (who worked at the White House), woke me up and said, "Sen. Dole is on the phone for you."

I had never spoken to Sen. Dole before, and didn't think that he knew me.

When I picked up the telephone and said hello, he snapped, "Ken Rietz, I understand you want my job." I told him I did not know what he was talking about. He told me he was looking at an article in the *Miami Herald*, which stated that I was going to be the next Republican national chairman and had written a re-organization plan for the RNC. He added that he wanted to say two things, "First, I want a copy of that plan. Second, you will never be chairman of the Republican National Committee."

I thanked the Senator for his call and told him that I could not give him a copy of the plan. "If you want it," I said, "you will have to get it from the White House."

"Fine," he said, "just remember, you will never be chairman of the Republican National Committee."

From "Robert Dole May be Out as GOP Chief" by Loye Miller Jr. in *The Miami Herald*, Tuesday, Nov. 14, 1972:

WASHINGTON – Sen. Robert Dole may be replaced as the national chairman of the Republican Party by early next year.

One who has urged such a change is Sen. William Brock of Tennessee, who has excellent connections at the White House.

Brock served as head of the Nixon campaign's youth division and chose the division's staff chief, political consultant Kenneth Rietz.

In recent days, Brock and Rietz have worked feverishly on proposed blueprints for a new 'more professionalized' national party staff setup headed by a political technician. They presented the proposal to top presidential aide H. R. Haldeman…

Seasoned Republican political technicians are scarce. Brock is reported to have highly recommended thirty-three (sic thirty-one) year-old tactician Rietz (who managed Brock's 1968 (sic 1970) Senate campaign).

In the end, Dole was right. But this was just the beginning of an all too public debate about the RNC chairmanship.

The day after hearing from Sen. Dole, I told Haldeman about the call and asked him what I should do. He said, "Ignore it, we'll take care of it." I believed him and went back to work on the inauguration. Neither he nor I thought Dole would start using the newspapers to fight his battle to stay, but he did. Soon *The Washington Post* was carrying the story that Dole was under fire, but determined to keep his job.

A few weeks later, the president called Dole to the White House for a chat about the national chairmanship. The plan was for Nixon to ask Dole to step down, and of course, Dole would. No one ever refused the president.

But this was Bob Dole. He not only said no to the president, but after he emerged from the White House, he told the waiting news media that the president had asked him to step down and he had refused.

It grew worse. Dole was talking to the press, and the press was calling me. I was refusing their calls. The whole thing was being played out on the pages of *The Washington Post*, including the article "GOP Divided On The Future" by staff writer Lou Cannon.

Party Chairman Bob Dole has made it clear that he wants to stay on and will step down only if asked to do so directly by the president. Last week he called senatorial colleague William

Brock and suggested that the Tennessee senator was "meddling" in Republican National Committee affairs. He did so after reading a newspaper account that a Brock protégé, Ken Rietz, who was director of the Nixon youth effort, would be named as Dole's replacement.

I couldn't blame Bob Dole. He was up for re-election in Kansas, and the last thing he needed was to be dumped as national chairman by the president. He wanted to stay and was willing to fight. While I wanted the job, I was not willing to take on Dole in the press, and Haldeman was telling me to keep my cool and it would all work out.

United Press International, in "GOP Chief Dole Getting Set to Leave" on Dec. 2, 1972, reported,

> An authoritative Republican source said Dole's exit probably would come no later than the GOP National Committee meeting Jan. 19 and would coincide with Mr. Nixon's commitment to shift White House staffers to the committee.
>
> Dole was reported anxious to avoid the appearance of a departure under pressure that might hurt his re-election chances in Kansas in 1974.

Charles Bartlett wrote in the *Chattanooga Times*:

> The elections have left no one disposed to be kind to national chairmen but the winning Republican, Sen. Robert Dole is being accorded no more civility than Jean Westwood, the losing Democrat.
>
> Both are on their way out but Dole is being dumped with an abruptness …
>
> The Kansas senator was asking for a few more months as party chairman, a transitional period to get set for his own re-election contest.

The president called the House and Senate leadership and his Cabinet together for a special meeting at Camp David to discuss the future of the party. He excluded Dole and me. One of the advantages I had was that during the campaign, I'd had Bob Haldeman's son Hank, Jerry Ford's son Jack, and John Ehrlichman's daughter Jan and son Peter working for me. Jerry Ford was then House Republican leader and would be attending the meeting, as would Haldeman and Ehrlichman. I asked my former employees to call their parents and put in a good word.

Friends of mine who attended the meeting said it was a hot and heavy debate about the future of the party. In the end, a consensus was reached that Bob Dole should step down as the Republican national chairman. The next day, the president called Dole to the White House, told him about the meeting, and asked for his resignation. This time Dole agreed, but according to Haldeman, Dole said he would not step down "For Rietz. You can pick anyone else, but not Ken Rietz."

Haldeman called me with the news. "What we have decided to do," he said, "is move George Bush from the U.N. to RNC chairman. He wants to go to China, and we are not ready for that yet. We'll put you in as deputy chairman, and then when Bush goes to China, you'll move up." It sounded like a good plan. I agreed, but it didn't quite work out that way.

Bob Dole is one of the shrewdest and smartest politicians I know. He is a fierce fighter and did all he could to defend his position as Republican national chairman. Who could blame him? He was up for re-election and didn't want any negative perceptions in the press.

Bob Dole is also one of the most gracious people I know; a real gentleman with a great sense of humor and sense of purpose. In 1986, when Dole was putting a team together for his 1988 presidential campaign, I was surprised to get a call from him. I was living in San Diego at the time and running political campaigns in California and the West. "Ken," that famous voice said to me over the phone, "do you ever get to Washington?" I said yes and that I thought I would be there the following month. "Come and see me. I want to talk to you about my campaign," he said.

I was astonished. Then I reached for the phone, called Dole's Senate office, and asked for David Chew, a former YVP staff member who was now working there. I told David about the strange call I had received. "Doesn't he remember 1972, and the fight over the national chairmanship?" I asked. David laughed and said yes, he did remember. "In fact, when we talked about it, he said one of the reasons he wanted you in the campaign was that you tried to get him fired and you succeeded."

The next month, I met with Sen. Dole and talked to him about his campaign. I didn't join it, but we had a great discussion. To this day, we are good friends. He is someone I admire and respect, and I believe he would have been a terrific president.

Right after the inauguration, Nixon announced Bush as the chairman of the RNC, and me as the deputy chairman. I was excited about the job. The president asked me to put together a national campaign, called "The New Majority." Under this campaign umbrella would be the Republican Senatorial Campaign, Republican Congressional Campaign Committee, and the state campaign efforts. It was a big undertaking, which I jumped into with both feet. Since most of the plan came directly from the proposal Bill Brock and I had written, I knew how to make this change work, and it would require long hours and a lot of travel. I was looking forward to working with George Bush as chairman. I knew him from his time in Congress and had a good relationship with him. As we kicked off the campaign, George Bush was supportive and hopeful that the plan would work.

A front-page article in the *Nashville Banner*, dated Feb. 28, 1973, headlined "Ken Rietz Gets National GOP Position."

> Ken Rietz who managed Sen. Bill Brock's successful Tennessee campaign in 1970 and President Nixon's bid for the youth vote last year, now has another challenging job as director of the Republican National Committee's 'new majority campaign.'
>
> Rietz, 31, a Wisconsin native, will coordinate the 1973 and 1974 party activities, with the House and Senate campaign committees, which previously ran their own show with few links to Republican headquarters.

In a March 16, 1973, thirteen-page memorandum to RNC Chairman Bush, I outlined the "New Majority" plan as follows:

The New Majority Campaign must be manifested through election of Republicans to the Senate, Congress and Governorships. We must win elections to maintain a new majority coalition. Our goal should be majority control of the House and Senate as well as winning a majority of the Governors' races. To accomplish this objective we need to recruit better candidates, have better planned campaigns and manage the campaigns in a more efficient and scientific manner. This objective can be reached by setting up a campaign-oriented staff within the RNC and reorganizing some of the existing resources of the RNC, RCC, Senate Campaign Committee and the RGA.

The memo included recommendations for staffing, research, organization charts, targeting districts, candidate recruitment, campaign planning, a timetable, and a $750,000 budget. I presented the plan to Chairman Bush. When I finished, he looked at me and said, "Well, let's get started." We also began to implement the recommendations Bill Brock and I had made in our suggested reorganization plan.

In a *New York Times* article titled "Nixon Gives the GOP Chairman More Authority as White House Prepares for 1974 National Elections" and dated March 27, 1973, R. W. Apple Jr. wrote:

When a Republican Governor from the West called at the White House a few weeks ago to discuss a political matter, he was told he was in the wrong place. The people he wanted to see, he was told by the White House staff, were at the Republican National Committee.

Incidents like that are becoming more frequent, reflecting an unorthodox decision by President Nixon as he looks ahead to the 1974 Congressional elections. For the time being at least, the White House political operation has been disbanded, and the National Committee, under its new chairman, George Bush, has taken over the liaison and patronage roles.

As Watergate continued to build momentum with the media, pressure was beginning to show on a variety of fronts. Although my value at the RNC was clear to the White House, the RNC members did not as easily agree with my position. In fact, my role was somewhat controversial. Since I was responsible for the reorganization, and most of the committee staff were not used to this kind of reporting structure (much less reporting to anyone who was only thirty-two years old), there were numerous negative backroom conversations. There was also the Dole issue. Although Dole and I would later become friends, he was still stinging from being pushed out as chairman. In addition, there was resistance by the Senate and House committee staffs to be part of this overall change.

In the meantime, Watergate was capturing more and more of the front pages. Members of the former YVP staff were getting badgering phone calls and visits from both Woodward and Bernstein. They seemed convinced that we were part of the conspiracy, and both reporters were determined to get someone to talk. The problem was that we really had nothing to say about Watergate, but Woodward and Bernstein continued to pester, call, and show up to people's houses looking for a scoop.

I was worried. Looming in the back of my mind was the volunteer taxi driver I had recruited for Magruder to work in the Muskie campaign headquarters. I knew about it, and so did Jeb Magruder. From my standpoint, I believed that I had not done anything illegal, but, as a professional, I knew the press. Once it went public, this small incident would be a media disaster, especially now that I was deputy chairman of the RNC. I tried not to think about it.

Then one day my housemate, Stan Anderson, and I were playing tennis at Congressional Country Club with Peter Curtis and Linda Tuerra, both former tennis professionals. We were hitting the ball back and forth playing doubles, when someone came from the clubhouse to alert me that Jeb Magruder was on the line and needed to speak to me. "Those darn White House operators," I thought. "They can find you anywhere."

I picked up the phone and heard Jeb on the other end of the line, in a quiet, sad voice, say, "Ken, I wanted you to be one of the first to know that I am going to start telling the truth to the Justice Department tomorrow." There was a hollow silence. "Jeb, what does that mean?" I asked. He responded sadly, "I can't tell you anything, except to advise you that you should probably get an attorney." And he hung up.

I sat there, inside the clubhouse, stunned. I really didn't know what to do. Many things were rushing through my head. What I did understand was that my life was going to radically change. Getting myself together, I returned to the court, determined to continue the day. My friends bantered back and forth with some light talk about my call, and we began the game again.

I played a lot of tennis, including being on my high school and college tennis teams. I wasn't great, but usually I could be counted on to get the ball back. Not that day. I could neither see the ball nor hit it. My mind was on Watergate and what Magruder's phone call meant.

The next day, I took my first step and called Jerris Leonard, an attorney and close friend, whom I met when I ran Bill Steiger's campaign. He was from Wisconsin and had been a candidate for U.S. Senate. He had served as deputy attorney general, heading the Civil Rights Division of the Nixon Justice Department, and was now in private practice.

I met with Jerry and told him what I knew, which wasn't much at that stage. When I described the taxi driver volunteer activities, his only concern, and mine, was how it would affect the Republican Party if it became public. Jerry said he would find out what he could about the investigation from his sources, and we would get back together. He said he should call George Bush and brief him, and I agreed.

After about ten days of talking almost every day with Jerry and learning more and more about the investigation, we both became even more concerned. At the same time, George Bush was inquiring about what would happen if the press picked up the scent, which would lead back to the RNC. Jerry's advice was exactly this: "I think you should resign and get as far away from Washington as possible." His reasoning was simple. He said, "No one seems to know exactly where this investigation is going. In fact, they are talking about a blanket indictment of people at the White House and throughout the campaign. As deputy chairman of the RNC, you are a big target. You're exactly the kind of political operative the Democrats would like to get, so your best alternative is to get as far away from Washington as possible." He also told me the FBI had contacted him, and they wanted to meet with me.

This was not what I wanted to hear. I had worked too long and hard for this to happen. I didn't much like this advice. I had no money, no idea what to do with my career, and certainly no idea where I would get a job in California, which was where Jerry suggested I move. As he was my lawyer, I knew he was looking out for my best interests. I also knew enough about the exploding Watergate atmosphere in Washington that I decided he was right.

One of the cardinal rules for political consultants is that they should do everything possible not to become an issue. If they do, they need to take action to remove themselves from the campaign and the attention of the news media. I was faced with the dilemma of determining if I would become a negative issue for the RNC. If so, I would have to resign.

Years later, when John Dean wrote his book, *The Nixon Defense*, I discovered that George Bush had discussed my dilemma with the president.

> The cabinet meeting that morning focused on energy and its influence on foreign affairs, and not a word was said about Watergate. After it ended, George Bush, chairman of the Republican National Committee, asked the president if he might have a minute with him, and they spoke for twenty minutes in the Oval Office. Bush had just returned from a trip to California, where he had met with Governor Ronald Reagan. It was Bush who raised Watergate, telling the president, 'I'm feelin' for ya on this other stuff.' Bush had raised Watergate because he said he had his own problem: a fellow named Ken Rietz, who had been involved in the Nixon campaign and had been sent up to the RNC, where he had 'worked in the dirty trick department,' doing some 'espionage on Muskie and stuff like that.' Bush had told Rietz they had to figure out how to get him out of the RNC without jeopardizing any of his rights, and Nixon agreed that if there was a problem, Rietz should be let go. Bush said that if he could help Nixon in some way other than by wringing his hands, he was willing to do so. Nixon urged him to just keep saying that the president has taken charge, and as he walked Bush to the door, assured him it would soon pass.
>
> When Bush departed, Nixon requested that Haldeman

return to the Oval Office, where he told Haldeman the gist of the conversation with Bush. Haldeman thought the situation had arisen because Magruder was still "lashing out" and pulling others in to get a better deal for himself. But Haldeman cautioned that people like Rietz had to be careful, because Magruder had exaggerated his activities.

The President told them (Haldeman and Ehrlichman) that George Bush was letting Rietz go. Ehrlichman was aware that Rietz had paid the expenses of the spy they had working for presidential candidate Sen. Edmund Muskie as a chauffeur. 'Well, nothing wrong with that,' the President said. Ehrlichman thought Bush, whom Haldeman called 'Mr. Clean,' was overreacting.

The truth is that there was no dirty tricks department at either the Nixon campaign or the RNC. I had made one mistake. At Magruder's request, I had recruited a taxi driver to work as a volunteer in the Muskie campaign, and Magruder then transferred supervision of that volunteer to Gordon Liddy. For that single mistake, I had to sacrifice my dream job and (I thought) my future career in political consulting.

I needed time to think. Several years earlier, I had purchased a forty-acre farm with a small historic house in Westover, on the Eastern Shore of Maryland. I spent the weekend there, thinking about my future.

While at the farm, reflecting on the past few years, I remembered a conversation with Mike Curb I'd had during the campaign. He was a shareholder and president of MGM records, and had helped us recruit entertainers for the YVP campaign. At the 1972 convention, he secured Sammy Davis Jr. to headline the show, and Mike had performed with the Mike Curb Congregation. He and I had become friends. When I became involved with the inaugural activities, in recognition of his help, I arranged for Mike to be co-chairman of the inaugural and chairman of the youth concert. We spent a lot of time together planning the activities. During one of our dinners, he'd asked me if I thought my experience in the campaign for the hearts and minds of young people could translate into marketing records to those same kids. We'd had a fascinating discussion about the similarities, and he'd told me that if I wanted a job in California, to give him a call. In fact, Mike had said, "If you ever decide to leave Washington and politics, I would love to have you in the record business. Anybody who can sell Nixon to young people ought to be able to sell records."

I had thought nothing of it at the time, but since my attorney recommended I go to California, I knew Mike might have some ideas. I picked up the phone from my farm and called him. I left a message with his assistant, and several minutes later, I was surprised when he rang me back. Because of his executive position with MGM, I wanted to make sure he was aware of the details of my situation and the facts, versus what the media was saying. I outlined the series of events, including the details of the taxi driver. I told him that I believed the situation was going to be unpleasant when I resigned from the RNC, and there would probably be a lot of negative press. Then I said that I needed a job and would like to live in California.

Without hesitating, Mike told me to head straight for California and that I would have a job at MGM Records. He also told me that if I could get there by the end of the next week, I could accompany him on his business trip around the world. He planned to tour MGM facilities and interview potential artists for the company. I told him I would be there as soon as possible, but needed a few days to take care of a few things in Washington.

Then I called my attorney. Jerry Leonard was very pleased with my decision, and told me he would stay in touch and keep me informed of the status of the investigation. He said, "I will let you know when I need you."

The day after my call with Mike Curb and my lawyer, I wrote a short letter of resignation, saying I was leaving to pursue an opportunity in business. I handed it directly to George Bush. He thanked me politely and said the resignation would have to be announced to the press. I told him to handle it any way he thought best.

In Washington, timing is everything. In this case, my timing stunk.

While I had spent time thinking about whether or not to resign from the RNC to protect it from a potential taxi driver scandal, Bart Porter was telling a completely different story to Watergate investigators. Porter was keeper of the cash at the Committee for the Re-election of the President, and in an effort to explain the distribution of the hundreds of thousands of dollars, he told investigators that there was a "kiddie spy corps." He would later be convicted of lying to the FBI about the existence of this corps. Unfortunately, the news media linked me to the kiddie spy corps without proof, simply because I was in charge of the Nixon youth campaign. Consequently, the headlines the day after I resigned from the RNC carried a completely erroneous story.

From the Denver *Rocky Mountain News*, "GOP Campaign Official Linked to 'Kiddie Spy Ring,'" April 25, 1973:

> WASHINGTON - Kenneth Rietz, recently assigned to direct the 1974 Republican congressional campaign efforts, has resigned after being implicated in connection with formation of a 'kiddie spy corps' for the Nixon re-election campaign, White House sources said Tuesday.
>
> The sources said Senate investigators have been told by Herbert L. Porter, Nixon Campaign scheduling chief, that Rietz recruited young voters to carry on espionage activities against Democratic presidential candidates including George S. Mc-Govern. The sources said Rietz, who directed President Nixon's youth campaign, led a team of four or five paid youngsters at the Committee for the Re-election of the President who were directly involved in the espionage activities. Most of the other young spies, the sources said, apparently were volunteers.
>
> Operations reportedly included infiltrating McGovern campaign organizations in key states including California and New York, and working undercover for the Nixon Committee in antiwar movements.

Bart Porter lied to the FBI and went to prison. Unfortunately, the news media, for the next twenty years, did not connect the dots, and continued to link me to a kiddie spy corps that never existed.

From *The LA Times*, "Former Nixon Aide Porter Charged with Lying To FBI on Watergate," Jan. 22, 1974:

> WASHINGTON - Herbert L. Porter, who helped set up the toughest law-and-order speech President Nixon delivered in the

1970 election campaign, was charged Monday with lying to FBI agents investigating Watergate.

Porter, scheduling director of the Committee for the Re-election campaign of the President, virtually confessed during televised Senate hearings last June to the multiple offense of making false statements to the FBI, a federal grand jury and the Watergate trial.

During the Senate hearings, Porter told of helping concoct a story that G. Gordon Liddy, a re-election committee official convicted in the Watergate trial, had given college students $100,000 for infiltrating radical groups. The purpose was to hide money that the re-election committee was giving Liddy for 'dirty tricks.'

CHAPTER 15
Mike Curb & MGM

When I left Washington in May of 1973, I had no idea what lay ahead. Most of my career had been focused on what I loved best, political campaigns. After seven years of the high pressure world of political campaigns, I would have to start all over.

Mike Curb was giving me a great opportunity. I was not sure what I would be doing in the music business, of which I knew little. What I did understand was that the foundations of my success came directly through values instilled in me by my parents and the community in which I grew up. Those Midwest values served me well. I knew they would work anywhere. I was very lucky.

As I flew to California, I reflected on my life and the twists and turns that had taken me to this point. I had been a fairly good high school athlete, but not a great one. Cong. Walter Judd had appointed me to the prestigious U.S. Naval Academy, but before I could make an impact there, I had to leave mid-way through my first year for medical reasons. I had taken a job to earn money and then enrolled in George Washington University, only to leave after three years without a degree to join a political campaign, where I found my true calling. Once I had left GWU, I'd run a series of successful political campaigns for Bill Steiger, Bill Brock, Bill Mills, and then YVP for Nixon. I'd helped develop a plan for reorganizing the RNC. The president had considered me for the chairmanship of the RNC. In a compromise, I had been named deputy chairman under George Bush. Because of a mistake in judgment that I had made in 1971, I had to resign my position as deputy chairman and political director of the RNC. I was thirty-two, and was mentally preparing myself to start over.

I did not have a college degree, and everything I had learned about political campaigns, strategy, and communications was on the job. I had no idea if these skills would be valuable in the business I was joining. I thought that my career in politics was over. When Jeb Magruder had asked me if I knew how to plant a volunteer in Muskie's headquarters, I should have said no—but I didn't. I had temporarily lost sight of the reason I was brought into the re-election campaign—to win the youth vote. I had succumbed to ambition, wanting to make "the people across the street" happy, and I took the wrong road. I believe many people caught up in Watergate made the same kind of mistake.

Sitting in the plane, I wondered what the future would hold. Fortunately for me, there was Mike Curb.

If there ever was a self-made man, it was Mike. He was the son of an FBI agent, and grew up in a middle class neighborhood in the San Fernando Valley. A self-taught musician who played in church and in his own band in high school, Mike was not only interested in music, but was fascinated by the music business. Most days, after school, he had worked in a local record store (the kind that no longer exists). When he graduated from high school, Mike skipped college and began to pursue his music business career. While working full-time in a small local record store and playing in his band on weekends, Mike was looking for an opportunity to get into the recording business. That opportunity came with Eddie Ray.

When Mike met Eddie, a veteran record industry executive, his life took a turn toward success. Eddie had expertise in several facets of the commercial music industry, including record distribution, promotion/sales, record production, songwriting/music publishing, artist acquisition/development, business administration, and commercial music education, plus he was shrewd about copyrights. An African-American, he was an extraordinary man who had climbed the executive ladders at both mainstream and independent record labels. When he and Mike first met, Eddie's career spanned Aladdin Records, Capitol Records (Tower Record Division), Co-Burt Television Productions, Imperial Records, and Central Record Sales Companies, with artists such as Fats Domino, Slim Whitman, Allen Toussaint, Lou Rawls, Irma Thomas, and Harry Nilsson, among others. As a songwriter, Ray was co-writer of the hit song,

YVP Staff with President Nixon, Trisha & Ed Cox

YVP Rally at the 1972 Republican National Convention

Discussing RNC reorganization with Senator Brock and President Nixon

The Rietz kids, Ken, Dick, Marty, Ginger

In front of a piece of the Berlin Wall at the Reagan Library

Shooting an Evelle Younger commercial with Reagan and Ford

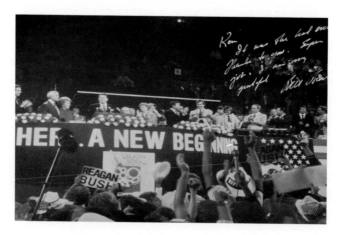

The 1980 Republican National Convention

With RNC Chairman Brock   *With Lt. Governor Curb and Susan Anton*

Shooting a Curb Commercial with Efrem Zimbalist, Jr.

With Mike Curb and his car at the Daytona 500

With Ursula and Jack Kemp

Ursula and Ken with Governor Pete Wilson and his wife Gail

Ursula and Ken with son KC

Nashville Banner.

State Edition

Ken Rietz Gets National GOP Position

By FRANK VAN DER LINDEN
Banner Bureau

Washington — Ken Rietz, who managed Sen. Bill Brock's successful Tennessee campaign in 1970 and President Nixon's bid for the youth vote last year, now has another challenging job as director of the Republican National Committee's "new majority campaign."

Rietz, 31, a Wisconsin native, will coordinate the 1973 and 1974 party activities with the House and Senate

By no mere coincidence, Brock heads the Senate campaign committee and one of his key aides on its staff is Bill Goodwin, the former Nashville public relations man who handled publicity in Rietz' camapgin for Brock.

Rietz went to Tennessee in October 1969, and stayed there, with his office in Nashville, until after Brock beat Democratic Sen. Albert Gore in the November 1970 election.

Republican National Chairman George Bush consulted Brock before appointing Rietz to his new job.

Rietz once was vice president of Allison, Treleavan & Rietz, Inc., a Washington-based political consultant firm which had a hand in Bush's own unsuccessful attempts to win a U.S. Senate seat in Texas.

"Ken will be a tremendous asset at the Republican National Committee as we go about the important business

Los Angeles Times

Late Racing

WEDNESDAY Morning Final

CIRCULATION: 1,034,329 DAILY / 1,332,879 SUNDAY — WEDNESDAY, NOVEMBER 8, 1978 — MF/142 PAGES / DAILY 20c

SPLIT TICKET ELECTED
Curb Wins Despite Landslide for Brown

Democrats Keeping Big Congress Margin

GOP Picking Up Two or Three Senate Seats and as Many as 15 in the House

BY JOHN H. AVERILL and PAUL HOUSTON
Times Staff Writers

WASHINGTON—The Democrats renewed their up-hours domination of Congress in election contests Tuesday that produced a larger than usual turnover to Senate seats and the defeat of the Senate's only black member, Edward W. Brooke (R-Mass.).

The voters, who turned out in unexpectedly large numbers, unseated four Senate Democratic incumbents and possibly one other plus two GOP senators. But there was little pattern

Deukmejian and Justice Bird Victors; Props. 5, 6 Go Down to Defeat

BY RICHARD BERGHOLZ
Times Political Writer

Jerry Brown won the smashing political victory he wanted Tuesday to project him as a major figure in national politics.

But the Democratic governor's relatively easy triumph over his Republican challenger, Atty. Gen. Evelle J. Younger, did not help enough marshal effort to carry along two members of his party's team.

Lt. Gov. Mervyn Dymally was defeated by 33-year-old record campaign executive Mike Curb, the Republican nominee.

And Rep. Yvonne Braithwaite Burke, the Democratic nominee for attorney general, fell to the challenge of Republican state Sen. George Deukmejian of Long Beach.

It is not unusual to have an election

Statewide Vote at Edition Time

Governor
61% Precincts Reporting

Gay Teacher

Democrats Keeping Big Congress Margin

Los Angeles Times

THURSDAY, NOVEMBER 9, 1978

Brown, Curb Pledge to Work Together

Both Say They Will Carry Out Mandate of the People, Put Differences Aside

BY LARRY STAMMER
Times Staff Writer

HE'LL SERVE WITH BROWN—An exuberant Mike Curb with wife Linda at news conference at their Trousdale Estates home the morning after his election as lieutenant governor.

Times photo by Ben Olender

Brown Sees Voters' Edict: Make the Promises Good

Governor Forecasts 'Massive Erosion of Public Confidence' if Politicians Fail on Economy Issue

BY GEORGE SKELTON
Times Sacramento Bureau Chief

Younger a Poor Candidate, State GOP Chief Says

BY KENNETH REICH
Times Political Writer

ANGIE DICKINSON and date, businessman Ken Reitz, at the wedding of producer Al Ruddy and society writer Wanda McDaniel in Beverly Hills. Angie joked: "Maybe I should run off and get married again, myself."

KEMP & BROCK TALKING WITH YOUTHFUL VOTERS IN WASHINGTON, D.C.

YOUTH DIVISION DIRECTOR KEN RIETZ

POLITICS

G.O.P. Reach to Youth

At Republican National Committee headquarters, the drive to re-elect Richard Nixon has yet to shift into high gear. In the offices of the Committee for the Re-Election of the President, the official campaign headquarters, some of the desks are still empty, awaiting the arrival of a staff—including Attorney General John Mitchell, who is expected to take up his old post as campaign manager. But one part of the Nixon drive has been operating at full tilt for weeks: the G.O.P. Youth Division is wasting no time going after the 25 million young men and women eligible to vote for the first time this fall. The early activity is spurred by the sound premise that the youth vote could be the key to a second term in office for President Nixon.

The Youth Division is headquartered in posh offices one block from the White House. There a staff of twelve professional political workers —all pointedly under 30—directs the most sophisticated youth campaign of any candidate. Its goal: to organize young volunteers across the country for doorbell ringing, voter registration and grass-roots organizing. With registration among the young currently running 2 to 1 Democratic, the G.O.P. hopes that its youthful volunteers can persuade enough of their contemporaries to vote Republican to offset the Democrats' nominal advantage.

To identify potential volunteers —and voters—the Youth Division relies on computerized analyses of young voters. The result is a carefully laid out plan that, unlike the strategies of most of the Democratic candidates,

does not rely primarily on college students. (Only one-fifth of the voters between 18 and 25 attend college.) While the G.O.P. has mapped speaking tours for Cabinet members and White House officials at key campuses across the country, the emphasis will be on noncollege youth. Traditionally less politicized and vocal than their collegiate counterparts, they have been somewhat overlooked by candidates in the past.

Like their parents, noncollege youth are primarily interested in the less glamorous economic and domestic issues: mortgage interest rates, unemployment, taxes for schools, government services. To reach them, the G.O.P. will send battalions of organizers into areas where new housing construction—and young families—is concentrated. G.O.P. statisticians have discovered that in California, for example, 2.4 million of the 2.5 million new voters live in ten of the state's 58 counties. G.O.P. bigwigs will visit vocational schools as well as universities.

Not Agnew. The scheme is the brainchild of one of the Republicans' most successful vote-getters among the young, Tennessee Senator William Brock. In his 1970 race against Albert Gore, Brock carried the youth vote by a 2-to-1 margin, despite Gore's dovish stance on the Viet Nam War. Brock won on 15 college campuses, losing just one and tying Gore in another. He is co-chairman of the Congressional Advisory Council for the Youth Division, and his former campaign manager, Kenneth Rietz, 30, is director of the Youth Division. With Brock on the advisory committee are ten Republican Congressmen primarily in their 30s and 40s, among them former Pro Quarterback Jack Kemp. A ce-

TIME, JANUARY 31, 1972

lebrity committee, including *My Three Sons* Star Stanley Livingston and Miami Dolphin Linebacker Nick Buoniconti, has been set up to provide the glitter for rallies and letterheads.

The real work is done by Rietz and his paid staff of twelve. Although no figures are available on the cost of the youth campaign, Rietz admits that his budget is generous and his latitude wide: "This is no back-of-the-bus thing." At this stage of the campaign, he and his people are concentrating on registration. An elaborate record-keeping system involving triplicate forms and follow-up letters and phone calls has been set up for each potential supporter contacted by volunteers. The staff is studiedly silent about Spiro Agnew, brushing aside questions about the Vice President with a curt statement: "The important thing is to re-elect the President." That Agnew's attacks on students will be a liability in campaigning among the young was underscored at a meeting of youthful Nixon supporters in Pennsylvania last week. When asked which Administration officials would be welcome campaigners, one youth replied: "Don't send Agnew."

Even the carefully honed Youth Division cannot overcome all of the antipathies young people feel about Nixon—his somewhat gray and cold image, the drawback of some key figures in his Administration, for example. Rietz and his young colleagues do not expect to elect the President on the basis of the youth vote, but they hope to prevent that vote from defeating him. Says one: "Let's face it —Nixon isn't going to carry the college vote. But the margin by which he loses it is important, and we're cutting that down."

TIME, JANUARY 31, 1972

GOP convention show 'made in Santa Barbara'

Continued From Page A-1

1970 Brock for Senate Campaign

"For the first time in 20 years we are spending more on human resources than on defense." *Richard Nixon*

PRESIDENT NIXON
NOW MORE THAN EVER

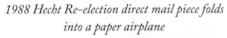

*1988 Hecht Re-election direct mail piece folds
into a paper airplane*

AUG 28 1972

August 26, 1972

Dear Ken:

You and the YVPs are to be congratulated
on the underlined job you did in Miami.

Their enthusiasm and excitement was
contagious to everyone on the floor, in
the audience and on television. Your rallies,
caucuses and overall organization were superb -
truly a job well done.

Best personal regards.

Yours sincerely,

John D. Ehrlichman
Assistant to the President
for Domestic Affairs

Mr. Ken Rietz
Young Voters for the President
1701 Pennsylvania Avenue, N. W.
Washington, D. C. 20006

THE REPRESENTATIVE
OF THE
UNITED STATES OF AMERICA
TO THE
UNITED NATIONS
at Camp David

GEORGE BUSH
AMBASSADOR

8-8-72

Jimmy— Ken Rietz did
a first class job at Camp
David briefing cabinet &
staff. The only one to get

applause — (Magruder, Malek, Stans,
Mosgregor)
Optimistic but realistic
credible —

Damn good job —

Thought you'd like to
know it — GB

THE WHITE HOUSE
WASHINGTON

SEP 12 1972

9/8/72

Dear Ken —
    Just a note to say "well done."
You and Tom Bell made outstanding
contributions to the success of the
'72 convention. I am particularly
grateful for the excellent cooperation
you gave me personally. The YUP
program certainly was the best
of the event and I know how
hard you worked putting it
together. Keep up the good
work.

                    your friend,

                    B.T.

THE WHITE HOUSE
WASHINGTON

January 22, 1973

Dear Ken:

I want to thank you for the fine contribution
you made to the Nation's most successful
Inaugural celebration.

Your name is becoming synonymous with
outstanding performance - most recently
the Young Voters for the President, now
the President's Inauguration. Keep up the
good work.

With best regards,

                    Sincerely,

                    H. R. Haldeman
                    Assistant to the President

Mr. Ken Rietz
Group Director
Inaugural Committee '73
Second and T Streets, SW.
Washington, D.C.

FEDERAL COMMUNICATIONS COMMISSION
WASHINGTON

September 9, 1975

Mr. Kenneth Rietz
9255 Sunset Blvd., Suite 710
Los Angeles, California 90069

Dear Ken:

The Fifth International Tchaikovsky Competition program
is a distinguished example of quality programming that
combines education and entertainment. In my opinion, it
was excellent in concept, performance and production.

The program brought into American homes a great
competitive concert of the most talented young classical
artists in the world.

Congratulations to you and WMAL-TV for presenting this
example of quality programming that reflects credit on
American TV broadcasting.

                    Sincerely,

                    James H. Quello
                    Commissioner

CC: Thomas B. Cookerly,
    General Manager, WMAL-TV
    Cliff Mezey

Ken Rietz

and

Palisades Communications

lacking its usual drawing power of suspense. One strategy used to rekindle the element of surprise, Rietz advised the GOP's to hold off on announcing the running mate. Rietz is quoted nationally as saying that "the whole idea is to make the event into a TV production instead of a convention."

From a detailed analysis of the 1976 convention, Rietz and 1980 convention chairman, California Lieutenant Governor Mike Curb, sought to identify and avoid earlier mistakes. Their tight direction of the July fete was designed to keep the television programmers focused on the Republicans as often and as flatteringly as possible. Speech makers were instructed to keep it short since the television cameras attention strayed away from the podium after eight or ten minutes in '76. Spotlights rather than a fully-lit Cobo Hall gave network producers a good target and kept the focus where Rietz and company wanted it. Rietz was also responsible for developing the convention theme, "Together, A New Beginning," plied in song and speeches throughout the proceedings. Special quickie films capturing the TV camera's eye for their entirety, were produced. The convention was also cut substantially in length to fit neatly into prime-time network programming. This trim weave of production planning provided the backdrop for the blockbuster lineup that replaced the usual excitement over nominees and platform planks. Susan Anton, Buddy Ebsen, Michael Landon, Vicki Lawrence, Wayne Newton, Donnie and Marie Osmond, Jimmy Stewart, Lyle Waggoner, Efrem Zimbalist, Jr. and others glittered for the Republican Party and added to the 20-hour volume of live network coverage.

Although recognizing that they were "walking a fine line between entertainment and political activity," Rietz claims that through his group's efforts, Reagan increased his lead in the all-powerful Harris poll by 16 points from gavel to gavel

photo courtesy of News-Press

In a city replete with media packagers who put together campaigns as varied in scope as they are themselves varied in size Ken Rietz & Company and its sister company, Palisades Communications, stands out. Youthful creative director Rietz has most recently been in the public eye for his production and programming of the 1980 Republican National Convention in Detroit. To produce that highly polished razzle-dazzle, Rietz employed his full complement of creative services including marketing studies, film production, campaign planning, media placement, writing, creative design, production and public relations. Rietz himself was involved in the entertainment industry for five years which gives him unique contacts in the area of creating special music and producing special events.

Anyone who caught the convention could see Rietz' touch. With Reagan's nomination assured by convention time, Rietz was given the difficult task of making a no-contest situation dynamic. He designed a spectacle that attracted the television audience to a political event

in Detroit.

Not everyone has required as extensive media packaging as did the GOP Convention. Palisades Communications has helped American Samoa promote its tourism and industrial possibilities simply by producing documentary film. Thrifty Drug and Discount stores reportedly benefitted greatly from Palisades' design for a new approach to their television advertising. The California Water Foundation boasts of playing a key role in the passage of the Peripheral Canal legislation due to Palisades' public relations campaign designed for them. Lieutenant Governor Curb enjoys the benefits of Palisades' public relations expertise. Local clients include Santa Barbara Aviation and MacElhenny, Levy and Company for whom they recently completed a market research study.

Whether you have a National Convention to put together or just need a little creative advice, Chamber members Ken Rietz & Company and Palisades Communications will help you solve your problem.

Santa Barbra Chamber of Commerce Publication

WASHINGTONIAN

What I've Learned: Don't Hide It

When an executive discovered he was going blind, he was scared and tried to fake it. Then he got to work to help others like him.

By Ken Adelman | June 1, 2008

"I did okay in my career," Ken Rietz says. "Having tunnel vision forced me to have tunnel focus on my problems." Photograph by Matthew Worden.

One day in 1985, Ken Rietz was driving in Los Angeles. "I was calmly turning a corner on La Cienega Boulevard," he says, "and almost ran over a family crossing the street."

The public-relations and political-campaign manager realized that his eye disease, retinitis pigmentosa, was heading toward blindness.

"I didn't hit anybody," Rietz says, "But I never drove a car again."

I excelled at faking it. Being in public relations and advertising, I figured that if people knew I couldn't see, they'd be more reluctant to hire me.

All that changed 20 years ago when I met Ursula, now my wife. After a year with her, tripping over everything, I told her about my vision problem. She urged me to tell everyone.

Until then, I had told nobody. I just went through life stumbling and banging into things. People thought I was just awkward or sometimes rude. They'd come up to me at a cocktail party, and I wouldn't even say hello. When someone extended his or her hand to shake, I ignored it because by then I'd lost all peripheral vision and couldn't even see below my nose.

When Ursula urged me to start telling people, everything changed. Instead of considering me rude and awkward, they thought I was overcoming a big obstacle.

Why didn't you do that from the start?

I was afraid to—partly because of my pride but largely because of my business. Going blind is a bad image. Clients and potential clients would look at me differently—or so I thought. As it turned out, no one ever did.

What did you do about reading?

I can still read—but barely, out of one eye, one word at a time, with computer-generated enlarged type. I lack any field of vision.

How could you work in public relations all those years? Isn't your profession all about visuals?

Until I retired in 2006, I worked for Burson-Marsteller, which gave me great support. I'd walk in to pitch new business while holding a staff person's arm.

During my years in public relations, I always concentrated on strategy. You don't need perfect sight to do that, because working out a strategy happens in the mind, requiring vision rather than sight.

What have you learned about being disabled?

The biggest lesson I've learned about coping with a disability is this: You can. You can cope successfully if you adopt a positive attitude, research the field to find out the best treatment, and adjust your life to your new condition.

Rietz is married to Ursula Landsrath, "who takes care of all our dogs, our farm, and generally manages our life." A son from a previous marriage, K.C., works in real estate in Fort Lauderdale.

Rietz lives in Delaplane, Virginia, 50 miles west of Washington. His office is in the basement of a Colonial-era church that was set for demolition before Rietz bought and restored it. It's now registered with the Virginia Trust as a historic building.

He talked in the church's basement about what he's learned.

This article is from the June 2008 issue of The Washingtonian. For more articles from the issue, click here.

xvi | *Photo Section*

"Heart of Stone," which became a national number one hit during the '50s. Eddie would later hold an executive position at MGM Records, and was appointed by President Reagan and confirmed by the U.S. Senate to serve as a commissioner of the U.S. Copyright Royalty Tribunal in Washington, D.C.

Eddie Ray liked the young musician, and asked him to work on the score for a teen movie. Mike jumped at the chance to get his foot in the door; always the shrewd businessman, he said he would do it for part ownership of the music. Mike's understanding of the music business paid off. He was a pioneer. Starting small, he ended up writing the music for some well-known films, including *Kelly's Heroes* and *The Big Bounce*. He also wrote a commercial called "You Meet the Nicest People on a Honda." Soon, he was making money in the business he loved. Then, he met the Osmond Family.

The Mike Curb Congregation was performing on the Andy Williams TV show when the young Osmond Family made a guest appearance. Mike became their record producer, and a series of huge hits followed. He leveraged that success into a share of MGM Records, where he was named president at the age of twenty-four.

When it came to music, Mike had an incredible memory. You could mention any song, and he would tell you the name of the artist, the composer, the producer, and the record label. During his 1982 campaign for governor, *San Francisco Chronicle* columnist Larry Liebert tested Curb and wrote:

> 'Who recorded 'He's a Rebel?' I asked Lieutenant Governor Mike Curb. Sometimes you have to ask the tough questions in this business.
>
> 'The Crystals, on Philles Records, 1962,' the Republican candidate for governor shot back without hesitation. It was written by Gene Pitney. Remember Gene Pitney?'
>
> Curb was equally swift at identifying one of my personal favorites, 'Hats off to Larry.' He said, 'Del Shannon on Bigtop records, a pink colored label. It would have been 1961.'

I did not know much about what Mike did professionally. He was extremely smart about people, marketing, and sales. Music was just one of his many talents. He wrote hundreds of songs, and had the ability to hear a song and recognize it as a potential hit. In the industry, he was considered to have "great ears." Because he was a producer, arranger, and musician, he was able to hear a song, and in his mind, associate it with an appropriate artist.

However, Mike's strongest suit was knowing what a good deal looked like. No one could negotiate deal points like him. He would read a contract, and then, facing the opposing lawyer, negotiate the entire thing without looking at it or at notes again. I witnessed him outmaneuver many of the music industries' best known attorneys.

In the early 1970s, Mike was in the middle of restructuring and resurrecting MGM Records, which had seen huge losses in the late '60s. He was not without controversy. His strong values, based on faith, and his anti-drug approach had led to a number of controversial (but profitable) artists being released from their contracts or not renewed.

Mike produced the Osmond's early hits. He knew that Marie Osmond and the song "Paper Roses" would be a good fit. Later, he conceived the idea of the Donnie and Marie duo. Mike also helped convince Kenny Rogers to turn to country music, and brought the Four Seasons back to prominence. He produced Sammy Davis Jr.'s biggest hit, "Candy Man," and worked with Steve and Edie Gorme, Andy Williams, Eddie Arnold, and Sean Cassidy. When I joined MGM, Mike was negotiating a deal with the Dutch-German conglomerate Polygram for them to purchase MGM Records.

With all of the business transactions going on, Mike always had time for politics. From his role in the campaign to his part with various aspects of the YVP, and most importantly, with his involvement in the convention, he continued to keep his foot in politics. I thought it was just his hobby, never more than an avid interest. He continued recruiting celebrities at Republican campaigns, where he was always available and supportive.

On the other hand, I knew nothing about the music business. The extent of my association with music was that I enjoyed listening to it. I was clueless about the process of launching an artist's career and all the other facets I was soon to learn from Mike. As he was so willing to teach me, I failed to realize that he had another agenda. He was forgiving my lack of expertise in the music business as he was interested in learning about political campaigns.

His goal, all along, was to run for political office. He never mentioned this, and it was not evident to me at the time. Mike had obviously realized that some of our work needed the same abilities. Selling a product or a candidate boiled down to the same kind of expertise.

California was also unknown to me. Having spent little time there, I did not know much about the environment and culture, nor did I know much about L.A. I arrived with a sense of excitement and trepidation. I brought lots of suits and ties, the typical uniform in Washington. I stood out immediately among the leather jacket, open-necked, gold chain world of the music business. I soon shed the suits and ties in favor of the more casual look of the entertainment industry.

The day after I arrived at MGM Records, Mike and I set off on his scheduled trip around the world. Although I had spent one week in Acapulco and time in St. Thomas, I had never really traveled outside the U.S., so this would be a new experience for me.

The tour was comprised of stops integral to the MGM business plan. Our first visit was to Japan, where Mike was a participant in the Tokyo Music Festival. We headed to the Middle East, and then on to Hamburg, Germany. Mike had scheduled meetings there with his potential German partners, Polygram. Seated in first class on every flight was a far cry from my days on the campaign trail with stale sandwiches and buses. On that first trip around the world in 1973, Mike showed an incredible interest in the mechanics of a political campaign. While I talked to him about the music business, he asked me questions about politics. It became increasingly obvious to me that Mike had something other than my expertise in youth marketing in mind when he offered me a job at MGM. We were learning from each other. It was this dynamic that strengthened our relationship.

In the beginning, we both thought this trip would be a good way for me to learn more about Mike and the music business while escaping the spotlight of the Watergate press coverage. It didn't quite work out that way.

While on our world tour, newspapers around the U.S. continued to have a field day, linking my resignation from the RNC to the so-called kiddie spy corps.

For three days, I was the subject of articles that were largely untrue.

This led to more articles in the news magazines, and the story began to get international coverage. It caused some very uncomfortable questions for Mike when we arrived in Hamburg.

When he arrived at the meeting, the Polygram executives had a copy of the international version of *Time Magazine*. Not only was I in the news, but so was my new employer, MGM Records. Getting out of Washington, getting out of the country, and getting out of the news hadn't worked. The negative press had followed me.

This was the first time Mike would have to defend me against my so-called Watergate connection. It would not, however, be the last. His future bosses at Polygram asked him to fire me, but he refused, and we returned to Los Angeles. I was always grateful for the way Mike defended me. He was a loyal friend, even during huge challenges.

One of the most difficult and disappointing meetings Mike and I attended was later in L.A. with the Polygram executives. They were determined to cut our artist roster to a specific number, and asked us to list the artists in order of preference. At the end of our list were two artists that we felt strongly about, but they were just beyond the number the Polygram executives told us we could keep. Mike and I didn't give up; we argued vigorously. In the end, we lost, and had to cut both Kenny Rogers, who had just recorded his first country album, and Neil Sedaka, who had just recorded his *Sedaka's Back* album. Giving up both artists and their albums was extremely disappointing. Both of them went on to make more money for their new record companies than Polygram paid for MGM Records.

My experience working in the music business with Mike was like nothing I had done previously or since. As they say out West, the entertainment business is entertaining, but it's not a business. The musicians are talented, eccentric, and obsessed with their music. Most of the contracts, deals, and negotiations were not run in a businesslike manner. Music in the mid-'70s was just starting to become a big revenue-generator.

I was introduced to a new vocabulary, with phrases like "take a meeting" and "pencil me in." Major deals were made at breakfasts and lunches at the Polo Lounge in the Beverly Hills Hotel. Mike and I usually started our business day with breakfast there. In those pre-cell phone days, having a phone on your table at the Polo Lounge was a real convenience. While having breakfast, Mike could call the MGM Records office in New York and conduct meetings by telephone. Many times our breakfast would stretch into the lunch hour, and we would continue at the same table. Most of the music industry, in those days, had the same schedule, and many of the executives also started their days at the Polo Lounge. We always joked that we could probably make any kind of record deal sitting right there, in our usual booth.

At one of those lunches, we were meeting with Mel Tillis to negotiate a new contract. Mel speaks with a halting stutter, but sings without stuttering. He was there without his manager, trying to make a point. He was having a difficult time getting the words out. I said to him, "Mel, just sing it." The rest of the meeting went without a hitch. We talked and Mel sang.

In my political life, I worked with many politicians with big egos. However, I don't think any of their egos match the size of most I met in the music business. It is probably essential to have a big ego to get out in front of thousands of people and entertain. The difference I found was that while politicians are generally interested in the world and things going on around them, in contrast, entertainers, by and large, are focused on themselves. When meeting socially or for a business reason, the conversation is generally about themselves and their careers. One of the exceptions was my friend Angie Dickinson. She loved books, and was constantly reading biographies, autobiographies, and political history. Although she was a Democrat, I enjoyed discussing politics with her.

A good example of self-absorption was at dinner we had one evening at Mike's home with Sammy Davis Jr. Sammy and I had become friends, and he always introduced me as a "member of his family." I found him to be generous, warm, and friendly, as well as an incredible entertainer. One night, a group of us had seen his show at Harrah's in Reno and then went to dinner in the hotel. Sammy walked by, saw me, and joined the group, a thrill for everyone there. He also picked up the tab. This was not unusual for him. One night, at dinner in London, one of our group admired his new camera and he immediately gave it to her. This generosity, to all those around him, is one of the reasons he was almost bankrupt when he died.

One night at Mike's house, we gathered with our record promotion team to pick a single for release as a follow up to "Candy Man." We recorded a new album and listened to it twice, while drinking wine. At about 10 p.m., we sat down to dinner. There were about ten of us, we had been drinking quite a bit, and the conversation around the table was getting louder and louder. Suddenly, Sammy stood up, pounded on the glass table and shouted, "No one is listening to me. I don't want anyone at this table to talk to anyone but me." He sat down to a completely silent room. The rest of the night belonged to Sammy.

My next obstacle while trying to build my career at MGM Records would be the Watergate FBI investigations and interviews. My interviews with the FBI were a real eye opener. They gave me an understanding of why people accept immunity and then testify against their colleagues. At least, in my experience, it would have been easy to cut a deal and tell the prosecutors what they wanted to hear. Not that I knew it in advance, but I learned what they wanted to hear during the many hours of the interview process. They were constantly offering immunity.

In my case, they wanted me to testify against Charles Colson, someone with whom I'd had very little contact; quite frankly, I didn't know much about him. However, after at least ten hours of interviews by FBI agents, I would have been an idiot not to know the answers they wanted to their questions. They were telling me the answers by asking the questions over and over in different ways. So much for our justice system.

In the end, they told me they could grant me immunity if I told them the story they were looking for. They said I should "think about all we have been talking about." I said no to their offer of immunity. I told them I didn't need to think about it and had nothing to say and nothing to hide. Because of the outcome with the FBI, I was then asked to testify at the Watergate Grand Jury, something I was not looking forward to. Since the investigation was underway, I had no idea how long it would take or when I would be asked to return to D.C. I knew, as the press continued to escalate the stories, the pressure was building. I was aware that it was going to be a difficult situation.

I returned to California. As I continued to work long hours with Mike, I watched the press frenzy about Watergate continue to build. Early one morning, Marilyn Johnson called me from Washington and told me there was bad news. Cong. Bill Mills had committed suicide.

I had spoken with Bill just a few days before. He was distraught about *The Washington Post* articles describing the transfer of $25,000 to his campaign from the White House slush fund. He asked me for the details about the transfer to his campaign treasurer, who had died in an automobile accident. I assured him the cash had all been there, and that he and the campaign had done nothing wrong as long as the money had been accounted for. At this, Bill was silent. Then he said that *The Washington Post* had been "hounding him" and hung up.

The morning of Bill's death, Mike Curb and I were having breakfast, as usual, at the Polo Lounge. We finished eating around 10 a.m., and were about to leave when Mike received a call from his office. His assistant was quite clear on the phone: "We have started to get press calls about the death of a Washington congressman. You might ask Ken what this is all about." I told Mike about Mills' suicide. We immediately decided to go to the office and figure out what was going on.

As we approached the MGM Records office building on Sunset Boulevard, we could see a group of reporters camped out with TV cameras and tape recorders. We made a quick decision and drove right past them to Mike's home in the hills above Beverly Hills. From there I called Marilyn Johnson, who was still working at the RNC, to get more information. She gave me the sketchy details. Bill Mills had taken his own life in his garage with a shotgun.

From *The Washington Post*, May 23, 1973, under the headline "$25,000 Gift to Rep. Mills Unreported":

> A $25,000 cash contribution from secret funds of the Finance Committee to Re-elect the President that was funneled to the 1971 campaign of Rep. William O. Mills (R-Md.) was not reported to Maryland's Board of Elections in apparent violation of state law.
>
> Several intermediaries said yesterday they helped deliver the cash in an envelope to Mills' campaign manager before the May

25, 1971 special election in which Mills was elected to Congress from Maryland's Eastern Shore, succeeding Secretary of Interior Rogers C. Morton.

The next few days were a jumble of emotions for me. I had not been back to Washington since I met with the FBI, but I knew I had to go to the funeral. The press were calling, and I dodged most of their calls. Like it or not, as Bill Mills' campaign manager, I was back in the news in Washington. Again, Mike Curb was steadfast in his support.

The funeral was sad. How could anyone explain this tragedy? I couldn't. But the press were there with their questions. One prominent reporter even asked if he could ride to the cemetery with me and ask a few questions on the way. I refused this rude and inappropriate request. All I wanted to do was pay my respects to the family and go back to California.

This would not be my last Watergate related trip to Washington. That October, I was called to testify before the Watergate Grand Jury. At the time, with all the investigations concerning Watergate and the numerous press leaks, being called to testify before the grand jury was scary.

I flew to Washington the day before I was scheduled to testify. Jerry and I spent the entire evening going over hypothetical questions. Jerry cautioned me to answer every question honestly, but only the questions that I was asked. "Whatever you do, don't volunteer information beyond exactly the question they ask you." I spent a restless night in a hotel, but felt somewhat prepared. As Jerry and I took the car service to the courthouse, nothing could have prepared me for what lay ahead. Flashbulbs and a gaggle of reporters yelling questions were waiting for me. Thinking back, I should have expected it, but I was not prepared for the magnitude of the press feeding frenzy. We pushed our way through; ignoring their questions, we entered the courthouse.

Jerry had prepared me as well as possible. He told me repeatedly to answer truthfully. He warned me that the prosecutors would be looking for lies and deceit. "Answer honestly. If you don't remember, do not make it up; state that you do not know or that you do not remember." He knew I would be bombarded with hypothetical questions, and cautioned me to answer truthfully or not at all. He kept warning me that they were after people who were not telling the truth. He alerted me that the questions were designed to test my memory, and to prompt me to talk about things of which I might no longer have a clear memory. Jerry would be correct on all points.

When testifying before a grand jury, one is not permitted to have an attorney present. He waits outside while the client is, in fact, bombarded by hypothetical questions from the prosecutors. Despite Jerry having prepared me well, it was still an interrogation I will never forget.

As I recall, the majority of questions were all along the same track as my FBI interviews. They wanted information about Chuck Colson. The prosecutor, repeatedly and in numerous ways, kept going over my relationship with Colson and his role, if any, in the Watergate break-in. I could not figure out why they were asking me those questions. I did not work at the White House and, except for one phone call, had no contact with Colson. Since I had nothing to contribute, I'm sure that everyone was rather frustrated with the way the questioning was going. However, I stayed consistent with the information that I gave in the previous FBI interviews.

At one point, the prosecution team asked if I would like to consult with my attorney waiting outside. They informed me that it was not an issue, but that if I so desired, they would stop the session. They added that it was perfectly normal to do so. I immediately recognized the trap. A stopped session would have gone on record and would appear that I needed to speak with my attorney. If it were not for my years of working with the press, this seemingly kind offer from the prosecutor could have been misinterpreted.

I responded without missing a beat, and said I did not need to seek counsel from my attorney or want to stop the session. I added that I would do all right just answering the questions honestly. The reality was that stopping the session to go outside and speak to my attorney would seem suspicious to the jurors. In addition, since the Watergate Grand Jury sessions were constantly leaked to the press, I knew asking for any pause in the proceedings would make it into *The Washington Post*. It was unfortunate how they had access to information, and it was obvious they had a source on the inside. Someone was leaking. The Post had access to everything from the grand jury, the FBI, and the Senate Watergate Committee. They were reporting on secret sessions while they were taking place.

I didn't need to speak to Jerry Leonard, and didn't need any more false press accounts linking me to Watergate. I had nothing to hide and continued responding to the questions.

I think I was in front of the grand jury for about two hours. I don't remember having any great difficulty in responding to any question, with the exception of saying, "I don't know" or "I don't recall" many times. As I left the courthouse, we once more had to make it through the crowd of reporters. They kept yelling their questions as Jerry and I smiled and drove off without responding. I was happy to be heading back to California.

In the end, I had nothing to add to the investigation, and was not indicted or required to testify before the Senate Watergate Committee. My only real problem came from the constant press coverage of the infamous but nonexistent kiddie spy corps. It was an untrue story that would haunt me for years. During almost every campaign in which I worked during the next twenty years, the story appeared in the local newspaper. Unfortunately, it was never reported that this story began when Bart Porter lied to an FBI agent about the funds he was distributing. Porter needed an excuse for the money that had been used for other purposes. He later pled guilty to lying to an FBI agent, and served time in prison. One of the lies to which he pleaded guilty was about the funding of the kiddie spy corps. To this day, the press has not linked that lie to the countless articles about me heading that fictitious spy ring.

CHAPTER 16
Curb Productions

Late in 1973, Mike Curb sold his share in MGM Records and we left to create Mike Curb Productions. The Osmonds was the first act he signed. Mike's goal for the company was to sign new emerging artists or those artists neglected by their current label. He wanted to build a new kind of operation.

With the Osmonds as our key client, my life in the music business included weekends in Provo, Utah, where they lived. We also spent time watching our entertainers perform in Las Vegas. Our schedule included breakfasts, lunches, and dinners with artists we signed or with whom we were negotiating. Most evenings, by 9 p.m., we were in a recording studio where Mike was producing a new record or mixing an album. The hours were long, but I was no stranger to long hours and hard work. Mike was focused on building the new business, and seemed to need very little sleep. We started early and worked late.

The first few years flew by, and I learned an enormous amount working with Mike. One of my favorite people to work with was Don Costa. Don was a well-known composer, arranger, producer, conductor, and an extremely talented musician. He worked as a producer and an arranger for us when he wasn't traveling as Frank Sinatra's conductor. Don and Nelson Riddle were the two conductors Frank Sinatra preferred. Don was a gregarious Italian who enjoyed life, worked long hours, and ate too much.

One night we were in the studio, recording an album with Andy Williams. There was a full orchestra, and Don Costa had created some exceptional arrangements. I was seated next to Don in the booth as the orchestra ran through the song. Suddenly, he jumped up and yelled, "Stop!" It was as if someone had slapped him in the face. He shouted, "The third violin got it wrong." To this day, I marvel that Don, or any musician for that matter, could hear a chord with an entire orchestra playing and identify a wrong note. But he did. I was impressed.

Another night in the studio, as we all sat around discussing the recording and arrangements, Don had a heart attack. He thought he was having a bout of indigestion. Because Don loved to eat, I didn't question his complaint, and later simply drove him home. The next day, Don called me from the hospital, and I went to see him immediately. As I was sitting with him talking about the options he faced, the telephone in his hospital room rang. It was Frank Sinatra.

I didn't hear the other end of the conversation, but I did hear Don say, "Yes, Frank." Then again, he would pause and say, "Yes, Frank." This happened several more times, and finally Don hung up. He looked at me and said, "Frank is sending his plane, and I am going to Houston to see Dr. DeBakey."

In the 1970s, open-heart surgery was new. Dr. Michael E. DeBakey was the pioneer and widely respected expert in this field. Frank arranged for Dr. DeBakey to handle the operation. Frank also ensured accommodations for Don Costa and his wife.

Several weeks later, Don called me from Houston to tell me he was coming home. He asked me to pick him up at the L.A. airport. As I waited for the plane, I saw Jilly Rizzo, Frank Sinatra's bodyguard and driver. When I asked him why he was meeting the plane, he said he was taking someone to Palm Springs to see Frank. I thought it was an unusual coincidence.

When Don came off the plane in his wheelchair, it became clear for whom Jilly was waiting. Don greeted me and then introduced me to the gentleman pushing his wheelchair, Dr. DeBakey. Jilly was taking the doctor to Palm Springs to see Frank Sinatra. I was taking Don to his home.

In the years since, I have heard many good and bad stories about Frank Sinatra. As far as I am concerned, that one story tells it all. He looked after his friend Don as if he were a member of his family.

Our relationship with the Osmonds gave me my first opportunity to produce a television program. I had written and produced numerous TV commercials and short political programs, but not a full-length program.

So, when the Osmonds started talking about their desire to go to the Soviet Union to perform in a series of concerts, I became very interested. They asked me to make inquiries about the possibility of a tour. I opened up a dialogue with Russian officials in Washington and started talking about the potential tour behind the Iron Curtain. We also proposed producing a TV show that would be broadcast in both countries. These conversations continued for a number of months, and by Christmas 1973, it looked like we had the green light.

The Soviet press got wind of the story, and ran a series of articles in the U.S.S.R. that were less than flattering to the Osmonds. They falsely claimed that the parents manipulated the kids to make money. Soon the trip was canceled. I received apologies from the officials with whom I had dealt in Washington. They assured me that I would have another opportunity.

By May, I had pretty much forgotten about the whole thing when I received a call from my Soviet contact in Washington. He told me he had another project for me, and wondered if I would be interested in shooting a documentary on the Fifth International Tchaikovsky competition. I agreed without hesitation, and then asked him the date of the event. He told me it was in two weeks. I told him that would present a few challenges, but that I would go to work immediately to assemble a crew, director, etc. He said, "No, Ken. We only want you. We will provide the crew, director, and everything else you will need, including your official papers."

I was stunned. I knew nothing about Tchaikovsky or classical music, had not been to the U.S.S.R., and never produced a full-length TV program. I was faced with two choices—going for it or forgetting about it. I went for it.

I arrived in Moscow with no idea of what I would find. I only knew that I was going behind the Iron Curtain and would be met by an interpreter. After a few tense minutes, I was greeted by a nice young man who spoke broken English. He would be my companion for the next two weeks.

The director and crew I was provided were very professional; however, they didn't speak a word of English, and I didn't speak Russian. I ended up drawing a lot of pictures to show the shots I hoped to get. I needed some interviews of the competition participants, and asked my interpreter to do them. His English was unintelligible, so I gave up on that idea and did the interviews myself. My imagination, persistence, a little luck, and the U.S. dollar allowed me to make a success from a potential disaster.

I decided to follow an American through the competition, to tell the story of what goes on behind the scenes and on stage. I chose an attractive young violinist from Colorado, Eugene Fodor. No American violinist had ever won the competition, but I thought this young, rugged violin player from Colorado would make a good subject. I was lucky and so was he. Although they refused to reward first place to an American, Fodor was awarded second place, along with two other competitors. That year, there was no award for first place in the violin competition.

I discovered that they were recording the concerts in stereo each night, to release as an album to the public. I found the engineer, and we soon reached an agreement that allowed me to walk away with a duplicate recording. I knew, if all else failed, as long as I had a good quality recording of the music, I would be able to build a documentary.

By the end of my two weeks, I had met quite a number of Russian public officials. On my last day, the head of the Young Communist League asked me to have lunch with him. That's when I saw how the other half lived.

He took me to an incredible restaurant. After eating mostly borscht for two weeks, I could not believe the great food (and, of course, great vodka) in this restaurant. I sat with three Russians. The plan was to have lunch and go directly to the airport for my flight to London. To celebrate my departure, the three Russians took turns toasting me. Each time, of course, I reciprocated. We were drinking water glasses full of vodka without ice. To this day, I remember going to the restaurant, having a great meal, and toasting my hosts. I do not remember arriving at the airport or getting on the plane; I woke up as we were landing in London. My only hope was that I had not done anything to embarrass the U.S.

The documentary was a success. It was broadcast in the Soviet Union and on PBS in the United States.

Mike and I had a somewhat regular Saturday tennis game at the Bel Air Country Club or the Mulholland Tennis Club with Andy Williams and his brother Don. Mike and Andy were very good tennis players. Don and I were not quite on their level. We could keep up pretty well, and we played a good competitive game. As a group, we were paired up nicely, and it made for a good match. This was before I discovered my problem with RP. I remember one day that my failing sight almost caused me a real embarrassment.

On this particular day, Mike, Don, and I arrived at the court, and Andy was hitting with someone. As we walked by, Andy turned and said to us, "Hey, you guys know John." We said hello and John left the court as we started to warm up, but he stayed on and watched. At this point, I had no idea who he was. I had a hard time seeing him as he sat in the shade. Our match began to be competitive. After the first set, we took a brief break, and John and Andy began a conversation. When I heard his voice, the same voice I heard each night on TV, I knew instantly it was Johnny Carson. Thank God, I had not done my usual, "I'm sorry, I didn't get your name."

In fact, by now, things with my eyesight were starting to deteriorate. Tennis was the first real issue that led me to see a doctor. During one of those games, I was having trouble finding the ball on the court after the point. I was fumbling around, and I felt like a dunce as Mike directed me toward the ball. They thought it was a joke, since the ball was plainly at my feet. I could see a ball coming at me, but not on the ground. Once everyone realized it was not a joke, they encouraged me to get my eyes checked.

Based on a recommendation, I saw a specialist. The doctor gave me the typical eye exam and told me I had 20/20 vision. He recommended that I stop worrying about it. A month later, I was back again for another exam, explaining that I was still having trouble finding the tennis ball on the court. He looked again, couldn't find any reason for my dilemma, and sent me away. Several months later, I was back once more, with the same complaint.

During this examination, the doctor looked into the back of my eye and discovered RP. He explained that Retinitis Pigmentosa was a rare eye disease that caused tunnel vision and ultimately blindness. He said little was known about it, and there was no cure. I'll never forget his response when I asked him what I should do. He looked at me and said, "See as much of the world as you can, while you can."

My mind was racing as I drove back to Mike Curb Productions on Sunset Boulevard. I was thirty-four and losing my eyesight. Nothing, it seemed, could be done. I decided three things. First, I would not tell anyone except those to whom I was very close. Second, I would seek other opinions and learn as much as possible about RP. Third, I would continue to pursue my career in the music business while I tried to find a way back into political consulting.

CHAPTER 17
Back to Politics (1976, Mike Curb, Younger)

After President Nixon resigned, the Republican Party struggled with its perception. The brand was damaged, and many thought it was permanent. The disillusion was widespread among Republicans and their candidates, who suffered and lost elections as a result.

It was a memo circulated from then White House staffer J. Robinson West to James Connor that finally triggered a series of wake-up calls across the country. The memo recapped a meeting with David K. Wilson, who at the time was co-chairman of the Republican National Finance Committee. It outlined the incompetence of the party leadership and criticized the lack of political campaign expertise. The memo included a series of follow-up comments, which criticized the lack of understanding related to messaging on television and in media campaigns. Now housed in the Gerald R. Ford Library, the memo's outline actually reinforced many of the suggestions Bill Brock and I had made in our "New Majority" plan.

Although unaware of the memo, I had kept in close contact with colleagues and was aware of the turmoil at the RNC. I was active with the local Los Angeles Republican Party, and saw an opportunity for both Mike and me to help. First, I encouraged him to become active in fundraising for the Los Angeles County Republican Party. The county needed some new blood, and I thought Mike could help the committee and build his Republican credentials at the same time.

Once he became involved, Mike was a big hit with the party elders in L.A. He was young, a successful businessman, and rich. He also came from an industry that was glamorous and exciting. Soon he was having dinner regularly with Holmes Tuttle, Justin Dart, and Republican State Chairman

Gordon Luce. They liked being with Mike and attending his celebrity dinners, and he was willing to give donations to their causes when asked.

I briefed Mike about the two most important things necessary to win a Republican nomination for office in California. The first was raising money, and the second was building support with the party faithful at the grassroots level. One route in California was directly through the Republican Women's Federation, which provided the backbone of volunteer support for the party. Many of the women had the ears of the party elders. Mike was young, handsome, and energetic, which helped with the women's organizations.

Both the elders and the women took to Mike immediately. The money folks liked his record of success at a young age (he was in his early thirties), and the women volunteers liked his youthful looks and enthusiasm. Mike could spend hours charming "the little old ladies," as they were called. He was polite, attentive, and patient.

By 1975, Mike was a well-recognized, active Republican. He was sought after in Republican circles for supplying entertainment for the big dinners and making financial contributions to candidates. He was a welcome speaker and dinner guest. We began to talk seriously about which political office he would like to pursue. One day, I asked him if he was a registered Republican. To my surprise, he responded that he wasn't even registered to vote. Within the next twenty-four hours, at my insistence, he became a registered voter. Unfortunately, his failure to register when he turned eighteen would haunt him in his campaign to become governor of California.

That year, the Reagan for President Campaign began to heat up, and Mike was at the center of the California effort. (Reagan would run against President Ford for the 1976 Republican nomination.) Reagan was viewed as the anti-Washington establishment candidate, and had a powerful team around him. His time as governor had allowed him to build a strong network across the Republican Party. However, money was an issue. Holmes Tuttle asked Mike to help raise money and recruit people from the entertainment community. Mike jumped at the chance.

I felt the Reagan for President campaign would allow Mike to meet the major Republican financial contributors he would need for his own campaign. It would also strengthen his Republican credentials, and that would be useful in a Republican primary. I was excited about the opportunity to personally be involved in another presidential campaign, after believing I was no longer a viable player.

When the Reagan campaign stalled and began to run out of money, Lyn Nofziger and Mike Deaver turned to Mike and asked him to finance the production of a thirty-minute TV program where Reagan would pitch for funds. Mike provided the seed money. Reagan went on the air, and the money started to roll in. Katherine Anderson, the assistant to the campaign controller, told me years later that there were so many envelopes with money arriving at the post office box, "I could barely get the bags into my car." That would be the last time Reagan had trouble raising money. Although he lost the nomination to Jerry Ford, he built the organization necessary to capture the nomination four years later.

For me, the 1976 Reagan presidential campaign marked my true re-entry into the political world. I volunteered to help the campaign, at first with the volunteer core, and then based on my experience, Mike Deaver asked me to be part of the advance team for Reagan's announcement tour. I was excited to be back in the game. My main responsibilities were to help set up events in Florida, North Carolina, New Hampshire, and, of course, California.

I viewed the '76 election campaign as a way for me to resurrect my political career. I knew if Mike Curb was going to run, I would be involved in his campaign. I also knew I had to ensure that my negative press from 1973 would not hinder Mike's campaign. To do that would require a few steps on my part. First, I thought it important to be involved in a high profile campaign before Mike's. The Reagan presidential run offered me that opportunity. Second, I wanted to set the record straight. The only way to do that was with a reporter. After doing some research, I decided on *The L.A. Times* and Ken Reich to do the interview and write the story.

I met with Ken at a coffee shop on Sunset Boulevard. I told him he could ask me any question about my involvement in the Nixon campaign, and I would answer truthfully. In an interview that lasted almost three hours, Ken grilled me about everything that had been covered by the Watergate Senate Committee and leaked from the FBI and Watergate Grand Jury. I answered all of his questions without hesitation. The article Ken wrote was lengthy, informative, and accurate. It pulled no punches. For years, when reporters asked me about my involvement with Watergate activities, I would simply refer them to that article.

I worked with the Reagan advance team, setting up events for his tour announcing his campaign for president. Reagan's formal declaration of candidacy was in Washington, D.C. The rallies we set up were in the initial primary states. In Miami, for the rally, we had selected an outdoor site at a Holiday Inn near the airport. Reagan had lots of support in Florida, and we expected a good turnout. At the beginning of the rally, being the lead advance person, it was my job to move Reagan along the rope line as he shook hands with his supporters. The plan was to then head to the podium, where Reagan would give his announcement speech. As I moved along the rope, it was exciting to see so many people coming out to support him. Suddenly, I saw a man, about two people deep into the crowd, pull out something that looked like a gun. Before I could yell, "GUN," I looked back to see where Reagan had been seconds before. He was gone. Turning my head in the gunman's direction, I saw four Secret Servicemen on top of him. The gun turned out to be plastic. If I had peripheral vision, I would not have needed to turn my head to see all the action. RP was destroying my outer vision and leaving me with a tunnel of sight.

The fascinating aspect of this was Reagan himself. I had been in his presence many times. In every situation, not only did he remain calm, he kept everyone else calm. Calmly, he said, "Let's continue with our rally." After about twenty minutes, Reagan came to the podium and gave his announcement speech to great cheers from an appreciative crowd.

It was setting up the announcement rally in North Carolina where I first met Charlie Black. He was a young staff member of a senator from North Carolina, working as a volunteer on our advance team. Charlie and I met on the tarmac of the Charlotte airport. We were looking for an appropriate site to hold the airport rally. Charlie became a lifelong friend, and is now recognized as one of the Republican Party's best political strategists.

Governor Reagan lost the Republican nomination by a close vote at a contested national convention in Kansas City. When he lost the effort to pick off delegates from the Mississippi delegation, he lost the nomination.

While with Reagan at that convention in Kansas City, Mike Curb ran for Republican National Committeeman from California. Each state has three representatives to the RNC—a committeeman, a committeewoman, and the Republican state chair. The California delegation elected Mike, adding to his Republican credentials.

Holmes Tuttle was encouraging Mike to run for governor, since Jerry Brown was up for re-election in 1978. Jerry Brown was the California Democrat the Republicans hated most, and Holmes insisted this was a great opportunity for Mike. Holmes was so enthusiastic that he got the Reagan "kitchen cabinet" together, and they appealed to Mike to run for governor. Mike was flattered and anxious to please his new friends. I, on the other hand, was skeptical and concerned about him being able to win the governorship. I told Mike that I didn't think he could jump from the music business to governor without experience. I also thought Jerry Brown would be a tough contender, a lot harder to beat than Mike's friends were predicting. I told Mike that he was only in his early thirties and would have plenty of time to run for the top position. It was more important for him to win his first campaign and he should consider running for lieutenant governor.

Mervyn Dymally, who had been a mostly invisible lieutenant governor, was up for re-election, and I thought he would be easier to beat than Brown. At the time, the major responsibility for lieutenant governor was economic development. With Mike's business background, this opportunity was much more suited for his candidacy, and I felt that this campaign would not be as expensive or extensive as a governor's race. If he won, it would also provide him flexibility for future campaigns.

Although it was difficult to argue with the big money guys, Mike made the right decision and announced he would run for lieutenant governor in the 1978 election. At his first, star-studded fundraiser at the Century Plaza Hotel, he raised a million dollars. In those days, even in California, that was unheard of for a campaign for lieutenant governor.

Mike's first challenge was to win the Republican nomination in the primary. He had some stiff competition from Republican office holders with more political experience.

While we were in the early stages of Mike's campaign, I was approached by Evelle Younger to run his campaign for governor, running against Brown. Evelle was the attorney general of California and was a Reagan ally. The problem Younger had from the beginning was fundraising. He was not part of the establishment, and as attorney general, he had not been pro-business. Instead, he had built a record of being pro-environment and pro-consumer, neither attractive to the business community. In his early years, he had been an FBI agent and was one of the first TV judges. His show had been very popular in L.A., and he had a large following in southern California. Brown, at this time, was at the height of his popularity, and I knew a campaign against him would be difficult. Also, very rarely did political consultants manage two state-wide campaigns at the same time. This would be a challenge.

Since I had committed to Mike first, I wanted to make sure he was okay with me running a dual campaign. At this point, Mike was leading in the Republican primary, as was Younger. In the polls we were taking, testing the general election, Curb was slightly ahead of Dymally, while Younger was running behind Brown in double digits. It would take some unique tactics to close the gap for Younger while maintaining the lead for Curb, but Mike was secure in what we had planned for his campaign. He saw the potential to close the gap for Younger, which would be great for the Republican Party. Once Mike agreed, I took on Shel Lytton as my deputy campaign manager. Shel had been an assistant attorney general under Younger, and counsel to President Ford's California 1976 campaign.

This dual campaign manager position created a lot of problems for me. I was also writing and producing all of the commercials and handling the paid media for both candidates. My dual role was not popular with my political consulting colleagues. In a column for the *San Francisco Chronicle*, with the headline, "Outsider in Charge of 2 GOP Races," Larry Liebert wrote:

> Republican party leaders tend to use unflattering adjectives to describe Ken Rietz, words like 'arrogant' and 'Machiavellian' … they are just as commonly balanced by a consensus that Rietz is one of the best campaign technicians around.
>
> He'd better be if the Republican party is to stand a chance in November's election. The 37-year-old with the undiplomatic

manner and extraordinary savvy as a campaign expert is simultaneously managing Attorney General Evelle Younger's race for governor and record tycoon Mike Curb's race for lieutenant governor.

'I do what I think has to be done to win,' Rietz said in an interview at the Younger-Curb campaign headquarters in Los Angeles. 'I don't get into a campaign to create a good reputation for myself.

'And there's my personality,' Rietz adds. 'I'm not outgoing. I don't enjoy cocktail parties and glad-handing and mixing with a lot of people.'

There's even a medical explanation: Rietz lacks peripheral vision. 'A lot of people think I'm rude because I never see them,' said Rietz, who stands an imposing six-foot-one.

If there is a single explanation for Rietz' compensating image as a savvy professional, it is that he is unflappable. He seldom gives in to campaign panic and seldom deviates from his original strategy or stops to regret a mistake.

'He never looks back,' Curb said with admiration.

Younger won a three-way primary against San Diego Mayor Pete Wilson and Ken Maddy, a young, attractive state senator from Fresno. The race split pretty much along geographic lines, with Maddy winning up north and Wilson winning in the south. Younger carried the vote-rich center of the state, including Los Angeles County.

The problem was that, although Younger had won the primary, he was way behind Brown. Curb won his primary and had a legitimate chance to win the general election. In his first run for office, Mike was a good candidate and easy to work with. Younger, on the other hand, had been through the political wars, served two terms as attorney general, and felt his time had come. He was surrounded by well-intentioned advisers who generally told him what he wanted to hear.

One of the things that made Mike successful in business is his tremendous focus. He also works hard and is willing to take chances. These qualities helped make him a terrific candidate for office. He was also very competitive, and would do what was necessary to win. That meant raising a lot of money, something at which Mike excelled.

Throughout both campaigns, we leveraged our internal resources. Most of the commercials and materials for the candidates were produced through my company, Palisades Communications. This provided us a way to carefully coordinate the messages and keep careful track of the budget.

With Younger, our strategy was to attack Brown on the issues and bring to the forefront Brown's greater ambitions for the presidency. We used commercials on radio and television and began to close our gap with voters, but Younger was often his own worst enemy. Although he was known as a good public servant and was an effective attorney general, Younger had a drinking problem. It took me a while to figure that out. One day, at a reception, I discovered that the wine I thought he was drinking was actually Scotch. It was his habit to drink straight Scotch in a wine glass. Many of his speeches after lunch were meandering affairs with little focus.

I recall one speech in particular, in agriculture-rich Fresno. We arrived by bus, and I briefed Younger on the speech as well as the question and answer period to follow. At the time, there was a proposal to build a pipeline called the "peripheral canal" from northern California to Los Angeles that would transport water from the north and central California to the south. This was, of course, not popular in northern California or the Central Valley, where water was essential for agriculture. While Younger supported the canal, I admonished him not to mention it in his speech, nor during in the Q & A. He assured me he would not.

After a longer than normal reception before, and a few glasses of "wine" during lunch, Younger rose to speak. The California press corps was traveling with us, and I expected Younger to give a hard-hitting law and order speech. Instead, he got up and endorsed the building of the peripheral canal. He lost sight of the important law and order message of the campaign, and fallen into the peripheral canal trap. His statement also made balancing the Curb and Younger campaigns more difficult, as Curb had come out firmly against building the canal project.

Evelle had a friend in Beverly Hills, a lawyer who represented Aaron

Spelling. Spelling offered to help us with our TV commercials, and we scheduled a meeting at the lawyer's office so we could talk about content and logistics. Besides Evelle, Shel, and myself, the lawyer invited Aaron and several other people.

As we sat down in the informal conference area, we were asked for our drink preferences. It was about 5 p.m., and an after work cocktail seemed like a good idea. As the drinks were being passed out, a very pretty young woman walked in and said, "We are all set up in the boardroom," and then walked out. I didn't get it. Soon, however, our lawyer friend left the room, and we continued to talk. When he returned about twenty minutes later, he smiled and said, "Would anyone else like to go see the girls?"

There I was, in a meeting with the California attorney general, and a couple of call girls were plying their trade in the adjoining room. While both Shel and I decided to pass, we often talked about the strange situation. That was show business in Hollywood.

Aaron Spelling did produce some very beautiful commercials for us. He used the set of the TV show *Vegas* in Las Vegas. I don't think anyone had the quality of spots in that campaign that we did. Unfortunately, we didn't have the money to air them effectively, or the candidate to win the race.

The best commercial we made for Mike Curb was aimed at the Hispanic community. Mike's grandmother had lived in Mexico, and his sister spoke fluent Spanish. We shot a commercial with Carole looking into the camera and telling her grandmother's story in Spanish. As a result, Mike received a larger share of the Hispanic vote than was usual for a Republican candidate.

A positive thing Younger helped accomplish during the campaign was bringing together President Ford and Gov. Reagan, who had opposed each other for the 1976 Republican nomination for president. Under the headline "Ford, Reagan Unite to Aid Younger," *The San Diego Union* reported:

> Hoping to stem Evelle J. Younger's slide in the polls, former President Gerald R. Ford yesterday had his first private meeting in two years with his biggest intra party rival, former California Gov. Ronald Reagan, and pledged with Reagan to campaign for Younger's gubernatorial candidacy.

He was brought to Ford's new home here (Rancho Mirage) to tape three television commercials - one of them boosting Younger.

Although the major contributors put pressure on Mike Curb to distance himself from Younger, who was trailing in the polls, Curb was steadfast in his support of the joint campaign. An article in *The Valley News*, under the headline, "Joint Campaign with Younger Ok'd by Curb" said:

> Michael Curb, Republican candidate for lieutenant governor, said Friday he has no misgivings about merging his campaign with gubernatorial candidate Evelle J. Younger, even though Curb has forged ahead in recent polls and Younger is losing ground.
>
> 'We both made a commitment to run a joint campaign and we intend to keep it,' Curb told a breakfast meeting of Los Angeles political reporters Friday.
>
> He conceded that the recent California Field Poll, which showed Gov. Edmund G. Brown Jr. widening his lead over Younger from 5 percent to 14 percent, will probably hurt the joint Younger-Curb fund-raising effort.
>
> Curb, who moved ahead of Lt. Gov. Mervyn M. Dymally by 2 percent in the same poll, was asked if his chances would be better if he were on his own.
>
> 'To tell you the truth,' he said, 'I really haven't thought about it.'

Younger's problems began when he announced he would take a vacation immediately following the June primary. Shel and I argued against the vacation, and said he should begin his general election campaign immediately after the primary. His other advisors urged him to go, as he needed a rest. After winning the primary, he and his wife Mildred, who was his most influential advisor, went to Hawaii.

Jerry Brown used that vacation to turn the tables on Younger. He created a series of very catchy radio commercials, complete with Hawaiian music, saying that Evelle Younger was off on a fancy Hawaiian vacation while he, Jerry Brown, was looking after the problems of the state. He flooded the airwaves with these very memorable commercials. Brown also cleverly co-opted Proposition 13 from Younger, endorsing this very popular anti-property tax initiative. When, after two weeks, Younger returned from his vacation, he was more than twenty points behind in the race, and we never caught up. Brown won in a landslide. The consolation for Shel and me was that our other candidate, Mike Curb, won a history-making victory.

Compared to Younger, Mike was exactly the type of political candidate with whom consultants want to work. Mike's Republican primary was close, but in the multi-candidate race, after a rough and tumble campaign with Lt. Gov. Dymally, Mike won. He became the first lieutenant governor in almost one hundred years elected from the opposite party of the governor. The November 8, 1978 *Los Angeles Times* front page banner headline blared, "Split Ticket Elected." The sub-headline was "Curb Wins Despite Landslide for Brown." Jerry Brown, the Democrat, had a Republican lieutenant governor, which was not good news for Brown, who had his sights on running for president in 1980.

The California Constitution makes the lieutenant governor the acting governor, with full powers, whenever the governor leaves the state.

CALIFORNIA CONSTITUTION

ARTICLE 5 EXECUTIVE

SEC. 10. The Lieutenant Governor shall become Governor when a vacancy occurs in the office of Governor.

The Lieutenant Governor shall act as Governor during the impeachment, absence from the State, or other temporary disability of the Governor or of a Governor-elect who fails to take office.

* * * * *

The Supreme Court has exclusive jurisdiction to determine all questions arising under this section.

This would prove to be the undoing of Jerry Brown in his run for president. Since Brown had given little support to Dymally in his campaign against Curb, he would suffer. Brown's self-absorption with his own ambition created problems down the road.

With the advice of Ed Meese, who later became President Reagan's attorney general, Mike used his "acting governor" authority while Brown was out of state campaigning for president. Mike took the opportunity, during the governor's absences, to sign legislation into law that Brown did not support. In addition, Mike made appointments that Brown did not want, including Armand Arabian in one high profile judicial appointment.

It was the kind of thing that amused Californians and created national news. Lt. Gov. Mike Curb would wait in his office until Gov. Jerry Brown left California air space on his way to campaign in New Hampshire or Wisconsin. When he received word that Brown was out of the state and the powers of the governorship had transferred to him, Curb would sign bills into law and make appointments. When the governor returned, he would rescind the appointments and try to undo the legislation.

Mike achieved more as lieutenant governor than most. He signed into law the "Rob a Home, Go to Prison" legislation that Brown refused to sign. He appointed the California Agriculture Commission, which dealt with migrant worker exposure to pesticides. He ordered out the National Guard during a flood in southern California. He became the best-known lieutenant governor in the nation. His fellow lieutenant governors, from both parties, elected him chairman of the National Lieutenant Governors Association.

Governor Brown decided to put an end to Mike's activities. He sued his lieutenant governor to strip his powers, and took it to the California Supreme Court. Curb hired Ted Olson (later an official in the Reagan and Bush administrations) to argue his case. Shel Lytton, Curb's chief of staff and a talented courtroom lawyer, assisted with the case. Curb won the case before the California Supreme Court, and Jerry Brown's campaign for president fizzled. Brown had lost sight of his road to the presidency when he didn't protect his flank by supporting Dymally for lieutenant governor. Mike Curb had used his four years in office to build his name identification, create a solid base of support with the volunteers, and continue to build his financial base.

All campaigns have humorous moments. If they didn't, those of us who earned our living running them wouldn't continue for so many years. In those times, the money just wasn't that great. During the Younger campaign for governor, I came to know Jerry Brown's chief of staff, Gray Davis, quite well. Gray would become California's governor years later, but in those days he was a young, ambitious, hard charger, running Brown's re-election campaign.

We had decided it was not in our interest to have Younger debate Brown. At the same time, we needed to make it look as if we wanted to debate. So we challenged Brown to debate, and set up a series of meetings to "work out the details." These meetings became known in the press corps as "the meetings to debate the debate."

The Associated Press described our meetings this way in an article titled "Debate Over Debates":

> The debate over the gubernatorial debates remained only a war of words today with still no assurance that they will ever occur.
>
> In the latest verbal battle, Attorney General Evelle Younger's campaign manager, Ken Rietz, accused Gov. Edmund G. Brown Jr.'s camp Wednesday of 'making a mockery of the debate' by rolling in seemingly insurmountable stumbling blocks.
>
> Brown's campaign director, Gray Davis, countered by calling Rietz a 'born-again debater,' since opinion polls have showed Younger trailing Brown, but he offered to meet privately with Rietz to settle the issue.

I would arrive at these debate meetings with Shel Lytton. Gray Davis would attend with several of his staff. The press would stake out the location and wait for us to emerge with an agreement. Although the Brown campaign wanted debates, we did not. We only wanted to delay the inevitable and make it appear that we were anxious to debate.

Even in those early days, Gray was very concerned about his public image. That led to a practical joke by me.

The first meeting ran about three hours. We reached no conclusion about the number of debates or where they would be held. The only agreement we came to was that we would meet again the following week.

As the meeting was breaking up, Gray came over to me. He said, "The press has been camped outside our door for a couple of hours, and we should talk to them. Do you want to go first or should I?" I told Gray he could go first. We left the room and headed for the anxious news media. I watched as Gray talked, and then I had my turn.

When we met a week later, as I had a reputation as a good media coach, the first thing Gray asked me was how I thought he did. I looked at him and said, "Gray, I thought you did really well. The only problem you have is when you look into the camera, you tilt your head to the right. You should try harder to keep your body straight."

I'm sure Gray thought about that comment all through our debate meeting. After I talked to the press first, he went before the cameras. He was trying so hard not to tilt right that he was overcompensating by leaning heavily to the left. He really looked terrible. Of course, he hadn't been tilting to the right in the first place. Now, he was overcorrecting a problem that he actually didn't have. Shel and I had a good laugh at Gray's expense.

In the weeks that followed, Gray caught on to my little practical joke, and he did just fine on his own. We came to know each other and actually became friends. When he ran for the State Assembly a few years later, he asked me to be chairman of Republicans for Davis. Grinning, I told him I would do it only, "as long as you don't tell anyone." He laughed and, of course, added my name to his campaign letterhead.

CHAPTER 18
The 1980 Republican National Convention

When President Ford was defeated in 1976, the National Republican Party was in a tailspin. It had lost the White House and the Senate. The Democrats controlled the Congress, most of the governorships, and the state legislatures. The party needed rebuilding from the bottom up, and it needed to reevaluate its message to the voters. Most importantly, the Republican Party needed new leadership.

I was also disappointed that Sen. Brock lost his Senate seat in that 1976 election. He was caught up in the Democrat sweep following Nixon's resignation. In addition, Brock had refused to disclose his tax returns, and that became an issue. Bill Brock and his family were adamant about privacy. In the end, between his refusal to disclose those returns and the Carter candidacy from neighboring Georgia, he lost voter approval.

Throughout his career in the House and in the Senate, Brock was a youthful leader. He was a thoughtful hard-charger who had been active in young Republican politics. After his loss, Bill and his wife Muffet visited me in California to discuss his future options. He had been in public office for fourteen years, and had been the conservative favorite to seek the presidency before Nixon's resignation. Now he was out of office and needed to find a new path forward. During our week-long discussions in a friend's beachfront cottage, we settled on Bill going back to what he felt most strongly about. He wanted the Republican Party to be re-born, and thought that he could provide the leadership. He decided to run for Republican national chairman when the RNC met in January 1977.

Brock's former chief of staff and close friend, Bill Timmons, ran the "syndicate" of young Republicans. Over the past few years, this group had selected the National Young Republican chairman on a regular basis. They would provide a valuable resource of conservative activist volunteers in a campaign for Republican national chairman. Brock's opponent would be a Texan who had supported Ford—James Baker.

In January 1977, when the RNC gathered to select the new chairman, the debate was fierce, with the old guard favoring Baker and the young leadership supporting Brock. After multiple ballots, Brock won, and one of his biggest supporters was Mike Curb, the Republican national committeeman from California. Bill Brock was a superior choice and would end up being one of the best chairmen to lead the Republican Party. He understood grassroots politics, believed in reaching out to the minority community, and was not afraid of new ideas.

At the RNC, Brock set up issues counsels to bring the party's best minds together to discuss positions it should take on future issues. He established concord conferences across the country, designed to recruit young people and find young candidates for the future. He recruited an experienced staff of proven political campaign strategists, including Charlie Black and Dennis Whitfield. To fuel the campaigns, he established an aggressive fund-raising operation.

The result of his four-year tenure at the RNC was a turn-around of the party at the local and national levels. In 1976, the party's candidates had taken a beating at the polls; it left Republicans holding only thirty-eight seats in the Senate, barely a third of the seats in the House, only twelve of the nation's governorships, and control of only seventeen of the ninety-eight partisan state legislative bodies. By the end of the 1980 elections, the picture had changed dramatically. The Republicans had elected a president, taken the majority in the Senate for the first time in over twenty-five years, gained thirty-three seats in the House, added four new Republican governors, and picked up more than two hundred new seats in state legislatures. With Reagan heading the ticket, November 4, 1980, marked the biggest political turnaround in nearly fifty years of American history.

As the 1980 Republican National Convention approached, Bill was determined to make it a different and more meaningful experience. To emphasize the efforts he was leading to attract the Black vote, Brock chose

Detroit as the site for the convention. The effort to change both the image and the actuality of the Republican Party as it related to minorities, women, and blue collar Americans was clear, focused, and determined.

To add some life and excitement to what had been a pretty dull process, Bill turned to Mike Curb and me. Mike would serve as the program chairman of the convention, and I was the program director. Mike and I worked for about a year, putting together the plans and the program for the convention. We were in charge of everything that would happen on the podium except the nomination process and the acceptance speeches. Both Mike and I were well versed in broadcast media, and knew there had to be some changes to facilitate our message reaching the public on television. We knew that thousands of members of the press corps would attend, representing local communities throughout the country. The program we were planning had to be aimed at them, as well as the three networks and one new cable channel (CNN) that would cover the convention.

We began our research by analyzing the tapes of the 1976 convention. We looked at them minute by minute, and compared the activities on the convention podium with what the TV networks were covering. Based on this study, we made several changes to the traditional program. To attract viewers the first night (Monday), we scheduled former President Ford to speak, and moved the keynote address to the second night (Tuesday). We found that generally Tuesday night had the lowest viewership, and by moving the keynote speech, we hoped to attract additional viewers. To keep the convention moving and the viewers engaged, we asked that speakers limit their speeches to fewer than ten minutes. We also planned each night of the four-day convention to end no later than 11 p.m. eastern time.

The San Rafael Independent Journal, under the headline, "Waltz for GOP Convention," described our planning this way:

> The nuts and bolts job of making the convention interesting to national TV viewers belongs to Curb's chief of staff, Ken Rietz, now one of the GOP's first-string political pros. Rietz is executive director of the convention program committee.
>
> Because Reagan figures to have the nomination nailed down

long before the convention, Rietz doesn't have much of a suspense element to work with in planning the program.

But, with convention manager Bob Carter, he's analyzed hours of videotapes of past conventions and has devised a strategy he thinks will keep the camera eye focused on the podium from gavel to gavel.

'We view our job as making what's going on, on the podium so interesting that the networks will have to cover it,' Rietz said.

The 1976 convention in Kansas City offered some outstanding horrible examples of creating dead time around the podium, including an entire Tuesday that put everyone to sleep and a long prime time pause for snapping a group photo. Rietz doesn't plan to repeat those mistakes.

He believes he's got a socko opening night act in an address by former President Gerald Ford, so he's altering tradition by moving the keynote speech by Michigan Rep. Guy A. Vander Jagt back to Tuesday to keep the momentum going.

Our most important goal was to showcase Gov. Ronald Reagan. The first step was producing an arrival rally at his Detroit hotel the first day of the convention. We would broadcast Reagan's arrival at the rally to the delegates in the convention hall, so they would get their first look at the next Republican nominee on the big screen. We asked L.A. producer Tim Swift to coordinate this; he had handled events for the Mike Curb for Lt. Gov. campaign. Reagan would also appear in the convention hall at the podium Wednesday and Thursday nights during prime time.

One night, Bill Brock and I were asked to have dinner with Bill Casey, the future director of the CIA, who was playing a prominent role in the Reagan campaign. He wanted to give us his thoughts about the convention. Ed Meese would join the three of us at dinner.

As we entered the restaurant at the L.A. airport Marriott, where the Reagan campaign was headquartered, Ed Meese tugged at my arm to hold me back. He told me Bill Casey wanted to talk about the convention theme, and had some concerns that we needed something fresh. Casey was suggesting "A Fresh Start." Ed said, "As you know, that's a laundry detergent. So, please be prepared to guide him toward another theme."

I didn't say much during dinner as I thought about a potential theme. I needed to be ready when Casey suggested his. We talked about the convention goals and how we had to bring the party back together; how it would take everyone working together to win in November, and how the nation needed a fresh start, after four years of Carter.

As we arrived at the theme discussion, Casey pitched his idea of "A Fresh Start." He was a pretty heavy drinker, and the more he drank, the more determined he became about his suggested theme. As diplomatically as possible, I finally said, "I think the concept of fresh start is important, but it doesn't include the 'together' theme we need. How about, 'Together, a new beginning.'?"

Casey sat back in silence. He said, "What about 'Together, a fresh start.'?" Bill Brock and Ed Meese chimed in, and the theme became, "Together… A New Beginning."

Having developed the convention theme and keeping in mind Brock's request to make the convention entertaining, we put together a one-hour live theme program. The show opened with the Mike Curb Congregation singing the song Mike had composed, "Together, A New Beginning." In the three-minute song, Mike managed to mention all fifty states, and the state delegations cheered wildly when they heard theirs. Other performers in the show were Susan Anton, Buddy Ebsen, Vicki Lawrence, Wayne Newton, the Osmonds, Lyle Waggoner, and Efrem Zimbalist Jr. The show also included welcome remarks by Detroit Hall of Fame hockey player Gordy Howe, perhaps the most popular Detroit athlete ever. Our pre-taped segments were provided by Michael Landon and Jimmy Stewart. Stewart, looking into the camera, set the tone for the convention, saying:

> Now there are a couple of words that have run all through American history. We hear them in our great documents, in all our literature of patriotism because they represent the ideals for which we stand.

Those words are liberty and justice and they're very fine words and standing for fine ideals and I doubt if any of us could describe America without using one or the other or both of them.

Well now in 1980, in the opening of this convention, we're starting to add five more words to these two.

Five more ideals that'll augment the liberty and guarantee the justice and I'd like to tell you these five words because they can lead us all to a rebirth of harmony and a national pride in the years ahead.

The words are family, neighborhood, work, peace and freedom.

Family, that's where it all starts, with people who share a roof, a name and a heritage of memories.

Families are the core of the country and the neighborhood they live in is a collection of all the marvelous diversity that makes up the face of America. It took work to achieve the things we love about our country and it's gonna take more work to keep them.

And the hardest work of all will be to turn us around, back on to the road of optimism and growth where we belong.

And at the end of that road are the ultimate goals of all humanity, peace now and forever and the freedom we all deserve to enjoy it.

Now here you have family, neighborhood, work, peace and freedom. They're five pretty good words and if we respect them, they just might return the favor and honor us by sticking around for a few years.

Certainly for the next four.

Tim Swift also helped us recruit celebrities to sing the national anthem at each session, including Glen Campbell, Pat Boone, Tonya Tucker, and Wayne Newton. Although the theme did not receive end-to-end coverage by the networks, it energized the delegates, and nationally, the coverage by the media was better than expected.

One example was the following article from the *St. Petersburg Times*:

> If you switched on television late Monday night, you might not have recognized the network shows as coverage of the Republican National Convention.
>
> You probably would have figured you had tuned into a variety extravaganza. A parade of flashy show biz celebrities, led by singers Donnie and Marie Osmond, were entertaining viewers and, presumably, voters.
>
> Welcome to politics, 1980 style.
>
> Without most Americans being fully aware of what was happening, political substance years ago started taking second place to the politicians' media image.
>
> How true this has become was revealed by Republican National Committee program director Ken Rietz, who helped make the 1980 Republican convention into a slickly packaged show designed to hook 90-million TV viewers.

Along with all the details of producing the convention, Mike and I had a series of speeches for which we were responsible. That meant spending a lot of time in Detroit, including the three months leading up to the convention. As Gov. Reagan became the obvious winner of the nomination, we began to work closely with his staff. We wanted to be sure he received a good convention "bounce."

One of the changes we made was rejecting the standard format for national political conventions, which previously were used as a forum for attack. We wanted the viewers to receive a positive impression leading up to the speech by Gov. Reagan. We asked the speakers to talk about the future, rather than the past.

In 1976, Reagan had been the anti-establishment candidate running against President Ford for the nomination. Because this was Reagan's convention, with delegates who had supported him in the primaries against Ford, we were worried about their reactions to some of our more moderate speakers, like former President Ford and Henry Kissinger. Concerned about how this conservative audience would receive them, we solved the problem by carefully orchestrating the introduction of each.

In Kissinger's case, he was introduced by one of the more conservative senators. In fact, the senator gave such an impassioned, conservative plea that Kissinger told our people backstage that he would not walk out while the senator was still at the podium. I was in our skybox, orchestrating the various elements, when Gary Hunt called me from backstage. He told me Kissinger would not go out there with the senator still at the podium. I told Gary to physically push him out if he had to. We needed to keep the program on schedule.

For President Ford's introduction, Hollywood producer Chuck Ashman and I created a very dramatic five-minute film, *The Ford Presidency*. Without a narrator and with a soundtrack of the popular song "What I Did for Love," Ashman showed Ford working in Washington and spending time with his family at the White House. It worked. When Ford walked out to speak, the audience was on its feet, cheering.

One of the videos I enjoyed shooting was with ninety-year old Alf Landon, who had been the Republican nominee for president in1936. Alf was beloved by many, especially the grassroots in the party. (Alf's daughter, Nancy Kassebaum, later elected to the Senate, married former Sen. Howard Baker.)

Since teleprompters were so new at the time, we wanted to make sure all of our speakers were comfortable with the technology and that each individual speech was timely and would play well with the audience. We also wanted each speech to stay on message and emphasize our "Together, A New Beginning" theme. Since each speech was put on a teleprompter, we received copies ahead of time, allowing us to review them. I assigned my friend, Tully Plesser, to read each speech in advance and make sure they were on message.

Early one morning, Tully came to me with a frantic look on his face.

He said, "Ken, better look at this invocation Billy Graham is scheduled to give." As he was pushing the paper into my hands, I couldn't imagine what Billy Graham would say that could possibly be controversial, but I thought I should humor Tully. When I looked at the invocation, I could see the problem. Graham had a line that looked innocent enough: "Lord, please keep our hostages in Iran." I knew what he was trying to say—keep them safe—but I also knew how it might play in the media. The question was how to tell Graham. I decided to talk to him when he did his practice run-through, and approached him cautiously. When I pointed to the phrase, he immediately knew the problem. "I better change that," he said. I sighed with relief.

We didn't have too many other problems with our scripts. The convention ran on schedule and on theme, until we got to the selection of the vice presidential nominee.

Reagan was undecided about his running mate. Paul Laxalt was a longtime friend and had conservative support. George H. W. Bush had run a good campaign against Reagan for the nomination, coming in second. Unexpectedly, there was a suggestion that former President Ford, running as the candidate for vice president, would bring the kind of experience to the ticket that Reagan needed. Many Washington politicians viewed Reagan as an actor who had been accidently elected governor of California. The selection of Reagan's running mate was up in the air, and things at the convention hall were in turmoil.

Our plan called for Reagan to announce his choice during his first appearance in the hall on Wednesday night. As the time approached for him to appear, I received a phone call at my place on the podium from Bill Timmons, who was the convention manager for the Reagan campaign. He said, "Ken, we have run into a little snag, and there is going to be a delay in the announcement." He hung up. There I was, with the hall full of the Republican faithful, the news media in full action, network TV grinding away, and I had no speaker to put on the podium. We had carefully planned this time for Reagan's appearance.

I did the only thing I could. I asked the band to begin playing, and hoped the delegates would begin cheering in anticipation. They did. I received two more calls from Timmons, asking me to keep the delay going. We did. For forty-five minutes, we did nothing in the convention hall except create noise with the band and the delegates.

I have no idea what went on behind the scenes and how it was settled. All I know is that it was a very long forty-five minutes. Finally, Timmons called me with the news that Reagan was on his way to the podium, and I was to find George Bush. I did, and soon after, Reagan walked onto the podium with Bush. Following a short introduction by Reagan, the nominating formalities of the vice presidential candidacy were under way. The last night of the convention, Bush would speak first, followed by Reagan. Our two nominees would accept their party's nomination and establish the theme for the remaining campaign. The delegates were brimming with enthusiasm, and the networks were ready to carry every word.

We established a policy with all three networks of not having a major speaker walk out to the podium or begin speaking while they were on a commercial break. That night, just as Bush walked out on the stage, the networks went to a commercial break. I told the band to begin playing. While the delegates cheered and Bush stood waving to the crowd, I watched the monitors so that I could stop the band when the networks came out of their break. That would quiet the crowd.

The networks were still out when I received a call in the skybox from Jolly Gissel, who was manning my post on the podium. He said quickly, "Mrs. Reagan thinks the applause has gone on long enough." I said, "Jolly, the networks are still on a commercial break. Bush cannot start his speech yet." Two more times, Jolly called me with Nancy Reagan standing at his elbow. Finally, out of frustration, I yelled into the phone, "Jolly, you tell Mrs. Reagan that she can run the White House when they get there, I'm running this program." Just then, the networks came back. I cued the band to stop, and Bush began to speak. I'm sure Jolly did not repeat my comments to Nancy Reagan—but I was never invited to the White House while she was there.

I only met Nancy Reagan once; she was there when we were meeting with Gov. Reagan to plan the convention and get his comments at their home in Los Angeles. After reviewing the program with them, they both asked a number of questions about speakers and made some suggestions.

Then, the governor made the most important comment of all, something I would remember for meetings and events I have set up since. He said, "Remember, Ken, always leave them wanting more." He was right, and we did.

Of all the candidates with whom I have had the opportunity to work, President Reagan was one of the few who never lost sight of who he was and what he stood for. He was a man of principal and determination. He loved his country, and was always gracious to those around him. Reagan was appreciative to everyone, no matter the rank. He was grounded in his own vision of what the world should be. Those who worked closely with him shared his vision.

While there were tense moments in the preparation and production of the convention, it was a huge success. RNC Chairman Brock's vision had worked. The party closed the convention more united than ever. By the end of the convention, Reagan had a sixteen point bounce in the Harris poll. Following the election, Brock would join the Reagan Administration, first as U.S. Trade representative and then as secretary of Labor.

CHAPTER 19
Curb Runs for Governor

As lieutenant governor, Mike Curb had taken the steps he needed to position himself to run for governor. He courted the big money crowd and worked to elect President Reagan. He now had the all-important name identification needed in California. He became well-known by making appointments while Gov. Brown was out of state campaigning for president. He played a prominent role at the 1980 Republican Convention and worked the grassroots Republican organizations. He had the backing of the Reagan finance organization and the leaders of the California Republican Women's Federation.

I had encouraged Mike to meet with prominent Republicans prior to his announcement of running for governor and to seek their advice about the up-coming campaign. One of the most prominent in California was former President Richard Nixon. After his resignation, Nixon had moved to San Clemente to write his books and escape the spotlight. Since I was still in touch with many from the Nixon organization, I contacted Maurice Stans, a close friend of the former president and former secretary of Commerce. I asked him to help schedule an appointment with Nixon, and Stans was happy to help. He, Mike, and I headed for San Clemente.

Joining us at the meeting was Ken Khachigian, an advisor to Nixon. Ken was also a close friend and adviser to the California attorney general, George Deukmeijian, who had not announced his campaign for governor, and was, at that time, keeping his options open.

During the meeting, Nixon was at his best. Relaxed and outgoing, he loved to talk about politics, and his knowledge of the California political situation was unmatched. We talked about issues and county Republican leaders. He gave us his analysis on winning against the Democrats, and spoke about what we needed to do. It was an informative and exciting meeting. At the end, while we were walking out, after Ken Khachigian left the room, Nixon paused and said to me, "Beware of the attorney general." We continued to walk toward our car. Obviously, Nixon knew what he could not say in front of Ken, which was that the attorney general was planning to run for governor. We knew that he would be a tough opponent, and the meeting with Nixon changed our view of the race.

I'm not sure how long Mike had nurtured the ambition to be governor of California, but he had it as long as I knew him. He had his sights set on it, and nothing, no setback of any kind, would deter him.

Unlike most young politicians, Mike did not immerse himself in issues. In fact, when I first started working with him, I was surprised that he didn't subscribe to a single national news magazine. His whole world was the music business. I was concerned that in his campaign for governor, he would need to be informed about all current issues, worldwide. I encouraged him to take up reading news magazines, as well as the local press like *The L.A. Times*. Once Mike realized the importance of being up-to-date on current affairs and issues, he became consumed with getting it right. Not only did he read, he started reaching out to experts on specific California topics.

Mike had gained his reputation and much of his fortune in the music world through his musical talent and understanding of the business. He was a good negotiator, and felt he could apply the same talents to politics. But politics differs from business in many aspects. Mike believed he could talk some of his opponents out of the primary, and thought he had a better chance of winning with less people running. Mike and I disagreed on this. I felt, as did my friend Lyn Nofziger, that the more candidates there were in the Republican primary, the better Mike's chances were of winning.

Working through George Gorton, who was managing the Pete Wilson campaign for governor, we suggested that Wilson would be better off in the Senate race. We told Gorton that if Wilson changed to that race, we could help him raise money. It took several weeks before Gorton called me privately and asked, "Are you sure you want to do this?" Although I was skeptical, Curb was determined. In the end, Wilson dropped out of the race for governor and ran for the U. S. Senate. This was a mistake for us. Wilson was a moderate like Deukmejian. Instead of two, we now had one, and that allowed the moderates to coalesce around one candidate. In the end, we lost by less than one percent to Deukmejian, when he should have been splitting his vote with Wilson. For Wilson, it was a brilliant move. He ended up in the U.S. Senate.

Mike had lost sight of one of the basic rules of California politics: a crowded field always favored the conservative candidate in a Republican primary. In this case, the conservative was Mike Curb.

There were other flaws in our campaign that contributed to our less than one percent loss. The Deukmejian campaign exploited our mistakes, and also used a last minute negative advertising campaign to distort Mike Curb's record. They stole the election out from under us.

The press corps in California did not like Mike Curb. He was a newcomer to politics, and had won his first campaign for statewide office. He was wealthy, and he looked even younger than his thirty-six years. He had taken on Jerry Brown, making appointments in his absence. Mike was also uncomfortable with the press and did not spend a lot of time courting them, nor did he go to the bars in Sacramento to hang out with them. The press was offended by this. Standard practice for other politicians in Sacramento was to spend time in the bars with the news media, drinking and schmoozing. The mistakes made with the press during Curb's run toward the primary fueled Deukmejian's campaign, which did a very good job of exploiting them.

We had decided to formally announce Mike's candidacy for governor at the fall state Republican convention in Palm Springs in 1981, the year before the election. We had raised a lot of money, which would give us a head start on the other candidates. At this point, the field of candidates was crowded. Our plan was to hold a press conference in Palm Springs and then, using several airplanes, take the news media on a tour of the state's major media markets.

Mike had worked hard on a list of endorsements that he wanted to release just before the convention. His thought was this would show strength and discourage the other candidates. The list was of several hundred Republican leaders, and we mailed it to the delegates who would attend the convention.

Like all such lists, there were people who had told Mike they supported him. Unfortunately, some were surprised when they saw their names in print. Linda Breakstone, a tenacious reporter for *The L.A. Herald Examiner*, decided to call those on the list and see how many she could find who were lukewarm toward Curb. She found several and wrote a story for the paper the Friday before the convention, challenging the list.

Linda was an attractive young woman. There had been a rumor about her involvement with a staff member in the Deukmejian campaign. This was not something to which I paid any attention, as politics did spawn strange bedfellows. The Breakstone article, however, promised to cause us a major headache at the press conference. When Shel Lytton and I briefed Mike before he went out to meet the press, we stressed he should stay away from the issue and merely mention that some people might have changed their mind since they committed, and that this was their right; he should get off the subject and on to other things.

I'm not sure why Mike responded the way he did at the press conference. Perhaps it was because Linda positioned herself right at the front of the room, where Mike had to look at her. In any event, as I watched from the back of the room where I normally stood during a press conference, Mike created a memorable moment in California politics. When asked by another reporter about the Breakstone story, he looked at her and then at me in the back of the room and said, "I have been told not to mention this, but Ken, this time I can't take your advice." Then he launched into a description of what he called an unhealthy relationship between Linda and a member of the Deukmejian staff. It was a media-relations nightmare.

When Mike finished and left the stage, the press flocked around me, asking me what advice I had given Mike. I politely excused myself and went to meet Mike and Shel. That was when Mike made his next media relations mistake.

He told me to kick Linda off the press plane scheduled to leave that afternoon. He did not want her traveling with the campaign. Shel and I argued, to no avail. I went to meet Linda. When I told her she would have to find her own transportation, she said, "Ken, are you sure you want to do this?" I wasn't sure, but had to do it. Linda said, "Okay, but I think you have made a mistake." She was right.

The next day, the only coverage of our carefully orchestrated press conference were headlines that read, "Curb Kicks Reporter off Press Plane." And, everywhere we showed up, there was Linda. Using commercial transportation, she attended all the events. She played it to the hilt. She sat in the front row at the press conferences and smiled for the cameras. Her colleagues in the media peppered Mike with questions about why he had kicked her off the plane. By the afternoon, I convinced Mike to let her ride with the press plane. He finally agreed. It was still a media-relations disaster, but we were back on track and back on message.

This incident is still replayed at cocktail parties in California when politicians and consultants get together. The real winner of the episode was Linda Breakstone, who became a recognized political reporter and went on to a successful TV journalism career.

By the spring of 1982, we were running ahead in the polls. Our advertising campaign was effective, and Mike had grown as a candidate. He was hardworking and an incredible fundraiser. In California, that counts for a lot.

A *Los Angeles Times* article by William Endicott, headlined "Curb Seizes Initiative from Deukmejian on 'Gut Issues,'" described our progress this way:

> Up until a few weeks ago, Atty. Gen. George Deukmejian had what he and his advisers thought was a sure-fire formula for success in his race for the Republican nomination for governor against Lt. Gov. Mike Curb: Keep the focus on the "persona" of the two candidates.
>
> The idea was that when potential GOP voters drew a distinction between the mature, stable and experienced Deukmejian and the boyish-looking, compulsive and inexperienced Curb, there would be no doubt whom they would choose.
>
> But over the last few weeks a funny thing has happened to the attorney general on his way to the June 8 primary. While he was busy trying to convince voters of his "maturity, integrity, stability and experience," Curb slipped in and changed the campaign agenda.
>
> The lieutenant governor has seized the initiative on the "gut issues" that are likely to pull conservatives to the polls next month

and has won a flurry of grudging acknowledgments that, despite a long-standing public image as a lightweight, he can talk welfare, crime and other issues with the best of them.

We were on our way to an event in Los Angeles when Shel received a call; Linda Breakstone was going to do it to us again. She had discovered, with the help of the Deukmejian campaign, that Mike had not registered to vote until just before he ran for lieutenant governor. She was going to ask him about it at the next stop.

As we rode in the car toward the event, Shel and I talked to Mike about what he should say. We told him to be apologetic, and to say it was a mistake not to register when he turned eighteen. He should encourage all young people not to make the same mistake. Mike agreed.

When we arrived at the event, the cameras were waiting; someone at the Deukmejian campaign had probably tipped them off. And there was Linda. Shel and I were confidant Mike would handle it just as we had rehearsed. We watched as Mike made his way through the throng of reporters—then came the question. Shel and I smiled at each other, knowing we had re-hearsed the right answer.

Maybe it was because Linda was there, but Mike looked into the cameras and said, "You know, in those days I was running my own business and just didn't take the time to register. I was too busy."

The headlines the next day were easy to predict, and they blared across the state—Curb too busy to vote. We were in full damage control mode, but it still took several weeks for us to get back on track. We would also see Mike's statement in Deukmejian ads.

It was a rough and tumble campaign. Deukmejian used his position as attorney general to try to destroy Curb's reputation. He had launched an investigation of Curb's record company's involvement with organized crime. There was no basis for the investigation, but the leaks to the news media from the AG's office were like a thousand cuts to Curb's reputation. When-ever we brought forward a new issue, the Deukmejian campaign would leak false information about this so-called investigation. Despite the ups and downs, we entered the final week ahead in all the polls. Unfortunately, some in our campaign took their eyes off the ball and started to think about the general election. When I asked our pollster, Dick Wirthlin, for his advice on whether we should go positive or negative during the final weekend, he advised me to start thinking ahead and building positive momentum for the general election.

At the same time, the Deukmejian team was focused on winning the primary. Years later, Lance Tarrance, their pollster, told me that despite the fact they were behind that final week, they thought they could win by attacking Curb, because his negative rating was so high. And that's exactly what they did.

At lunch one day with James Carville in Washington, I asked him which Republican consultant he disliked going up against. He answered very quickly, "Lance Tarrance, because he knows how to interpret a poll and understands strategy." I learned how good Lance was in that 1982 campaign against us. I would use Lance in all campaigns after that. In addition to the presidential campaigns he has worked on, Lance has conducted public opinion studies for national corporations, foundations, and elected leaders of the Senate, House of Representatives, and state governments.

I'm convinced we could have overcome the last minute attacks in the press. What we could not overcome was the last minute Deukmejian TV ad blitz. We had made the decision to end the campaign on a positive note. The Deukmejian team, led by pollster Lance Tarrance, had decided to do just the opposite. The ad they used included a totally false statement, that Mike Curb had released the 'Onion Field Killer.' This referred to a famous killer who had been paroled while Mike was acting governor. However, Mike had absolutely nothing to do with the parole.

That weekend was a miserable one for me. We had entered the week ahead, but I had allowed us to take our eyes off the ball. The Deukmejian campaign had a very carefully orchestrated attack plan, and although I knew it was having an impact, I thought we could hang on. As I watched our positive TV campaign and the negative attack of the Onion Field Killer ad, my concern grew. Despite the negative press we received that weekend, it was that dishonest ad that did us in. We lost the election by less than one percent.

Notwithstanding their negative attacks, it was probably my losing sight of the need to do everything possible to win the primary that lost the campaign. I had allowed myself to get talked into going easy on the negative and stressing the positive the last weekend in preparation for the general election. It was a mistake I would not make in future campaigns. I remembered what Nelson Rockefeller said in 1968. He was ahead in all the national polls going into the Miami GOP Convention, and then lost the nomination to Nixon. He said, "On the way to the presidency, I forgot to get nominated."

By 1982 I was beginning to notice a continuing deterioration in my eyesight. It was harder for me to find my way in a dark room. It was more difficult for me to drive at night. One day, while driving to my office, I stopped at a four-way stop sign in Beverly Hills. Although I had looked both ways, when I stepped on the gas, I ran into the side of a car crossing in front of me. I just had not seen it. My lack of peripheral vision had done me in.

Several years earlier, I had become a patient at the Jules Stein Eye Centre at U.C.L.A. Although not much was known about RP at the time, they welcomed me into their experimental program. They asked me to wear a colored contact lens in one eye and not the other. Each week they would examine my eye, to see if there had been any deterioration of the retina. In addition, they did a complete oral history of my childhood, in an attempt to determine how long I had had RP. The answer was that I'd had it from early childhood. I continued the experiments for several years, with the colored lenses switching from eye to eye. The theory, at the time, was that sunlight accelerated the deterioration. That turned out not to be the case.

I would continue to seek answers about RP. Las Vegas casino owner Steve Wynn, who suffers from the same disease, recommended that I visit Dr. Alan Crandall at the Moran Eye Center in Salt Lake City. Dr. Crandall helped me by removing cataracts from both eyes, but like all doctors at hospitals I visited, he said there was no solution to the impact of RP.

CHAPTER 20
Chic Hecht

One of the worst things about losing the primary was showing up the next morning for the unity breakfast, where we would all pledge our support to Deukmejian. We felt miserable, but Mike carried it off with a lot of style and class. Meanwhile, I sat at the breakfast trying to figure out what I would do next. It was June of the election year. My candidate had lost, and I was now without a client, as I had bet everything on Mike. In effect, my political consulting business was out of business for this campaign cycle.

Ed Rollins, President Reagan's political director, consoled me and said, "You should look at the Nevada Senate race where Sen. Howard Cannon (D) is running for reelection. I understand there may be a new Republican challenger there." I didn't really pay much attention to this remark. It was, after all, June, and I found it hard to believe that someone would be starting a campaign with only three months left before the September primary.

A few days later, as I sat in my Los Angeles office, I received a call from Lyn Nofziger, who was Rollins' boss at the White House. Lyn and I had been good friends since the '76 campaign. He was always thankful to Mike and me for helping him weather the storm during the Reagan campaign implosion in '76. He was one of the people in the Reagan White House with whom I got along well. Lyn told me that one of Sen. Paul Laxalt's friends in Nevada was thinking about running for the Senate, and that Paul would appreciate it if I would meet with him. His name was Chic Hecht.

I was very doubtful. Rick Fore, a wealthy businessman from northern Nevada, had been running for the Republican nomination for more than a year, and had already spent one million dollars on his campaign. He had

Roger Ailes and Stu Spencer advising him. These were the two biggest names in the world of Republican consultants.

Spencer-Roberts was considered the Republican pioneer in the campaign consulting business. The agency, founded in 1960, was connected with Nelson Rockefeller's 1964 campaign for president. Later, the firm would provide key consulting services for all of President Ronald Reagan's campaigns for governor. Roger Ailes had been the producer of the Mike Douglas TV show. Ailes was an expert on television, and at age twenty-eight, had been the producer of the 1968 election-eve telethon that many credit with turning the tide for Nixon.

However, I was a consultant without a campaign. I talked to Chic on the phone, and we agreed to meet.

Chic Hecht was from Las Vegas and had been a state senator. He was a merchant who owned several women's clothing stores and, at the time, ran a Western store at a casino called Sam's Town. Chic was Jewish, wealthy, about five foot eight, and spoke with a lisp. In the macho state of Nevada, that didn't exactly add up to a victory. I knew we were going to have to use different tactics to overcome some of the speaking issues, but Chic was a regular guy—a man's man, an easy-going, easy to meet guy, not a city slicker. This made up for a lot.

When I met with Chic in my L.A. office, I became a little more enthusiastic. The first thing he said to me was, "I want a California style campaign. The pros in Nevada only know one way to do it. I want my campaign to be media oriented, like they do it here."

We talked about the late start he was getting. The filing deadline was only three weeks away, and he hadn't raised any money or declared his candidacy. None of this fazed Chic; he said he was ready to go that day. When I asked him if he was willing to put money in himself, he asked me how much. I said a minimum of $500,000. He said, "Let's go. Tell me where to send it." That was the beginning of my most unusual campaign.

The first thing Chic wanted was to go to Washington and meet with his friend Paul Laxalt, to tell him he was going to run. We walked into Sen. Laxalt's office, and after a warm greeting, sat down across the desk from the senator. Paul looked at Chic and told him he had to learn the issues and take positions that would appeal to Nevadans. "For example," he said, "where are you going to stand on abortion?" At that, Chic turned to me and said, "What are we going to say about abortion?" I told him what I thought, and we continued with the question and answer session. Each time Paul asked him a question on an issue, Chic deferred to me. He was convinced that if he did everything I said, he would win.

We put together a campaign like Nevada had not seen before. It was media based, and we only did enough at the grassroots level to keep local Republican leaders happy. In Las Vegas, they were almost apoplectic about us using billboards instead of the small yard signs they were used to. They couldn't figure out why we were focusing on fundraising and TV advertising instead of having hundreds of volunteer events. At one point, Bob Brown, one of our advisory board members and a respected politician and newspaper publisher in Las Vegas, told me he thought it was the worst campaign he had ever seen, and that we couldn't possibly win. After we won, he wrote me a warm letter of apology.

I felt the keys to our campaign success would be raising money, an effective advertising effort, and keeping Chic Hecht out of contact with the press as much as possible. Our campaign was being discounted by most of the political pundits in Nevada, and that was just fine with me. I thought our best chance was to catch Fore by surprise; we limited most of the joint appearances and agreed to only one televised debate. We kept raising money, producing our TV spots, and waiting for our final six-week campaign push, when we would launch an all-out effort.

I spent most of my time in Las Vegas, and began to know the city and some of its characters. In fact, on my first day with Chic in Las Vegas, we had lunch at the Las Vegas Country Club. As we entered the club, Chic greeted many people, and it was obvious he was well liked. Then, just after we ordered lunch, he told me he wanted me to meet someone. We left our table to walk across the room, where an older gentleman was seated. Chic said hello, and then turned to me and said, "Ken, I would like you to meet Mo Dalitz." After we greeted each other, Mo told Chic he wanted to help him in his campaign, and handed him a check.

At the time, Mo Dalitz was one of the most notorious mob figures in

Las Vegas. When we returned to our table, Chic said, "As my campaign manager, you have your first decision to make. Do we keep the check?" Knowing that the key to victory would be how much we could raise, and that in Las Vegas the Dalitz name would not hurt us, I told Chic that if the check was good, he should deposit it. Ironically, years later, Mo was honored as the Las Vegas citizen of the year.

Our strategy for the final six weeks of the primary was to brand Rick Fore as an outsider and city slicker, while promoting Chic Hecht a man of the people. We would focus on his reputation as a businessman and Las Vegas state senator and maximize the vote there, while working hard to attract votes in the "cow counties," rural Nevada, where Chic's personality would be well received. Chic was one of the most humble, unassuming, and down-to-earth people, and voters connected with him. Meanwhile, the campaign would not focus nor spend a lot of time or money in northern Nevada, where Rick Fore lived and was part of the community. We knew we had to concentrate on areas like Clark County and the rural counties, where we could win the most votes with our limited timeline.

The other tactic we used was the endorsement spot, using radio and television. We had everyday people talking about Chic with positive messages and endorsements. This worked extremely well, and left a positive impression with the voters. We ran ads focusing on Rick Fore as a carpetbagger who had moved into Nevada a year earlier just to run for the Senate. *The Las Vegas Review Journal* ran a great editorial supporting Hecht, and called Fore an "empty suit." This was a reference to Rick's good looks and his lack of understanding of Nevada issues. The empty suit tag was just the kind of thing we needed for the rural counties in Nevada. It caught on.

We began the last six weeks twenty points behind, and won in a landslide. It wasn't even close. We caught everyone by surprise. A few months later, when I walked into Stu Spencer's office, he looked at me and said, "How the hell did you do that?" I simply smiled and said, "Damned if I know."

The Political Report described our primary campaign this way:

> Wealthy businessman Chic Hecht had to come from behind
> to win the GOP Senate nomination. Hecht served as the state

Senate Minority Leader under then Governor Paul Laxalt, but has not held political office since.

The early candidates in the Republican race were businessmen Rick Fore and Jack Kenney. But Fore had lived in the state for only a few years and both he and Kenney lacked legislative experience. But most voters remained undecided and then Hecht jumped into the fray.

Hecht was believed to have the support of Nevada Sen. Paul Laxalt, a close associate of the President and he did assemble a 'Reagan team' to assist his campaign. Former Reagan political aide Lyn Nofziger served as a consultant, while White House pollster Richard Wirthlin's firm conducted the survey research.

Fore was ambushed by Hecht's television advertising. Media producer Ken Rietz's commercials pointed out that Hecht had the legislative service and long-term residency in the state that Fore lacked. 'Hecht's advertising just shifted the campaign's emphasis,' Bailey Dotson, the Fore campaign manager, told the Report. Hecht won with 42%, while Fore and Kenney trailed with 27% and 19% respectively.

We had also caught Sen. Howard Cannon's campaign by surprise. For more than a year, they thought they would have northern Nevadan, Rick Fore, as their opponent. Now, with two months to go, they had Las Vegan Chic Hecht to run against. Cannon had been in office twenty-four years, and was an institution in Nevada. His campaign advisors felt there was no way that Hecht could beat him. Just like the Fore campaign, they underestimated us.

We used the same formula in the general election: raise as much money as possible and use it on television, do only as much grassroots work as we needed to do to keep the local Republicans happy, and have as few public appearances as possible. We decided not to challenge our opponent to debate. In the end, we agreed to only one debate, which was held in a rural county. We also branded Cannon as a big spending liberal, out-of-touch with Nevada. In the last two weeks of the campaign, the press started to recognize our strategy of keeping Hecht undercover, and began referring to him as the "shadow candidate."

We were bombarding the airwaves with spots critical of Cannon. As the polls began to tighten the last ten days, his campaign began to pay attention, but it was too late. We had the momentum. Nevada was Reagan country, and Hecht had the endorsement of the president, which included a TV spot and campaign appearance by him. Our negative TV ads eroded the voters' confidence in Cannon.

To keep Hecht occupied and out of sight of the news media, I suggested a simple strategy to him. I said, "Chic, the best thing you can do these last ten days is find contributors to play golf with." So, he played golf every day during those last ten days, and he was a happy candidate. It worked. He won.

An *Associated Press* story in *The Las Vegas Review-Journal*, dated November 6, 1982, with the headline "Santini Surprised by Hecht Victory," described our campaign:

> RENO – Rep. Jim Santini, contemplating a future as a mining industry lawyer, insisted Friday his primary campaign against Sen. Howard Cannon was not a major factor in Cannon's subsequent defeat.
>
> Santini, D-Nev., said in a telephone interview from his Washington office that Republican Chic Hecht beat Cannon by employing a 'masterful' strategy of 'political hide-and-seek.'
>
> 'His successful campaign represents a Nevada first,' Santini said. 'It's the first time that in a major state-wide race, a candidate was able to succeed on the basis of media advertisements alone.'

When Chic was sworn into the U.S. Senate, he asked me to go to Washington and be there for the ceremony. I met him in his new office, and he said, before the swearing in, that we should go see Paul Laxalt. We entered Sen. Laxalt's office and sat down in the two chairs across from his desk. Paul, charming as always, congratulated Chic, and then turned to me with a smile. He said, "Look, Ken, I asked you to help this guy, I didn't think you would get him elected." We all had a good laugh and went to the Senate floor for the ceremony.

About a week after the election, I received a phone call from someone in Las Vegas I had never met—Andy Tompkins. Andy was one of the pioneers of gambling in downtown Las Vegas. He had started with four slot machines, and had grown that into a small casino just one block off Main Street, downtown. His small casino was a favorite with local residents, and Andy was known as a successful character, as were a lot of the old-timers.

When I picked up the phone, Andy said, "Ken, you don't know me and I want you to know Chic Hecht is a close friend of mine. But, if you can get him elected to the U.S. Senate, I want you to work for me." The Lady Luck Casino became my first commercial account in Las Vegas, and Andy and his wife Susan became close friends. We laughed about that first phone call many times. While doing the advertising and public relations for the Lady Luck, it grew into a hotel with two towers and a large casino.

For the next six years, I spent half of my time in Las Vegas, commuting from San Diego. My commercial client list grew to include Sam's Town, Sam's Town Gold River, the Stardust, Binion's Horseshoe and the California Hotel.

CHAPTER 21
Chic Runs for Re-Election

As a senator, Chic Hecht had done a good job for his constituents. Generally, Nevadans liked him. He had established a service atmosphere in his Nevada office and with his staff, and this was a reflection of his character. It was what made him a successful merchant. His job approval rating always ran in the low fifty percent which was average for an incumbent senator. Chic also understood Republican Party alignments. He supported President Reagan on issues in the Senate, and sought Paul Laxalt's help on the important issues affecting Nevada. He made up for his lack of speaking skills with hard work. Most of all, he loved the job, and it showed.

Although some of his verbal gaffes were amusing, his constituents actually became used to them. One day, on a national televised interview, he referred to the proposed nuclear repository at Yucca Mountain in Nevada, which he opposed, as a "nuclear suppository." That gaffe received national press attention and made all the bloopers shows. I felt, however, his statement was fairly descriptive of what the nuclear power industry was trying to do to Nevada.

When Chic decided to run for re-election, he asked me to manage his campaign. But my situation, both personally and professionally, had changed. My vision issues were becoming more apparent. While I thought I could manage my deteriorating sight, it was no longer working. The situation had progressed to the point that I could no longer drive. In 1986, while I was driving in Los Angeles, I almost ran into an entire family making their way across the street. I was turning left off Santa Monica Boulevard, and because of my narrowing tunnel vision, I could not, peripherally, see the family. It was a real scare, and right then, I decided not to get behind the wheel again. The next day I stopped driving, and have not driven a car since.

I was going through my third divorce, and at forty-six, found myself broke and starting over again. It would have been easy for Chic to get someone else to run his re-election effort, but he stuck with me. He was a loyal friend who thought I could help him win what would be a tough campaign. For his confidence in me, during this difficult time in my life, I was always thankful. I was determined to do everything possible to help him win. I moved to a hotel in Las Vegas and took on only one other campaign that year.

Chic was also in a really tough position. In his re-election campaign in 1988, he would face the most popular governor in Nevada's recent history—Dick Bryan. This would be a challenging time for both of us.

Based on my experience in the 1982 Curb campaign, I decided to change pollsters for the Hecht campaign. Lance Tarrance had been an effective weapon against us in California, and I wanted him on our side in Nevada. I asked Lance to do his first survey in September in 1987, which showed we were twenty points behind Gov. Bryan. Working with Lance, we developed a strategy and plan for the campaign.

Las Vegas Review Journal political reporter John Ralston analyzed our effort in a post-election article:

> In September 1987, Republican consultants Ken Rietz and Lance Tarrance met to discuss how they could re-elect Chic Hecht, considered the nation's most vulnerable senator and already trailing by as much as thirty points in some polls.
>
> The strategy they arrived at was relatively simple: portray the low-profile and gaffe-prone Hecht as a 'fighter who works hard for the people of Nevada.'
>
> The campaign would play up Hecht's work on the 65 mph bill and his support of the Reagan administration's agenda of strong defense and low taxes while using Hecht's support of reprocessing to neutralize his weakness on the nuclear waste issue.
>
> The plan almost worked.

Aided by the serendipitous 'private jet' issue and the collapse of democratic presidential candidate Michael Dukakis' Nevada campaign, Hecht threw a scare into Bryan that few foresaw when the governor entered the race.

But in the end, both campaigns agree, Hecht's inability to quash the impression that he was not respected or taken seriously in Washington, D.C., because of his awkward public persona cost him the election. 'We were able to make the race competitive and pretty much call the tune as far as issues were concerned, but we were not able to overcome the big issue of respect,' Rietz said after the election. He added that while the campaign tried to 'soften the issue' with television testimonials from GOP senators, it proved not to be enough.

This time, we were able to raise the kind of money that had eluded us in the six years earlier. We had an aggressive advertising campaign that started earlier than anyone expected. Chic's service to his constituents was emphasized. We criticized Bryan's job as governor, and reminded voters that his ambition to be senator meant leaving the job before his term ended.

At the beginning of our run, many news articles were critical of Hecht. Some polls showed us, in the early months of 1988, as much as forty points behind. But we believed there were things about Bryan's term as governor that we could point out that would weaken him. Our research into Bryan's actions as governor found that he had purchased a private jet for Nevada. Previous governors had been satisfied with using a Nevada National Guard airplane when they needed to move from city to city in the state. This discovery proved to be great fodder for our campaign. We created a TV spot showing the plane, and the announcer called it Bryan's private jet. Our California direct mail specialist, Dave Ellis, created a piece that folded into a paper airplane. Across the front, the mailer said, "Governor Bryan has his own private plane, you should have one too." We sent the mail piece to every voter in Nevada.

It worked. Everywhere Bryan went, people asked him about his private jet. As he rode in parades, people would call out, "What about that airplane?"

When I saw him in Washington one day after the election, Bryan told me that it really drove him crazy.

Although we tried, this time we were unable to avoid public appearances. From time to time, Chic still tangled up his words. As we left one speech, a TV reporter from Reno asked if he could have a word with Chic. I agreed and then watched in dismay.

The reporter wanted to talk about counter-intelligence. It was common knowledge that Chic, who was Jewish, had served in Army Intelligence behind the Iron Curtain during the Cold War. The reporter asked his question. Instead of answering, Chic said, "You are confusing 'covert' and 'overt.' I was working as an overt operative." Of course, the opposite was true. Chic had been a covert operative. The reporter tried to correct him in order to help him out, but Chic refused to give in on his definition. It was all caught on tape. After the interview, I asked the reporter to downplay this natural mistake. The reporter would have none of it, and led the evening news with a story about the confused senator.

By the summer of 1988, despite the gaffes and the popularity of the governor, we were in a neck and neck campaign. A poll by Tarrance and Associates showed Bryan with forty-three percent, Hecht with forty-one percent, and sixteen percent undecided. Our campaign tactics were working.

Our weakness was in northern Nevada, normally a strong Republican area. I felt if we could get Vice President Bush to make an appearance there with Hecht in the last week of the campaign, we could pull it out. Unfortunately, Bush had other priorities at that time. He, of course, was campaigning for the presidency and had other obligations. It was a real shame, because I believe that an appearance by Bush in Reno would have clinched the race. As a result, we did not do as well as we should have in northern Nevada, and lost the race by one percent.

The following is from a column written by John Ralston for the *Las Vegas Sun*:

> Memories of 1988 came rushing back this week with the news of the accidental senator's passing.
>
> Chic Hecht was a kind and gracious man, a gentle soul who

showed, in 1982, when he was elected by fortuitous circumstances, and especially in 1988, when he barely lost a seat no one thought he had a chance to keep, that he was anything but mild-mannered when it came to the hurly-burly of campaigns.

People talk about how hundreds of votes separated Harry Reid from eventual victor Paul Laxalt in 1974 or John Ensign from ultimate winner Reid in 1998. And they still recall Hecht's improbable 1982 defeat of venerable Sen. Howard Cannon, after the opportunistic businessman entered the race at the eleventh hour and capitalized on a bruising Democratic primary.

But no Nevada Senate race was quite as spectacular as the 1988 clash between Hecht, the oratorically challenged anti-politician, and Gov. Richard Bryan, the smooth-as-message-points politician's politician.

Early polls showed Hecht trailing 40 points, an upside-down dynamic - an incumbent U.S. senator looking moribund. And yet the man many pundits considered an accident of history, a fluke to be corrected by one of the most graceful pols the state had seen, almost proved the oracles and the polls wrong again.

I remember Hecht as being almost imperturbable in the face of those polls.

He always had a ready smile and even a twinkle in his eye when he rolled out a line needling Bryan, some of them prepared by a cutthroat campaign team headed by Ken Rietz.

Although we lost, there was a silver lining for me. It was during that re-election campaign that I had the good fortune to meet Chic Hecht's next door neighbor, Ursula Landsrath. It would not have happened had she not decided to go to a barbeque fundraiser for Chic that was held in the fall of 1987 at Annabel Stanford's farm, close to Mt. Charleston. Ursula, to escape the scorching heat of Las Vegas, had decided to take her son into the country. It was her first political fundraiser.

By then, my eyesight had become even worse. Dim light and darkness were challenging for me. Although it was dark by the time the fundraiser kicked off, I could see Ursula, who was wearing a white top and white slacks. She was beautiful, interesting, and had a great laugh. She paid absolutely no attention to me. I kept her within earshot. I struck up a conversation with Ursula's son, Jensen, so I could sit near her.

Through our conversation, he spoke of his interest in attending the Naval Academy; he really wanted to go. When I mentioned my experience there and asked for a phone number in order to give him more information, he replied, "My mother has an unlisted number. I have to ask her." I heard him explain to his mother that he had met someone who had actually attended the Naval Academy, and begged to be allowed to give out the unlisted number. The more I spoke to her son, the more I wanted to get to know her; she had raised such a great person. My persistence paid off. Ursula and I spent a lot of time together during that campaign. Chic Hecht lost the election, but I gained a close friend and confidant, who later became my wife.

CHAPTER 22
Burson–Marsteller and Beyond

After the 1988 elections, I re-located to Las Vegas, moving into Ursula's home at the Desert Inn Country Club. She had moved to Las Vegas from Sydney, Australia in 1975. Ursula had been a fashion model, stunt-driver, and sky-diver, and in Las Vegas, she managed several businesses. We organized a small office in her home where I could work. In a very short time, Ursula was helping me run my small business.

I was writing and producing TV and radio spots for the Lady Luck Casino and its new hotel. At Binion's Horse Shoe, I was working with Jack Binion in an effort to get his annual *World Series of Poker* on television. We decided to produce a TV special on the finals ourselves, and were successful in placing it on ESPN. I was also working with local Nevada political candidates, providing them with strategic counsel and advertising services.

My eyesight was a growing problem. Although I could still move around by myself, I had no vision below my nose, so steps were a hazard, as were objects left on a floor where I was walking. My eyes also took an unusual amount of time to adjust when I went from bright light to a dimly lit interior. Ursula was a great help warning me about steps, although from time to time she forgot to say up or down. She also let me take her elbow when we went from the bright Las Vegas day into a restaurant or casino, and guided me through the crowded, meandering casinos to my meetings.

Because I could not meet people in my office, I talked with clients in their offices or at breakfast or lunch meetings. I selected a coffee shop for my breakfast meetings and the Elephant Bar for lunch, and was able to memorize the interior layout of both, which made it easier for me to find my way to a table or booth. I also developed the habit of showing up early.

It was more convenient for me to be seated at my table and allow my client to find me. While scanning a room with my small tunnel of light, I often missed people if I arrived late.

I was working with Mike Sloan, an executive at Circus Circus, on the gaming community's desire to widen I-15 at a choke point near Riverside, California. The gamers felt the slowdown and traffic jam at that point caused California gamblers to leave their casinos earlier and earlier on Sunday evenings. I went to Washington to meet with my friend Cong. Jerry Lewis, who represented Riverside, to discuss the potential of getting federal funds to help with the I-15 widening. While in D.C., I set up meetings with a couple of potential political clients. One of them insisted on meeting me at a restaurant to which I had never been. I was alone, so I decided when I arrived at the restaurant, I would go in the door, take a couple of steps, and then wait for my eyes to adjust. To my great surprise, immediately inside the door was a flight of stairs. I took one step inside and found myself rolling down a complete flight of stairs, coming to rest in front of the maître d's desk. Fortunately, I was early, the restaurant was fairly empty, and my potential client had not arrived. The maître d' helped me brush off my suit and led me carefully to my table. I had about fifteen minutes by myself to settle my nerves and recover from my fall. Despite my grand entrance I was successful in securing the client.

A few months later, I returned to Washington, this time with Ursula. Tom Bell had been hired by Burson-Marsteller, the largest public relations/public affairs firm in the world, to head its Washington office and lead the Global Public Affairs practice. Bill Brock and his wife Sandy, along with Sen. Howard Baker, were hosting a welcoming reception for Tom. We were invited, and I spent some time with Tom, catching up on the previous four to five years. On our way out, Tom asked me if I would be willing to do some consulting work for him at Burson-Marsteller. I told him that I was always looking for work, and would welcome the opportunity to work with him again.

In November 1989, I received a phone call from Tom Bell. He had grown from a young protégé of mine in the Brock and Nixon campaigns to an accomplished business and political strategist. He had been a critical force, helping organize and mobilize our Young Voters for President as well as organizing the 1973 Nixon inaugural balls. When he worked for me then, he was one of the younger members of our team, but definitely one of the best. We had a great relationship, and I could always count on Tom for his commitment and wonderful attitude. There was a Southern charm about him that was always backed up with exceptionally executed strategic plans. Tom would become CEO of Burson-Marsteller Worldwide, and later CEO of Young and Rubicam, Burson-Marsteller's parent company.

The call was direct, and Tom's inquiry went straight to the point, "Ken, are you interested in a little work?" I could hear a little mischief in his voice, and knowing Tom, I knew this would be something interesting. I told him that at this point in my career, I was looking more at roles where I could be a consultant, but since it was Tom, I wanted to know what he had in mind. He was one of the best sales people I ever met. Originally from Memphis, Tennessee, he had just a little Southern drawl. When he spoke, it was like listening to a low-key Southern preacher. He was believable and persuasive. Tom quickly responded that I could work as a consultant in the beginning, but that our working relationship might progress from there.

"Ken, I need you to get on a plane next Wednesday and come to Vancouver to pitch a potential client on Thursday." I replied, "Tom, are you aware that next Thursday is Thanksgiving?" Quick on the reply, Tom responded, "Ken, they don't celebrate Thanksgiving in Canada. Besides, they asked us to pitch on Thursday, so we pitch on Thursday." I paused, "Well, Tom, are you going to tell me what this is all about?" "No," he replied, "just meet me on Wednesday at the Four Seasons Hotel in Vancouver, and I will bring you up to date." I told him I would bring Ursula with me so that we could celebrate Thanksgiving together in Vancouver. He said, "That's a good idea," and added he would bring his wife Jennifer, so we could all celebrate together. The following Wednesday, Ursula and I flew to Vancouver.

That evening, Tom described the potential client and the challenge. It was a group of the thirteen largest forest companies in British Columbia. They were losing a public relations battle with environmentalist groups. More importantly, they were losing credibility with the general population of British Columbia. At the meeting the next day, each company would be represented by their CEO. After he went through a few of the details, he said to me, "We want to sell them a campaign-style program, so just do your regular campaign pitch, and you will see where it fits in with everything else we are presenting."

The next day, Tom led the pitch. He introduced the various members of the Burson-Marsteller Vancouver team. Several of the account representatives described B-M's capabilities and highlights of specific public relations campaigns. Then there was a pause. Tom looked around the room at the various CEOs and said, "The campaign we want to put together for you will be very different from any of the other campaigns you have experienced. We want to run this campaign just like political campaigns are run in the U.S."

Suddenly, there was energy in the room. He had their attention. Something new had just been put on the table. Tom went on to say, "To do that, we have brought in Ken Rietz, who has successfully run numerous campaigns in the U.S." Tom then turned to me and said, "Ken, why don't you take it from here?" I stood and did the same thing I had been doing for twenty-five years. I began the pitch with my traditional statement.

"Every campaign has to start with a goal. In this case, your goal is to overcome the negative publicity that you have suffered over the past ten years. You are going to have to rebuild the credibility of the industry with your various stakeholders and the public." I told them the campaign had to be based on research. We would have to determine who the best spokespeople were, and how best to communicate a positive message to all of BC. We needed a research-based strategy, which would have to be long-term to accomplish the campaign goals. We would need to develop a variety of tactics to implement the strategy.

Then I described a specific campaign in California that I had managed. I explained how the elements of research, strategy, tactics, and implementation fit together in a winning formula. Once I stopped, Tom Bell turned to the thirteen CEOs and said, "This is not going to be an inexpensive campaign." He told them the cost, and said it would take five years and require meeting with all thirteen of them once a month, to hear a progress report. He emphasized that the CEOs could not send substitutes to the monthly meetings.

Tom had an incredible way about him when he was pitching. He was able to make most people feel what he was telling them was what they should do. He was truly a great salesman. He smiled and asked if there were any questions. One of the CEOs asked if they could have some time alone in the room to discuss the plan. We left the room; just a short time later, we were called back. They had only one question: "If we decide to hire you today, who is going to lead the campaign here in Canada?"

Without even a hesitation, Tom looked at the CEOs and said, "Ken has brought his bags all packed and will be staying here, and is prepared to start the campaign tomorrow."

This, of course, was news to me. Without cracking a smile and with a straight face, I said, "Okay, Tom." That was how Burson-Marsteller won one of the largest accounts in its Los Angeles office. It was also the beginning of my Burson-Marsteller career, which included one year as a consultant and sixteen as a full-time employee.

I started the next day. We put the research component together quickly. One of the key elements of our research was the need to find a credible spokesperson or group that could speak on behalf of the industry. Our strategy was to create a citizens' group called the British Columbia Forest Alliance (BCFA), which would consist of local schoolteachers, college professors, students, housewives, forest workers, and others. BCFA would then become the vehicle for telling the truth about the industry and its forest practices. The second part of the strategy was to develop a code of best forest practices for the industry. A committee of the BCFA membership would write the code, to which the forest industry would agree. We lost one company because of this requirement. In the end, twelve companies agreed to the strategy.

As we needed to find a credible spokesperson for BCFA, I recruited the co-founder of Greenpeace International, Patrick Moore, who lived outside of Vancouver. He was well-known as the person in the well-known documentary film trying to stop hunters from clubbing seals to death. Patrick's father owned a sawmill, and he had an interest in keeping the forest industry in BC viable. When I spoke with Patrick, I promised him that if he joined the BCFA as co-chairman, he would chair the committee writing the code of practices for the industry. Although we would need to negotiate with the industry to gain their acceptance, it would be his code of practices. Patrick accepted the deal.

The second person recruited as co-chair was Jack Munro. He was retiring as president of the Forest Industry Workers Union, the largest union in Canada. He was not exactly known as a friend of the forest industry due to the contentious attitude between workers and management. Jack wanted to do something new, and was intrigued by the idea of the BCFA.

Ultimately, we recruited about 20,000 people, who paid ten dollars for membership in the organization. We set up a rapid response communications team, just like a political campaign, to respond to the claims and complaints of the environmental groups.

Our main vehicle to reach our target audiences and sway opinions was our thirty-minute television show. Produced by me and called *The Forest and The People*, it aired every Sunday night, just before *60 Minutes*. The show was focused on forest practices, and highlighted the economic benefits of the forest industry. I recruited Fanny Kiefer, a well-known environmental reporter, to be the host for the TV show. Fannie agreed, as long as we would not attack environmental groups. We never did. The show explored all facets of the industry and told the truth about their practices. In some cases this was not complimentary, but that was a necessary part of the story. The fact that we were telling the truth provided credibility for the TV show and the BCFA.

When the environmentalists claimed that BC was becoming the Brazil of the North by destroying its forests, we sent our camera crew, Patrick Moore, and several Alliance members to Brazil and taped a thirty-minute show. The documentary style footage clearly showed that there were no similarities. In Brazil, they were burning down the forests and reclaiming the land for pasture and other agricultural uses. This was unlike the practice in BC, where they harvested the forest and replanted three trees for every one cut down. When the environmentalists said BC should do selective cutting as in Sweden, we sent the camera crew and BCFA Citizens Board members there. Our TV program showed how impractical it would be to do selective cutting in BC.

Most people did not know that forest companies in BC replanted three to four trees for every tree they harvested. To emphasize this point, we set up a huge sign in downtown Vancouver with a running total of how many trees were replanted, minute by minute, each day. The numbers kept ticking up, showing the millions of trees being planted in BC each year. To highlight re-planting on Earth Day, we passed out seedlings with a note saying, "Plant a tree and help save the forest."

When we began our campaign in 1990, a survey showed that seventy-nine percent of people in BC felt the environmentalists acted responsibly. Only forty percent thought the forest industry had responsible practices. After just two years of our campaign, there was only a five-point gap between the activist groups and the forest industry. By 1994, sixty-two percent of people surveyed felt the industry was acting responsibly. Over seventy percent of those polled said they believed environmental concerns should be resolved slowly to avoid job losses. Our campaign had turned the perception of the forest industry from negative to positive. In the process, our group of forest companies committed to the BCFA and the code of practices had grown to seventeen. Throughout that time, I spent three days a week in Vancouver. Fortunately, Ursula was able to accompany me much of the time. That was my initiation into Burson-Marsteller.

In late 1990, Tom Bell asked me to join B-M full time. He wanted me to work out of the Los Angeles office and build a statewide Public Affairs practice. I would continue to supervise our BCFA campaign and commute weekly to Vancouver. Ursula and I discussed this new challenge, and decided to accept Tom's offer. Within a few weeks, I reported to the L.A. office as a vice president of B-M.

On my first day in L.A., a senior executive came into my office and asked me what I was doing there. I told her Tom Bell had asked me to build a California Public Affairs practice. She told me that B-M had no public affairs capability in that office, and she thought I was wasting my time. This, of course, fired up my competitive juices. Although I had never worked in a large public relations firm, I was determined to succeed. I did what I had been doing for years in California political campaigns. I researched the public affairs capabilities of all other PR firms in the state. I learned about their key people and their clients.

The strategy I developed focused on promoting our local people and capabilities, as well as the network of professionals available to us nationwide. B-M was the largest public relations/public affairs firm in the country, and we had a lot of talent to call on. I then went to work, touching base with my network of political contacts built up over the previous twenty years.

It didn't take long before we had some marquee public affairs clients, including McDonnell Douglas Corporation, Southern California Edison, Hollywood Park, and Morrison-Knudson. McDonnell Douglas was building the C-17 transport aircraft for the Defense Department. They had run into some problems with Congress when, during a test, a wing fell off. Some members of Congress had decided it was a waste of money, and were trying to terminate the development program.

Our effort to save the C-17 worked just like a political campaign. Through our research, we discovered there were hundreds of suppliers to the C-17 program, and they had thousands of employees. Many of them were small businesses in California and neighboring states, and many of the employees were minorities.

Through our phone bank and direct mail, we set up a contact program asking employees to help save the C-17 and their jobs by contacting the member of Congress in their district. Before long, the phones were ringing in specific congressional offices, and the tide began to turn. We also established a PR campaign that included allowing members of the news media to receive briefings and tours of this previously secret program. The campaign worked. Congress approved additional funding for the C-17. Today, it is a workhorse for the armed forces.

I was appointed president of B-M's California region in 1992. To enhance our L.A. reputation, we did pro bono work for the L.A. mayor's office and the L.A. Urban League. To strengthen our public affairs offering, I decided to open a B-M office in Sacramento.

Searching for someone to lead our Sacramento office, I called Rex Hime, whom I had met when he worked for Lt. Governor Mike Curb. Rex was running an association in Sacramento. He introduced me to an energetic, personable young woman named Gwyn Bicker. Gwyn and I hit it off immediately. She had a hearing disability she had overcome by learning to read lips. It became a standing joke that we were the blind and the deaf looking for the "dumb." Gwyn did a terrific job, and our office in Sacramento soon had numerous clients and fifteen employees. A few years later, Rex and Gwyn would marry. They now have two grown sons, Rex and Reagan.

I have come to the conclusion that my disability actually helped me in both my political and business careers. It made me focus on the problem in front of me and avoid distraction. It forced me to realize I could depend on others. As it became more difficult to read, I needed to memorize facts and numbers, which enhanced my memory. It made me more understanding, patient, compassionate, and aware of the problems facing others. It taught me to adjust to circumstances beyond my control. Often I thought of the old saying, "Do the best you can with the cards you were dealt."

By the fall of 1995, Tom Bell had been promoted to CEO of B-M/USA. He was reorganizing the company by practice. Tom asked me if I would be willing to relocate to Washington, D.C. and become chairman of the U.S. Public Affairs practice and CEO of the Washington region. Although Ursula was very reluctant, after long discussions, she and I decided to make the move. I was familiar with Washington, having attended college there and having worked in the House of Representatives for Bill Steiger and for President Nixon's re-election campaign.

I knew the key to building a successful Public Affairs practice was re-cruiting talented people, as I had done in California. I looked for someone with whom I could partner. Almost everyone I asked for a recommendation gave me the name of Cynthia Hudson, an employee in Washington of Rob-inson Lake. She was a Democrat who had worked in several presidential campaigns. After numerous discussions and negotiations, Cynthia agreed to join B-M to run our Washington Public Affairs practice. She would be my deputy, and soon became one of our most sought-after public affairs and crisis management communications professionals.

Cynthia and I created a campaign model we could use to sell and manage public affairs business. Based on our political campaign experience, it includ-ed research, strategy, message development, public relations, rapid response, stakeholder outreach, and grassroots mobilization. B-M had acquired Charlie Black's lobbying firm. His congressional outreach capability fit our model.

Charlie would also provide valuable strategic advice to our clients. As we needed an in-house grassroots mobilization capability, we acquired Direct Impact (DI), Washington's most successful grassroots company. We used the same campaign model for the next sixteen years at Burson-Marsteller.

During this period, we helped Allergen, the manufacturers of Botox, prevent states from creating an extra tax on their product. We helped the MGM Grand in Las Vegas stay union free. We were also hired by the Canadian government to manage a campaign creating a more sympathetic attitude in Washington, D.C. toward Canada-U.S. trade policies.

In all those sixteen years, moving around the world and heading various divisions of a multi-national company, my wife Ursula was my constant companion. She guided me through difficult airports and helped me navigate in hotels. Since I was colorblind, she made sure my ties and suits matched, and always had me at the right place at the right time.

For many years, I did not tell people about my loss of sight. I didn't want to be viewed as anything but whole, especially in my work environment. One day, Ursula convinced me otherwise. She told me that as long as I did not admit the loss of sight, people would think there was something else wrong with me. "It has become obvious you have a problem," she said. "You might as well tell people. They won't think any less of you. Besides, they won't think you rude when you ignore their outstretched hands or friendly nods."

Although I knew she was right, it was a hard thing for me to do. I was concerned about how clients would perceive me. I was worried that if they knew I was visually impaired, they would not hire me in the advertising, communications, and public affairs businesses. After all, most of what we did had a visual component.

However, once I started opening up to people, I found that many of my friends or their relatives also had disabilities. I had been wrong, and Ursula proved to be right. My staff responded with amazing sympathy. I was overwhelmed with their support. By opening up to my team, I found that many people had family members touched by vision problems, and it became an open discussion on several occasions. I actually learned from them. However, I did have a few Mr. Magoo moments.

One day, we were in Washington, D.C., preparing to pitch Iridium, a satellite phone company. We were in the lobby of a hotel, getting ready to go into a meeting room where thirty Iridium executives from around the world were seated. I was going to open the meeting, and Tom Bell was going to close it, as he often did. I took Cynthia Hudson's elbow, and although she was used to guiding me, she forgot to allow me enough room. She ran me straight into the side of the door, in front of the entire group. Cynthia was embarrassed by the accident and my head was ringing. Despite the awkward start, our pitch was a success.

However, Cynthia's most embarrassing moment when offering her elbow to me followed a meeting in a conference center outside New York City. She and I were seated together at a table during a long and boring program. When it was over, she encouraged the team to go to the bar to have a drink. As we walked into the dimly lit bar, I took her elbow so she could guide me. Her husband, Jim Lake Sr., was playing pool, so we went to the pool table. The waitress came over and took our drink order. When the drinks arrived, the waitress gave each of us our drinks, but left out Cynthia. The second round came, and again, no drink for Cynthia. Furious, Cynthia got up, stomped over to the bar, and demanded an explanation. As she was going towards the bar, I decided to take a shot on the pool table.

The bartender explained to Cynthia that she could not be served. He said that she obviously had had too much to drink, because when she entered the room, the person she was with was holding her elbow in order to hold her up. With great indignation, Cynthia looked at the bartender, turned to point at me, and said in a loud voice, "That person is blind." Just as she pointed over, I made a lucky shot and sank a ball. We all had a great laugh at Cynthia's expense.

By the fall of 1998, Tom Bell had been promoted to B-M CEO World-wide. Our business in Europe was not doing well. On the other hand, the Public Affairs practice in California that I had started and the U.S. Public Affairs practice I was leading were both highly successful. Tom asked me if I would be willing to spend a year in London as CEO of Europe. This was to be my most difficult decision at Burson-Marsteller. I had been familiar with Los Angeles and Washington. It had been relatively easy for me to navigate, even with fading eyesight, and in both places I had a good network of contacts. Although I had visited Europe, this would be a different experience and a completely new challenge. It was the first time in my professional life that I had trepidations and severe reservations. Could a blind person actually handle the necessary travel and analysis of documents and people? I later found out there were also a number of key executives at B-M who thought Tom Bell had lost his mind. After all, I was legally blind.

Ursula had spent quite a bit of time in Europe before we met. While she was not enthusiastic about yet another relocation, we agreed to take a chance and move to London.

Once I decided to move, I knew that I would have to level with the European staff about my disability. I wanted to make sure the team I worked with heard it from me; it was important that I disclose my situation to them. Over the first few months, while visiting the employees in our seventeen offices across Europe, at the beginning of my presentation, I would mention my vision limitations. I would discuss scenarios where my sight issues might have an impact. I would explain, "If you reach out your hand and I do not shake it, it means I cannot see it, as I have no vision below my nose. As I have no peripheral vision, when I pass you in the hall and do not acknowledge you, it is because I have not seen you." I found people to be extremely understanding.

There were some awkward but amusing moments. One time, in the London boardroom, we were having a senior staff meeting to discuss a particular client. In the middle of the discussion, I felt like having a Coke. I picked up the can and poured it on the table next to the glass. There was silence. Then one of my colleagues quickly took the glass and can to pour my drink, while another colleague cleaned up the mess. I apologized for the interruption, and the tension left the room as we all had a good laugh.

Another time, holding onto Ursula's elbow as she led me through Heathrow Airport, we were late for a plane. We were moving very fast, and I took a wider turn than I should have and banged my leg on a low metal and glass table. My pants were ripped and leg was bloody. We were told, very politely, that I could not board the plane with an injury. Of course, they were not aware of Ursula and how determined she could be. After a tense negotiation, we boarded the plane, and I made it to my meeting in Frankfurt on time, ripped pants and all.

Any corporate reorganization requires the firing of non-performers. To accomplish my job, I had to do my share. For that reason, behind my back, the staff referred to me as "Darth Vader." Within a year, however, I had put our European business on a solid foundation and hired a new CEO. Ursula and I returned to Washington, where I took on the responsibility of chief operating officer (COO) and vice-chairman worldwide. I would work out of both the Washington and New York offices, while continuing to lead the Global Public Affairs practice.

My last few years at Burson-Marsteller were challenging. I had lost the vision in my right eye, and the tunnel of light in my left had narrowed. I could still move around unaided in the D.C. and New York offices; outside of the office, my colleagues would offer their elbows and guide me. Young and Rubicam (our parent company) CEOs Tom Bell and later Mike Dolan had provided me with a driver in Washington, and allowed Ursula to travel with me. In New York, Ursula would take me to the office at 19th & Park Avenue South by taxi, and then walk the fifty blocks back to our apartment on the Upper East Side. In the evening, she would walk back to the office, and we would catch a taxi home. My assistant in D.C. would keep me up-to-date by reading my emails and other documents to me. Because Burson-Marsteller's founder, Harold Burson, had created a very collegial atmosphere, I was comfortable and productive, even though vision impaired, until I retired at age sixty-five.

EPILOGUE

In retirement, I get my political fix every few months at a luncheon in Washington organized by Dennis Whitfield. Attendees include Bill Brock, Bill Timmons, Stan Anderson, Mike Baroody, Tom Korologos, Charlie Black, and Jim Lake, Sr. We tell old campaign war stories and discuss current political activities. At this writing, the Republican nomination for president is at the top of most of our minds.

I have been receiving many phone calls from around the country from people concerned about the future of the Republican Party. Many say if Donald Trump is our nominee we will lose the presidential election, as well as our control of the Senate and House of Representatives. Others believe that Trump is attracting new people to the party, and if he is blocked from the nomination, we will lose those new voters and the election.

I'm not sure how it will turn out. I am sure, however, that the Republican Party will survive. In 1964, Senator Goldwater was our nominee. He lost in a landslide, and Republican office holders across the country were swept out of office. Just four years later, in 1968, Republicans won the presidency. The same thing happened in 1976, after Nixon resigned and President Ford pardoned him. Republicans lost elections across the country. In 1980, Republicans won the presidency, and the Reagan revolution was born. In both 1964 and 1976, the Republican Party had been declared dead. It wasn't true then, and isn't true today.

I have known most of my political pals for more than thirty years. They knew me when I could see. Today, they treat me no differently, except for offering their elbow when we walk somewhere and cutting my food when we dine together. Several have asked me what it feels like to be blind. The truth is that I don't feel different at all. I miss playing tennis, driving a car, seeing a TV show or a movie, seeing my son's face, and seeing the sparkle in Ursula's eyes or her expression when she jokes with me. But I see through her eyes, and take advantage of life as it is.

Going blind has been a gradual experience for me. More than forty years ago, when my eye doctor told me I had RP and there was no cure, I thought my ability to see would end quickly. It didn't. Instead, I had forty years to prepare for my eventual loss of sight. This hasn't made it any easier. It has made it slower.

Many of the new friends I have met through the Foundation Fighting Blindness did not have that same luxury. Blindness came on quickly for my mentor, Gordon Gund. On the other hand, RP patient and casino owner Steve Wynn, and California legislator Willie Brown had experiences similar to mine. The Foundation Fighting Blindness founded by Gordon Gund and Steve Wynn is a wonderful and much needed organization. It is making progress in discoveries that will assist people losing sight. Gene therapy and the artificial eye are just two research successes starting to show positive results.

Although I was aware that I would go blind, just as Dr. Alan Crandall predicted, it was important to me to carry on my daily activities. It was only when I visited unfamiliar places that I felt the impact of the loss of sight. At Dulles Airport or LAX, my memory helped me make it through the corridors. When going into a familiar restaurant or building, I was fine.

At first, I had trouble seeing in the dark. Then, progressively, I lost my peripheral vision. Eventually, people and objects became mere outlines, and now I only see shadows. I need someone to guide me from one place to another, but I can still read enlarged type with my left eye, one or two letters or numbers at a time. I know that one day I will not be able to see even that. I am preparing myself emotionally for the day I will need to carry a white cane.

There are new developments that may slow the progression of RP. Currently, I am in an experimental program at Emory University Hospital in Atlanta, under the direction of Dr. Timothy Olsen. They have implanted a capsule in my left eye. The capsule secretes a protein substance designed to slow the degeneration of my retina. Once it was implanted, my ability to read the eye chart with that eye improved about thirty percent. Since that time, my vision in that eye has remained constant. I now have 20/200 vision in a narrow tunnel that is 13 degrees, whereas normal is 180 degrees. I have no useful vision in my right eye.

To keep up-to-date, I use two services provided to the blind. *The Washington Ear* allows me to listen, on the telephone, to numerous publications, including *The Washington Post, The Wall Street Journal*, and major news magazines. The Library of Congress provides a wide range of digital books on request.

I have learned that people are more than willing to help when asked. It took a while for me to be comfortable asking for help. Now I no longer hesitate. There are some well-meaning people who try to steer me by pushing me in one direction or another. When they do, I remind them of the movie *Scent of a Woman,* in which Al Pacino explains that you lead a blind person, you do not try to steer them. Then I ask for their elbow.

In the darkness that is closing in, Ursula is my strength and best friend. Gordon Gund is my inspiration. Sometimes I feel like a UPS package being delivered from place to place, but I am blessed to be surrounded by a great group of supporters. I have my son, KC, family, and many friends.

Today, we live in the beautiful Virginia countryside in Fauquier County, at the foot of the Blue Ridge Mountains. We are in the middle of the Virginia Hunt Country, with open fields and old stone walls. There are nine Virginia wineries within five miles of our farm, and we are surrounded by the hallowed ground of our Civil War history. We feel, as did those who lived here before us, that we are only the caretakers of this little piece of heaven.

We spend our time raising money for the Animal Rescue Fund of Virginia, (ARF), a non-profit founded by Ursula to serve the needs of Virginia animal rescue organizations. I also spend time soliciting funds for the Foundation Fighting Blindness (FFB) and its annual fundraising dinner in Washington, D.C. I have served as co-chairman, with former Secretary of Labor Ann Korologos and former Secretary of Commerce Carlos Gutierrez

We are surrounded by friends who care about us as we care about them. I enjoy my time with family, friends, and our dogs, and keep my hand in local politics when asked. I often go out to breakfast or lunch with friends, who pick me up and drive. I take their elbows as they lead me through obstacles in the restaurants. They tell me about steps, they cut my food and generally look after me. Socially, we are active. With friends, we attend hunt breakfasts, go to steeplechase races, charitable events, and functions. We particularly enjoy the Upperville Colt and Horse Show, founded in 1853. It is the oldest continuous sporting event in the U.S. Although I cannot see the horses, I can participate by hearing the sounds of the horses' hooves, the excitement of the crowd, and the announcer. Ursula describes the horses and riders to me as they enter the ring, and I follow the sound of their progress on the course.

My good friend, Manuel (Manley) Johnson, a former vice-chairman of the Federal Reserve, has told me many times that he forgets that I am blind. Many people have echoed the same sentiment; I regard this as a compliment. In Manley's case, it may be because I help guide him. Whenever Manley and I are driving places locally, I constantly give him advice on directions: "Manley, you just missed that right turn back there… Manley, left here…" and so on. Perhaps it is because my other senses are heightened, or perhaps my sense of direction has never been impacted by the loss of sight.

Another good friend, Allen Richards, and I like to go to a local coffee shop for breakfast. Its owner, Kevin, is a mutual friend. One day, when we walked into the coffee shop, I held Allen's elbow as we navigated to the counter. After breakfast, I took his elbow again, and as we walked toward the door, we heard our waitress turn to Kevin and ask, "What's wrong with Allen's eyesight that Ken has to guide him?"

Ursula designed and built a beautiful home for us on top of a hill overlooking the historic Crooked Run Valley. Although I cannot see it, many of our visitors have told me of the spectacular, 360-degree view. The house has no steps, an open floor plan, and no complicated hallways. It is easy for me to navigate by myself, and the only time I am tripped up is when a dog becomes an obstacle. Our dogs keep us entertained and are ever vigilant. The cat, of course, runs the house. Every morning, I thank God that I found Ursula and we discovered the glorious place we now call home.

ACKNOWLEDGMENTS

There is no way for me to adequately acknowledge all the help of the wonderful volunteers and staff who have contributed to my success over the years. Many of them are mentioned in this book. To all of them, all I can say is thank you. I want to thank my parents, Catherine and Howard Rietz, who gave me the sense of confidence and support that would propel me to each new adventure. Mom always told me that I could do anything I wanted if I worked hard enough. Dad always stressed teamwork, and reminded me of President Truman's saying that "It is amazing what you can accomplish if you do not care who gets the credit." Both Mom and Dad were right.

This story would not have been the same without some great mentors. Thanks to Bill Brock, Fred Malek, Mike Curb, Tom Bell, Bill Steiger, Lyn Nofziger, and Gordon Gund.

Lots of people have helped put this book together. Thanks to Dr. Manuel (Manley) Johnson, Tom Bell, Shel Lytton, and Bill Brock for their thoughts on the final draft. Thanks also to Sandy Schwalb for proofreading it.

Thank you to those who have helped with research, including Dan Morrow, Heather Ray, Michaela Wilkerson, Andrew Richards, Chiara Parlagreco, Ryann Stout, and Jeremy Burns. Thanks to Kathy Durand for photographing the items in the appendix, and to her son Peter and Angelic Webber for organizing it.

APPENDIX

This information corresponds with the Photo Section

In a letter to the editor of the *West Allis Star*, a YVP convention participant described his experience in an article titled "Young GOP Convention Experiences."

(The following is an account of the Republican National Convention in Miami as seen by one of the young people attending. Steve, 16, is a student at Nathan Hale High School where he is an officer in the Student Council.)

It was 4:30 am and I had been sitting in this stuffy 8 x 20 room with dozens of others for 2 ½ hours. It was Saturday morning and I had flown out to Miami Friday night to attend the 1972 Republican National Convention as a member of the Young Voters for the President.

The hang up was that I had been confirmed just Friday morning and the organization hadn't time to find me a hotel room. By five I had a temporary room assignment so I could catch about 90 minutes of sleep before my first day. It started bright and early (or was that late?). At any rate I soon came to the conclusion that little naps here and there were to be part of my lifestyle down here, taken between the many youth oriented events we had going.

Paid Own Way

But I accepted this. I paid my own way, as all the others did, to come with the full knowledge and intent of being very busy most of the day and much of the night with much work and many educational and/or entertaining activities.

My typical day would include going to a rally or two to welcome people I was interested in, listening to noted administration and congressional officials and then just rapping with them and helping with our signs for the convention sessions.

I was among the group that got out to the airport to see and welcome the first family and Vice-President Agnew, which is a side of these human beings we don't get through the press.

I also was out as were all the YVPs to meet the President on his arrival. The rain that had been coming down for an hour ended when the "Spirit of '76" touched down.

On Sunday evening, the 20th, Ted Agnew, along with the first family, mingled with us at the dinner given the YVPs by the senior party, and I was touched by the contrast between my perception of him as a warm and compassionate man and the perception delivered by the media of him in the role of the vice president as being brash and hawkish.

In all our meetings with administration officials, the barriers were broken and we had honest and sincere two way communication.

We talked with John Ehrlichman, the President's chief domestic advisor; Bill Ruckleshaus, the energetic director of the Environmental Protection Agency; Barbara Franklin, in charge of executive recruitment of women for government positions and staff assistant to the President; George Bush, U. S. ambassador to the United Nations; Gov. Ronald Reagan; Sen. Bill Brock, the founder of Young Voters for the President; Rep. Gerald Ford, House minority leader; and numerous others of equal stature that I just can't mention. Everyone learned a lot more from these encounters than you find in textbook and lecture oriented schools, because there was dialog with the people that make the decisions.

Encountered Demonstrators

We had encounters with other people too. There were the Vietnam Veterans Against the War, who led generally peaceful demonstrations and there were Zippies and others who were not always as peaceful. The others did such things as tear apart about 20 cars down to heaps of junk at one intersection alone, stopped delegates and YVP buses and cars, slashing the tires and ripping out ignition systems, beating YVPs and older Miami residents, smashing windows wherever there were some and generally violating everybody's civil rights and physically injuring many.

I did not come away unscathed either by demonstrator elbows or misplaced or lingering pepper gas, CS gas and occasionally tear gas. The worst night was Wednesday, of course, and the next morning I found out a property of tear gas. It clings and collects. When I opened a pocket in my pants I got it right in the face. Mass contact between YVPs and demonstrators, which would have been disastrous, was avoided however, as we shipped out minutes before the demonstrators encircled our operations center.

In Convention Hall

Convention attendance obviously was the most interesting and desired part of our schedule, and I managed by luck to be in all three night sessions including the floor demonstration following the re-nomination of President Nixon.

Monday night, when all 3,200 or 3,500 of us were allowed to attend, shock waves went through the party but especially the press, which had always been caught up with the myth that if a person was under thirty, activist and excited, then he or she wants McGovern. With only a reassurance that we need not worry about interrupting the order of a heretofore relatively uneventful convention, we went in and demonstrated genuine enthusiasm for people that deserved it.

Charges by the press that we were rehearsed and controlled were totally untrue and asinine. Over 3,000 young people cannot possibly be controlled when none of them have any want to be controlled. In fact I saw many kids with completely different reactions than me. I would cheer, they would fall asleep and vice-versa.

In fact the national media even broadcast to millions completely inaccurate statements of what YVPs are. YVPs that attended that convention were for the most part independent. Republicans and Democrats that want the President re-elected and have been working in their home towns for several months and will continue to do so, organizing in schools, registering the young people having their first election and just talking.

Press And TV Wrong

So the fact that the TV commentators and national press were charging that we were shipped in to rehearse and yell on cue and then be sent home is a fabrication which covers up the fact that myth has been shattered.

As a sixteen year-old attending the Republican National Convention this has been the most exciting and educational experience of my life and though I only got two to three hours of sleep a night, I'd do it again and so would the rest of us, who believe in the president's total and long term efforts at a stable peace, rather than a short term euphoric peace, followed by a worsening world situation in which peace could be lost for a generation. I'm one of between 125,000 and 250,000 young bent on showing that our adulthood world is best served by the re-election of President Richard Nixon.

From left to right (Photo Section page xi), there was a student poring over a book. Above the words:

EDUCATION - The President is spending four billion dollars more than ever before on education, and he is making it possible for every qualified student to go to college who wants to. Also, he has "career education" programs to prepare college and non-college youths for jobs.

Underneath is an illustration headlined:

DRUGS - A three-pronged attack has been launched by the President against drugs: Education to prevent drug abuse in the first place, rehabilitation for those beyond prevention, and blockage of incoming drug supplies.

The third circle shows a young woman speaking into a telephone receiver with the words:

WOMEN - President Nixon signed the Equal Rights Amendment barring sex discrimination, tripled the number of women in top government positions and has the Equal Employment Opportunity Commission helping women in discrimination suits.

Below and centered under the photograph of the president is a rendition of a group of young, black people with the heading:

MINORITIES - 40% of Black students attended all-Black schools when the President took office. Today, only 12% do. And high school equivalency, college opportunities, and bi-lingual courses were set up for Spanish-Americans. President Nixon is a President for all Americans.

Curving upwards, now to the right, is a drawing of a group of people discussing an architectural plan with a government building in the background:

BIG GOVERNMENT is the heading. He wants the government to respond to the people. So President Nixon is working to make the bureaucracy smaller and better, and to return more tax money to the states that raised it.

As we move up around the photograph, the illustration is of a group of young men and women with the Capitol in the distance.

YOUTH INVOLVEMENT is the header. The President held the first White House Conference on Youth in history, got eighteen year-olds the vote and appointed more White House staff under thirty than any other President. He's listening to you.

Now in the top half of the poster, the illustration depicts young black and white men with the U.S. Armed Forces as the backdrop. Heading:

DRAFT - The President has made the draft fair to all, and cut down the waiting and uncertainty. Now he is working on an all-volunteer army which would mean no draft at all. (After Nixon ended the draft, the poster was revised.) Last, the rendering depicts flowers, mountains, a heron in flight and two fishermen in a small boat. The words read :

ENVIRONMENT - President Nixon established the Environmental Protection Agency, the first Federal Agency ever set up to defend our quality of life.

The last vignette completes the circle and ends at the banner above.

INDEX

A

B

E

Ehrlichman, Jan 68, 111

Ehrlichman, John 68, 84, 92, 111

Ehrlichman, Peter 68, 111, 117, 205

Ellis, Dave 182

F

Ford, Jack 68, 111

Ford, Gerald 68, 111, 140-142, 145, 148-149, 155-157, 161-162, 199, 205

G

Gissel, Jolly 163

Gore, Sen. Al, Sr. 7, 41-43, 45-54, 62

Gorton, George 10, 68, 75, 78-79, 85-86, 166

Gund, Gordon 29, 200-201

Gutierrez, Carlos 201

H

Hahn, Colleen Dedication

Haldeman, Bob 9, 48-49, 58, 68, 78-81, 84-86, 92, 97-98, 103-105, 107-111, 116-117

Haldeman, Hank 85-86

Harris, Angela 68, 78

Hecht, Chic 7, Chapters 20-21

Hime, Rex 193-194

Hudson, Cynthia 194, 196

Hunt, Gary 161

Hunt, E. Howard 62, 72

J

Johnson, Dr. Manuel (Manley) 202-203

Johnson, Marilyn 61, 63, 83, 93, 130

K

Kelly, Tom 19

Khachigian, Ken 165-166

Kiefer, Fanny 191

Korologos, Ann 201

L

Laird, Mel 12

Lake, (Dr.) Jim 196, 199

Landsrath, Ursula 184-187, 192, 195, 197-198, 200-202

LaRue, Fred 95-96

Laxalt, Paul 162, 173-175, 177-178, 180, 184

Leonard, Jerris (Jerry) 115, 116, 133

Lewis, (Cong.) Jerry 187

Liddy, G. Gordon 63, 71-72, 95, 117, 120

Lytton, Shel 145, 148-153, 168, 170, 203

M

MacFarland, Alf 51

Maddy, Ken 146

Magruder, Jeb 59, 61-64, 66-67, 71, 74, 77, 80, 82-85, 94-95, 102, 105, 114-115, 117, 122

Malek, Fred 61, 76-77, 94, 102, 105, 203

McCord, James 81

McGovern, George 65-66, 75, 82, 88, 96-97, 99-100, 119, 206

Meese, Ed 151, 157-158

S

T

W

Y